The UNIX Operating System

This book was prepared for phototypesetting by the author using the typesetting tools of the UNIX Operating System.

The UNIX† Operating System

KAARE CHRISTIAN

The Rockefeller University
New York, New York

† UNIX is a trademark of Bell Laboratories.

A Wiley-Interscience Publication

JOHN WILEY & SONS

New York   Chichester   Brisbane   Toronto   Singapore

Library of Congress Cataloging in Publication Data:

Christian, Kaare, 1954-
   The UNIX operating system.

   "A Wiley-Interscience publication."
   Includes index
   1. UNIX (Computer system) I. Title.
II. Title: U.N.I.X. operating system.
QA76.6.C456 1983 001.64'25 82-24811
ISBN 0-471-87542-2
ISBN 0-471-89052-9 (pbk.)

Printed in the United States of America

20 19 18 17 16 15 14 13 12

For Edward Josiah Bunker

Contents

PART 2   ADVANCED UNIX SYSTEM TOPICS

Preface

UNIX is the name of a family of computer operating systems. Many experts feel that the UNIX System is the most important development in computer operating systems in the past decade. The impact of the UNIX System is being compared with that of FORTRAN, the first major portable high-level programming language, or that of IBM's System/360, the first compatible series of computers spanning a wide performance range. The UNIX System is becoming increasingly important because it runs on a wide range of computers and because it has many applications.

Originally used on Digital Equipment Corporation minicomputers for computer science research, program development, and document preparation, current versions of the UNIX System are now available for computers as small and inexpensive as the Zilog Z-80 and computers as large as the Amdahl 470/V7. The UNIX System is now used for a large range of business, scientific, and industrial applications.

Operating systems are also called executives because they (like business executives) administer and control the operation of a complicated device. In the narrowest sense the UNIX System parcels computer time into a number of portions and allocates the portions among the various users. It also controls the flow of information between the central computer and the disks, tapes, terminals, and printers, and manages the long term storage of information.

In a broader sense the UNIX System is a large collection of programs that rely on the basic services just mentioned. The programs allow a user to create and examine files, to write and test new programs, to perform sophisticated document preparation, in short, to manage information. The UNIX System is simple, useful, and intelligible.

One of the most important advantages of the UNIX System is the fact that it runs on many types of computers. Ordinary programs that run on one type of computer (under the UNIX System) can usually be run on other types of computers with little or no modification. This allows companies that sell computer programs to produce a single product for a large market and it allows computer users to learn a single operating system that is applicable to many different machines. Even though this sounds simple and obvious it has taken three decades of work with computers to achieve.

The work of Ken Thompson and Dennis M. Ritchie at Bell Laboratories in the early 1970s started a revolution. In the mid-1970s the excitement spread to the academic community, which was seeking a solution to many difficulties of modern computer science. In the 1980s this phenomenon reached the business community, which sees the UNIX System as an important part of the struggle to provide better and longer-lasting software products and services.

The original goal of Thompson and Ritchie was to create a productive environment for pursuing computer science research. The original goal, and much more, has been achieved. Thompson and Ritchie have demonstrated that individuals can make important contributions in a difficult field, and the UNIX System has demonstrated that new and better ideas are eventually accepted in the marketplace.

During its first decade (1970 – 1980) the UNIX System was used primarily in academia and internally in the Bell System. This was a period of refinement and testing that proved beyond doubt this system's superiority in the domain of general purpose interactive operating systems. The current decade marks the UNIX System's entry into the commercial marketplace, where it is rapidly becoming the standard operating system for a wide range of computer systems performing many different applications.

In fairness to other systems, note that the UNIX System is weak in two major areas. At heart the UNIX System is an anarchist. The UNIX System works well if everybody on the system is doing something different but gets in trouble with applications where everybody is doing the same thing. If you know in advance what everybody is going to do (check processing systems, reservation systems, etc.), then you can optimize the system accordingly. The UNIX System is optimized to allow everybody to work independently.

The second weakness is in real-time systems. Real-time systems are used for controlling machinery, industrial processes, laboratory equipment, and the like. The computer has to react quickly as the machinery moves, the process advances, or the laboratory data arrives. It is certainly possible to adapt the UNIX System to perform most of these operations, but there are other operating systems that are better for real-time applications.

In the past most people learned to use the UNIX System informally. Most people outside of the Bell System who learned the UNIX Operating System in the mid-1970s can tell you the name of the person who tutored them. Bell Laboratories documented the UNIX System with *The Unix Programmer's Manual,* an admirably complete and accurate reference. Unfortunately the Bell Labs manual is too terse to be useful for novice and intermediate users. The other major source of information in this area is the set of scholarly journal articles which have provided computer scientists with detailed explanations of the UNIX System and its major programs.

Part 1 of this book provides the basic knowledge and introduces the basic ideas that novice and intermediate users need in order to use the UNIX System effectively. The chapters in Part 1 introduce you to interactive computing, explain the basic use of the shell and the editor, explain some of the ideas embodied in the UNIX file system, and survey the most useful utility programs. Examples are used constantly to illustrate the ideas and to show the power and flexibility of the UNIX System. You will become acquainted with the UNIX System much faster if you try the examples on your UNIX System.

The UNIX System manual is a good reference but a poor introduction. For instance, in my manual the entire description of the pwd (print working directory) command is "Pwd prints the path name of the working (current) directory." This book explains path names, explains the notion of a working directory, explains why and when you might want to know the name of the working directory, and provides examples of using pwd. Once you are familiar with the UNIX System you can expand your knowledge by using the manual, but in the beginning a gentler introduction is helpful.

Another function of this book is to distinguish the common and the generally useful facilities of the UNIX System, which is supplied with over 200 utility programs. However, only about 40 of these programs are considered general enough to warrant an individual description in this book. Chapters 7, 8, and 9 present these utility programs arranged by function. These same programs are also presented alphabetically in the Abridged UNIX System Manual at the end of this book.

Part 2 of this book presents a selection of information for intermediate and advanced users. Perhaps the most important topic in this part of the book is the Version 7 shell, the UNIX System's standard command interpreter. The shell is extremely important, yet it has not been adequately described in the literature. Other topics in the second part of this book include the internal organization of the UNIX System, information for programmers and managers, and introductory descriptions of some of the most innovative UNIX System programs.

The glossary of the UNIX System terminology preceding the Abridged the UNIX System Manual should be useful to most beginners.

I would like to thank Robert Schoenfeld, Owen Smith, and Paul Rosen of The Rockefeller University for their encouragement, comments and criticism, Tom Krausz and Eric Rosenthal of IMI Systems for their extremely helpful comments, and Edward Gershey of The Rockefeller University for his support. Ed Catmull and Alvy Ray Smith of Lucasfilm Ltd. generously supplied the cover artwork. Finally I would like to thank Jim Gaughan and Jenet McIver at John Wiley for their encouragement and assistance throughout this project.

Kaare Christian

New York, New York

The Cover Illustration

The illustration on the cover is a single frame of a one minute sequence known as the "Genesis Effect" from the motion picture *Star Trek II: The Wrath of Khan* from Paramount Pictures. Members of the Computer Group at Lucasfilm Ltd used computer graphics techniques to create the one minute sequence. No physical artwork or physical models were used — instead computers running the UNIX System created the 1620 images.

Computer graphics has progressed from simple black and white line drawing systems to sophisticated color animation systems. Most advanced computer animation systems are capable of creating impressive images — images which are obviously computer generated. At Lucasfilm the state of the art has advanced to the point where computer generated images are so "real" and "lifelike" that they can be smoothly intercut with images of reality.

The Genesis Sequence opens with a view of a dead planet as seen from a nearby spacecraft. The spacecraft fires a projectile at the planet — the result of the impact is a wall of fire which spreads across the planet, transforming the lifeless rock into a Garden of Eden. During the planet's evolution the spacecraft flies close by the surface to observe the dramatic biogenesis occurring on the planet. Finally the spacecraft pulls back to reveal the verdant planet, complete with rivers, plains, mountains, oceans, and atmosphere.

Alvy Ray Smith, the head of The Graphics Project at Lucasfilm, supervised the talented group that created the Genesis Sequence. He likes to think of the group as an "off-line rock group." He noted that "We work together on our individual instruments for months, and only later do we face the music. The point is that all members of the team are creative contributors and a project requires all of them."

Each frame of the Genesis Sequence was assembled from many pieces using computers running the UNIX System. First the background image was created and then the foreground images were sandwiched on top. It took the UNIX System up to five hours to perform all of the calculations for some of the most complicated frames, and up to 50 programs were used for some of the frames. Besides the complexity of the individual frames, the magicians at Lucasfilm had to worry about continuity from frame to frame and the constantly changing perspective as the spacecraft flew past the planet.

I am indebted to Ed Catmull, the director of the computer Division at Lucasfilm and Alvy Ray Smith, the Graphics Project Leader at Lucasfilm for supplying the cover image. The following members of the staff at Lucasfilm Ltd. were the principal creators of the Genesis Sequence:

Loren Carpenter	Fractal mountains, Atmosphere, Shockwave
Pat Cole	Projectile
Tom Duff	Cratered sphere, Texture-mapped sphere
Chris Evans	Painted the pull-away planet surface
Tom Porter	Stars, Compositing, Paint
Bill Reeves	Fires
Alvy Ray Smith	Concept, Direction

PART

1

UNDERSTANDING THE UNIX SYSTEM

CHAPTER

1

The History of the UNIX System

The UNIX System is one of the major advances in the progression of computers from the esoteric realm of high technology into the mainstream of people's daily activities. The UNIX Operating System has demonstrated that a powerful operating system can be largely machine independent, and the UNIX System has shown that powerful software tools can be used effectively by people in the course of using a computer to solve problems.

The UNIX System provides essentially the same services as those provided by all operating systems: it allows you to run programs, it provides a convenient and consistent interface to the wide variety of peripheral devices (printers, tapes, disks, terminals, etc.) that are connected to most computers, and it provides a file system for information management. The UNIX System's uniqueness is largely due to the way it evolved. We can best understand the system's growing popularity by adopting a historical perspective.

Part of the UNIX System's popularity is attributed to its portability, flexibility, and elegant design. Ironically, the UNIX System emerged from the attic of one of the strongest and most powerful corporate monoliths in the world: Bell Laboratories, the subsidiary research arm of AT&T. Most operating systems have been developed by computer manufacturers in order to sell computers. Since AT&T was not in the business of selling computers the UNIX System was not originally envisioned as a commercial product. The UNIX System has only become a commercial venture in response to the enormous demand that has developed.

In the late 1960s Bell Labs was involved with an operating system called Multics. Multics is a multiuser interactive system using a GE mainframe computer. Bell Labs withdrew from the Multics project in 1969, but Multics had a major influence on the UNIX System. In fact, the name UNIX is a play on the word Multics. One of the most striking differences between the UNIX System and Multics is complexity — the UNIX Operating System is relatively simple while Multics is extremely complex.

At about the same time as Bell's withdrawal from Multics, the "granddaddy of the UNIX System," Ken Thompson, began tinkering on a reject Digital Equipment Corporation PDP-7 minicomputer. Ostensibly, Thompson sought to create an operating system that could support the coordinated efforts of a team of programmers in a programming research environment. In retrospect this objective has been successfully accomplished. Also, in order to appease management, Thompson proposed that further UNIX System development be supported by Bell Labs in order to provide a document preparation tool for the Bell Labs patent organization. An early version of the UNIX System using a PDP-11/20 was eventually delivered to the Bell Laboratories patent organization in 1971.

From the very beginning two seemingly incompatible disciplines, programming and document preparation, have been the cornerstones of the UNIX System. In practice the UNIX System has demonstrated that text management tools are central to many disciplines, including programming. People have criticized the UNIX System for being just a fancy word processor. While there are applications that require operating systems other than the UNIX System, the focus on text manipulation has served to make it an extremely general purpose operating system. Text is an accepted medium for communication, a key feature for a general purpose interactive operating system.

Ken Thompson's original efforts culminated in the creation of an operating system, a PDP-7 assembler, and several assembly language utility programs. In 1973 Dennis Ritchie rewrote the UNIX System in the C programming language. C is a general purpose high level programming language that was developed by Ritchie. It has proven to be adaptable to many different types of computer architecture. If the UNIX System had not been rewritten in a high level language, it would have been chained to the machine (the outdated PDP-7) that it was developed on. Once the original assembly language programs had also been rewritten in C it was suddenly possible to move the entire UNIX System from one environment to another with a minimum of difficulty.

Operating systems have traditionally been tied to one computer or family of computers because they were written in assembly language. Although the UNIX System was not originally intended to be a portable operating system, once it was coded in C everything was in place to move it to other systems. The first move to a different type of computer was accomplished by Ritchie and Stephen Johnson in 1976 when they transported the UNIX System to the Interdata 8/32. Since then the UNIX System has been moved to a dozen or so architectures, ranging from single chip microprocessors such as the Zilog Z-80 and Z-8000, the Motorola MC68000, and the Intel 8086, to large mainframe computers such as IBM 370 and the Amdahl 470.

As Thompson gained acceptance from his colleagues and management during the early 1970s the UNIX System began to be used internally throughout the Bell System. As word of the operating system spread it generated interest at several prestigious academic institutions. In 1975 Western Electric started licensing the UNIX System. The fee was nominal for academic institutions, encouraging many of them to use and further develop the UNIX System. Because the UNIX System was looked upon so favorably by the academic high technology research communities, it was initially met with skepticism by the business community. Recently, the business community has realized the ease with which the UNIX System can be adopted for a wide variety of applications. Starting in the late 1970s a UNIX System industry has emerged to supply hardware, software, and related services.

The UNIX System has pioneered several important ideas. One of the most important innovations is the pipe, which has in turn led to the idea that complicated functions can be programmed as a set of programs working together. Typesetting provides the best example. The UNIX System contains several different typesetting programs, one for conventional chores, one for mathematics, one for tabular data, and one for diagrams. Pipe connections allow a user to use as many of these programs as are necessary. Each typesetting program does not duplicate the features in the other programs; instead there is a complementary relationship. Solving a complicated problem using a body of cooperating processes has proven to be convenient for both program developers and program users.

Another idea which has pervaded the UNIX System is the notion of a software tool. This idea is not unique to the UNIX System, but it certainly has been developed further here than in other systems. To simplify programming chores involving the recognition of a command language, the UNIX System has yacc and lex. These two programs allow a programmer to implement a command language interpreter by describing the command language in a tabular form rather than writing a unique interpreter for the language. Lex and yacc require study before they can be mastered, but once they are mastered they make it possible to conveniently program new applications involving command languages. Two other examples of sophisticated tools are Make and the Source Code Control System (SCCS). Make is used to specify the interdependencies in a software system so that the system can be maintained automatically. SCCS is used to track a software system throughout its mature lifetime so that old versions can be retrieved, and new versions can be documented.

At this point the UNIX System appears to be emerging as a standard operating system for general purpose use on a wide spectrum of computers. The UNIX System is not likely to be used widely in situations where a computer is used for a special purpose that lends itself to a specialized operating system (e.g., transaction processing, reservation systems, real-time systems). From a pragmatic point of view, the UNIX System is likely to be important in the years to come because it is widely used. At this point the UNIX System industry is in its infancy, and in monetary terms it cannot be compared with the industry that services some of the established mainframe operating systems. However, in the next few years the prospects are very good for the companies in the UNIX System service industry, and some industry analysts are predicting that the UNIX System industry may come to rival the support industries that exist today for the more established operating systems.

Another aspect of the UNIX System's future relates to its widespread acceptance and use in the academic computing community. Somewhat like the programming language ALGOL (and more recently PASCAL) is widely used in the academic literature to describe algorithms, the UNIX Operating System is being referenced widely in the literature whenever operating system topics are discussed. The UNIX System has become a standard against which new developments in operating systems are measured.

CHAPTER

2

Fundamentals

The difference between computers and most other machines is that computers are general purpose. The generality of computers is the central difficulty in learning to use a computer. As a first step in understanding the UNIX System, or any other operating system, you should have a general understanding of the building blocks that underlie a computer. This chapter presents some of these fundamentals.

One of the major functions of an operating system is to disguise the building blocks of computers. You don't have to understand motors and circuit theory to operate an electric appliance, and you shouldn't have to understand computer architecture to use a computer. However, a basic understanding of the fundamentals will make it easier to understand some of the ebb and flow of ideas in the following chapters. If you have some experience with computers, then you should probably skip to Chapter 3.

2.1 Low Level Functions

A typewriter is easy to use because there is a specific button to press in order to get a specific letter printed on the page. Common operations such as rolling the carriage up and returning to the start of the line are built into the mechanism even though they are quite complicated. The typewriter contains a mechanism that translates a keystroke into a series of mechanical events which produce the desired result. The purpose of the translator is to disguise the basic mechanical events in order to make the typewriter easy to use.

Let's get more specific in order to make this idea clear. When you strike the letter "a" on a typical typewriter keyboard the following events occur: (1) the ribbon raises; (2) the "a" striker bangs against the platen; (3) the ribbon lowers; (4) the assembly moves to the next print position (unless you are at the margin); and (5) the bell rings if you are a certain number of spaces from the right margin. The typewriter mechanism translates a key depression into a series of internal actions resulting in a letter being printed.

We can imagine a typewriter which lacks the mechanism that translates the keystrokes into the sequence of mechanical events. One of the meanings of the word "proto" is "the earliest form." Let's use the term prototypewriter to describe a machine that can perform all of the low level functions of a typewriter. A prototypewriter can raise and lower the ribbon, move the mechanism back and forth, bang the symbols against the platen, and so on. However, our imaginary prototypewriter lacks the high level capability of a typewriter to print a letter in response to a single keystroke. In order to use the prototypewriter you would have to memorize the sequence of primitive operations that are required to perform each advanced function (e.g., printing an "a"). One could argue that a prototypewriter is more powerful than a regular typewriter because it is more general purpose. You could make a prototypewriter type right to left, diagonally, or vertically. However, a prototypewriter would be tremendously awkward and I suspect that we will never see one on the market.

A computer is somewhat like a prototypewriter. It has potential for being very useful but it isn't endowed with a convenient high level control mechanism. It is easy to build a translator into a prototypewriter in order to create a convenient and useful device because a typewriter is a single purpose device. It is much harder to endow a computer with a convenient set of operations because computers are general purpose machines. The role of an operating system is to make it easy to use a general purpose computer. An operating system endows a computer with a set of useful functions just as the keyboard translator endows a prototypewriter with a set of useful operations.

2.2 Typical Computers

Many different types of computer are manufactured. Even though there is great variety among computers, the pressures of the marketplace and the path of technology have led to a certain standardization of the major functional units.

Basically a computer is a machine that follows a sequence of instructions. The instructions perform operations such as adding two numbers, moving some information from one location to another, or changing the sequence of instructions. The part of the computer that executes the instructions is called the processor (the central processing unit, abbreviated CPU), and the place where the instructions are stored is called the memory. The CPU is the part of a computer where information is manipulated, but relatively little information is stored in the CPU. The memory is the place where information is stored; each storage location in the memory is assigned a unique number called an address. The memory is often called the primary store (store as in storage) because it is the place the CPU acquires its instructions.

The major advantage of main memory is speed. Information can be retrieved very rapidly from the main memory of a computer. The disadvantages of the computer's main memory are that it has a limited capacity, it is relatively expensive, and on most computers the information in main memory is lost when the computer is turned off.

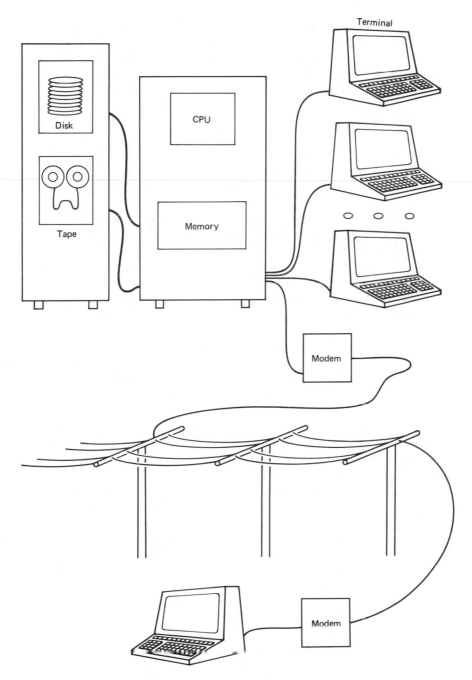

Figure 2.1. A typical computer.

Secondary storage has been developed to complement the abilities and drawbacks of the primary storage. The secondary storage has a relatively large capacity, it is relatively inexpensive, and it doesn't lose information when the computer is turned off. On most midsize computers, which often use the UNIX System, the secondary storage devices (also called mass storage devices) are usually disks and tapes. Disks and tapes store data magnetically, as do audio cassette tapes. The disadvantage of the secondary store is that the information stored there takes much longer to access than the information in primary store. Information is almost always moved from secondary store to the primary store

There are many analogies that attempt to explain the workings of a computer. My favorite is the cookbook analogy. A recipe is just a sequence of instructions for cooking something. When you follow the recipe you are doing the same thing that the CPU is doing when it is running a program. Just as there are many different recipes in a cookbook, there can be many different programs in a computer.

I suspect that computers seem so mysterious because they work electrically and they store information in patterns of ones and zeroes. If computers were able to read a cookbook and prepare meals (a much harder task), then people might not be so impressed.

A collection of information on a disk or a tape is called a file, and files are usually identified by names. The way that files are organized is one of the central features of a computer system. Disks and tapes usually contain many files (often thousands) so it is important for a computer to be able to locate a given file quickly. Therefore, computers maintain lists of files and their locations. You have to understand the basic organization of these lists in order to direct the computer to access files. This very important topic is discussed in Chapter 6.

You communicate with a computer by using a computer terminal. A computer terminal has a typewriterlike keyboard and an output device. A display terminal uses a television style output device, and a printing terminal uses a printer output device. A few terminals have displays and printers in one package. Some other names for display terminals are video terminals and CRT (cathode ray tube) terminals. Voice entry is still many years away, so if you want to use computers you should become familiar with the layout of the keyboard.

Computer terminals can be connected to the computer over telephone lines or by direct connections. Direct connections are preferable because they are faster but they work only when the computer terminal and the computer are physically close (within a mile or so).

A modem is a device that allows computers and terminals to communicate over great distances. Modems translate electrical signals into audible chirps and squeals that can be sent through the public telephone system.

2.3 Naked Machines

A computer without any programs to help the user is often called a naked machine. Very early computers were true naked machines. They were operated by actuating a series of switches. Operating systems were developed in response to the clumsiness of using switches to control a computer.

Operating complicated switches is a job for specialists — the computer elite. As computers have evolved, more and more effort has been expended in liberating computers from the clutches of the computer elite. Although the liberation is not yet complete (and probably never will be), great advances have been made. Operating systems are one of the major advances in making computers more accessible. Operating systems make it easier to use a computer, although they breed a new member of the computer elite — the operating systems specialist.

Today virtually all general purpose computer systems use operating systems to avoid the problems of the naked machine. The goal of an operating system is to increase the effectiveness of a general purpose computer. Special purpose computers such as the computers that run microwave ovens and sewing machines and industrial processes rarely use operating systems.

2.4 Operating Systems

An operating system is a program that manages the resources of a computer. Operating systems send information to the communication devices, manage the storage space on mass storage devices, load information into memory, and so on. In computer systems that allow several people to use the system simultaneously the operating system arbitrates the various requests in order to distribute the computer's resources fairly and effectively.

There is nothing mysterious about using a well-designed operating system. You just have to know how the system is organized. Unfortunately, some people have a bad impression of operating systems because some of the early operating systems were almost more of a hindrance than a help.

The complexity of operating systems usually varies with the complexity of the host computer system. Very simple computer systems usually have very simple operating systems. The simplest operating systems are called monitors and they have a very limited repertoire of functions.

Computers in the middle range of complexity, price, and performance are called minicomputers. The UNIX System was originally designed to run on minis, although now there are versions of the UNIX System for very small computers (microcomputers) and very large computers (maxicomputers). On some minicomputer operating systems only one program can be run at a time, whereas others allow several programs to run simultaneously. Running several programs at once is called multiprogramming and it is very difficult to achieve. Therefore, operating systems that don't include multiprogramming are usually much simpler than those that do.

The UNIX System is a moderately complex operating system. It is far simpler than the operating systems that run on maxicomputers, but it is has much more capability than most operating systems that run on microcomputers. For example, the UNIX System allows you to run several programs simultaneously.

2.5 Time-Sharing

Time-sharing is one of the techniques that has been developed for sharing a computer among several users. Computers that usually run just one program at a time such as home computers don't need time-sharing or any of the other multiprogramming methods. The goal of time-sharing is to give each user the illusion of exclusive use of the machine. Time-sharing works because modern computers can perform millions of operations in a second. At that rate a computer is able to devote thousands of operations to your tasks, and thousands to your neighbor's, and thousands to the job of coordinating everything — all in a single second.

In some computer systems you wait until the computer is ready to run your programs. However, in interactive computer systems the computer is always waiting for you to start a program. When you ask the computer to run a program it starts running immediately and the computer works diligently on it until it is finished. The computer may be doing some other operations concurrently, but basically your program starts as soon as you enter the command and the computer makes continuous progress.

Time-sharing works by dividing each unit of time into a number of slices. Each executing program receives a slice of time. When more programs are executing each program receives a smaller slice than when only a few programs are executing. Since computers are very fast devices they can switch rapidly from one job to another, creating the appearance that the computer is performing many tasks simultaneously. In fact the computer is making progress on one task and then switching to the next, and the next, and so on.

Some time-sharing systems become very inefficient when they are overloaded. Inefficiency strikes when the demand is so large that the computer spends all of its time switching between programs and very little time actually running programs.

2.6 The Kernel

Certain operating system functions are required many times each second. For example, the part of the UNIX System that is involved in switching from one program to another (time-sharing) is needed many times each second. In the UNIX System all of the functions that are needed immediately are constantly kept in memory. The memory resident part of an operating system is called the kernel.

Many operating system functions are needed only occasionally, such as the capability to move some information from one mass storage device to another. These types of function are provided by utilities, standard programs which are invoked upon demand by the computer users. In the UNIX System it is easy for people to add to the stock of utilities simply by writing a new and useful program.

In many operating systems the kernel contains a great many features. The UNIX System attempts to endow the kernel with relatively few features so that most operating system functions can be provided by utility programs. If you are curious about the kernel, then you should read Chapter 19. The UNIX System kernel is simple enough to be understood in principle by most users.

2.7 Programs

A program is a sequence of instructions that the computer follows in order to achieve a certain result. When a program is not being executed the sequence of instructions is stored in a mass storage device (usually a disk). To run the program a copy of the instructions must be loaded into memory.

While a program is running in the UNIX System it is called a process. If several people are running the same program at about the same time, then there are several processes but only one program.

Programs are important because they are the only interface between people and the power of computers. Most programs require some information from you and then they usually provide some information in return. In a well-designed system the machine spends more time working for you than you spend working for the machine.

Well-designed programs work flexibly. It would be foolish to write a program that changed the name of a file called "alex" to "alicia." The program would be used once and then discarded Instead there is a program that renames a file and it is your responsibility when you run the program to supply the two names.

Although well-designed programs work flexibly, all programs have limits. Sometimes the limits seem arbitrary. For example, you can't use the program that changes the names of files to change other types of names in the system, such as the name that you use in your dialogs with the UNIX System (your login name). When you use a program it is important to know what information the program requires from you, what the program can do, and what it cannot do.

Most UNIX System programs perform just one function. A complicated operation such as using the computer to write and distribute a memo requires a sequence of programs. It is up to you to decompose complicated operations (e.g., writing a memo) into a series of steps that correspond to the available set of programs. As you become proficient with the UNIX System you will realize that there are usually several different approaches to most complicated operations.

Programs can be divided into two general classes: utility programs and application programs. Utility programs usually perform general functions while application programs are designed for specific purposes. For example, a program that an accounting firm runs to automate its bookkeeping would be classified as an application program, whereas a program that displays the time would usually be considered a utility. Utilities are usually supplied with an operating system while application programs are often acquired separately.

One purpose of this book is to acquaint you with the most useful UNIX System utilities. Chapters 7, 8, and 9 present most of the UNIX System utility programs. The majority of these programs are simple, effective tools for performing simple functions. The presentation of the programs in these three chapters shows typical applications. The idea is to acquaint you with these programs, not to present an exhaustive treatment of each program. After reading the general descriptions in this book you should be able to learn the details of the utilities that you rely on from the documents supplied with your system.

2.8 The Shell and the Editor

Typical UNIX System users spend the majority of their time using two programs: the shell and the editor. To use the UNIX System flexibly you need to have a working knowledge of many other programs, but the greater part of your time will probably be spent using these two programs.

An editor is a program that allows you to create and modify text files. The standard UNIX System editor is an interactive program. You control the editor program by entering commands. There are editor commands to print lines of a file, commands to add text to a file, and commands to change text that has already been entered.

You will probably use the editor for a wide variety of functions. You might use the editor to create a file containing a message that you want to distribute electronically using the UNIX System's mail program, or you might want to use the editor to create a document or report that will be printed and distributed on paper.

You can acquire a basic working knowledge of the UNIX System editor in Chapter 5. A basic understanding will allow you to use the editor but if you plan to use the editor extensively then you should also become familiar with the advanced functions discussed in Chapter 10. The editor functions discussed in these two chapters work in the great majority of editors used in the UNIX System. The editor that is used at your system probably has several features that are not mentioned in this book so you should probably examine the manuals for your system in addition to Chapters 5 and 10.

The shell is one of the most important programs in the UNIX System. Like the editor, the shell is an interactive program. You control the shell by entering commands which the shell interprets (decodes) and executes. Therefore, the technical name for the shell is command interpreter.

The function of a command interpreter is to execute the commands that you enter. For instance, if you want to run the program that prints the date and time on your screen, you enter the command "date" and the shell then arranges for that program to be executed by the UNIX System.

On many systems the command interpreter is a part of the internal structure of the operating system. In the UNIX System, however, the shell is just an ordinary program, similar to the date program or any other program that runs in the UNIX System. The only thing that is special about the shell is the fact that it is central to most of your interactions with the UNIX System. If you are a typical user, then you will spend much of your time entering commands. The shell has many features that you can use to increase your effectiveness.

The UNIX System is really a tool for information management. The power of the UNIX System stems from its ability to let programs work together to produce the information that you need. On most computer systems each program is a world unto itself. In the UNIX System most programs are simple tools that can be combined with other programs to produce more powerful tools.

The shell is the key to coordinating and combining UNIX System programs. Several chapters present the features of the shell. About half of Chapter 3 is a very simple introduction to the shell. Chapter 4 focuses entirely on the shell as an interactive command interpreter. The information in Chapter 4 may seem dry on first reading; try to work through it a second time after you have some experience with the UNIX System.

Besides being an interactive command interpreter, the shell is also a very sophisticated programming language. Most users ignore the programming language features of the shell simply because most users are not computer programmers. However, if you want to use the shell as a programming language, read Chapter 13 and work through the examples given in Chapter 14.

CHAPTER

3

UNIX System Basics

Learning about a new computer system is like visiting a foreign country — the experience is intimidating at first. Even though the UNIX System is designed to be a friendly and supportive operating system, as a novice you will often be frustrated. The purpose of this chapter is to help you survive and understand your first encounter with the UNIX System.

Some people want to read a short paragraph that will tell them everything they need to know in order to use the UNIX System. Perhaps a typewriter or a toaster can be described briefly but a computer operating system can't. To use the UNIX System effectively you have to master a fairly large body of knowledge. However, most of the ideas are straightforward and if you are patient, you will soon be an effective UNIX System user.

The UNIX System is harder to use than a toaster, but then it does more than a toaster. Learning the UNIX System is somewhat like learning a complex skill such as swimming or bicycle riding. At first none of your reflexes seem appropriate but eventually the skill is mastered.

This chapter discusses some of the basic rules for using the UNIX System. You should skip this chapter if you are already familiar with the UNIX System.

3.1 Logging In

The first thing that you have to do to use the UNIX System is to log in. The purpose of the logging in is twofold: to let the UNIX System verify your right to use the system and to let the UNIX System set up your environment. In computer systems that allow access over the telephone it is very important to restrict use to authorized people, and in computer systems where the users are charged it is important to know who is using the computer so that the billing can accurately reflect use. One of the functions of the UNIX System is to manage the computer resource so that several people can share the computer. In order to do this the UNIX System maintains a separate environment for each user. The UNIX System remembers who each user is, when each logged in, how much computer

16

time each has used, what files each owns, what files are immediately accessible, what type of a terminal is being used, and so on.

In most single-user computer systems (most home computers) there is no login procedure because physical access to the hardware confirms your right to use the system. In batch operating systems there is no formal login process; instead each submitted job is identified for billing and scheduling purposes. In the UNIX System once you have completed the login process you don't have to identify yourself each time you run a program.

Before you can log in for the first time the system administrator or some local UNIX System guru must create your account. It is usually simple to set up an account at a UNIX System installation that doesn't charge the users for computer time. Setting up an account at installations that charge for computer time is more difficult because information about billing and money is required.

From your point of view the major issue in setting up an account is deciding on your login name. The login name is the name that you want to use during your interactions with the UNIX System. Short, lower case names are usually easiest. Many people use their initials or nickname. The names "Betsy," "kc," and "m" are all acceptable.

Once you have an account you can try logging in. If you are using a dial-up terminal, you should set the full-duplex/half-duplex switch to full and you should set the speed of the terminal to the correct speed. Dial the number of the computer and wait for the beep. When you hear the beep you should place the handset in the acoustic coupler or hit "HOLD" on a multiline phone or "ONLINE" on a data phone. The exact scheme depends on what telephone hardware you have. Things are easier from a hardwired terminal − simply strike return or Control-d once or twice in order to get a fresh "login:" message.

Once you have established a connection the computer will type something on your terminal. If the message is

login:

or something similar, then the communication speeds (of the terminal and the computer) are synchronized and you can go ahead and enter your login name. If the message on your screen is garbled, then hit the break key on your terminal. The break causes the UNIX System to change its communication speed in an attempt to synchronize with your terminal. The UNIX System will type a fresh message. If the message is garbled, try hitting the break key again. The UNIX System usually cycles through a list of four or five speeds in order to synchronize speed with your terminal. If after four or five attempts you can't get the UNIX System to print a clear "login:" message on your terminal you should seek the help of a resident expert.

Eventually you should see the "login:" message. Enter your login name and hit return. After a brief pause the UNIX System may ask for your password. A password is a secret word that you enter in order to confirm your identity. Enter your password and hit return.

During most of your interactions with the UNIX System you will see each character that you type. However, while you are entering your password the UNIX System will try to maintain the privacy of your password by not echoing the characters that you are typing. The UNIX System is listening, but not echoing. You must type your password very carefully because you will not see it as it is entered. If you make a typing mistake you will probably have to restart the login process from the beginning.

Once you have entered your password the system checks it. If it passes inspection, then the login process will continue. If the check fails, then you will be asked to enter your login name and password again. On some systems the password system is not used. Some systems have an additional layer of security: they require you to enter a dial-up password before you are asked to enter your login name and personal password.

The UNIX System may print several messages at the end of the login process. The messages will probably divulge news about system scheduling, new programs, users meeting, and so forth. After the messages the UNIX System will print a prompt to indicate that the system is ready to accept your commands. The default prompt is usually a currency symbol ($) (or a percent symbol on older systems). You can now enter commands and interact with the UNIX System.

3.2 Some Simple Commands

The best way to learn abut the UNIX System is to use it. Type the UNIX System command

    date

and hit return. The system should display the date and time. On the line following the date the system will display a new prompt to indicate that it is ready for another command. You should always wait for a prompt before entering a UNIX System command. Throughout this book we print commands without showing the UNIX System prompt because the prompt varies from system to system and because the prompt is not part of what you type in order to run the command.

Since you always have to hit return (or newline) at the end of your command from this point forward we will refrain from mentioning it. However, whenever you enter a command you have to complete it with a carriage return or newline. Whenever we print a command in this book you should remember the carriage return (or newline) at the end of the line. We don't use the clumsy notation <CR> or <RETURN> at the end of each printed command to indicate the presence of a carriage return.

Next type the command

    who

The system should display a list of the people who are currently using the system along with the time they first logged in and the identification name of the terminal they are using. Notice that your login name is in the list. Type the command

echo hello

The system should display the message "hello". In this command the word "echo" is the name of the command and the word "hello" is an argument to the command. Arguments to commands are used to supply additional information to a command. The echo command simply repeats its arguments. Several uses for the echo command will be seen later in this book. In the UNIX System commands and their arguments (there can be several arguments) are separated by spaces or tabs. The white space (spaces or tabs) is extremely important. If you enter the command

echohello

you will get an error message.

In the UNIX System capitalization is also extremely important. The UNIX System understands that lower case letters are different from upper case letters. The names of most UNIX System commands are written in lower case. If you enter the command

Echo hello

you will get an error message because there is no command named "Echo".

Date, who, and echo are three of the most common UNIX System commands. A command is a request for the UNIX System to do something. The UNIX System dialogue usually works as shown above. Following a prompt, you type in a command followed by a return, then the UNIX System attempts to perform the command. When the UNIX System has finished running the command it displays a fresh prompt. Figure 3.1 shows the beginning of a UNIX System dialog.

3.3 Files and Directories

A file is a named collection of information. You will use numerous files in your interactions with the UNIX System. The term "file" is extremely well chosen. A computer file is completely analogous to a paper file stored in a filing cabinet. Computer files have names, they have lengths, they can get bigger and smaller, they can be created and discarded, and they can be examined.

It is impossible to exaggerate the importance of files in the UNIX System. Every time you run a program you are accessing a file. Most of the programs that you run then access more files — often files that you have mentioned on the command line.

While there may be thousands of files in a UNIX System, only a few of the files are visible at one time. In the UNIX System files are clustered into groups called directories. Each directory has a name, for example, the full name of the directory that contains most of my files is '/usa/kc'. Throughout this book the

```
login: kc
Password:
NOTICE —The system will be down
from 17:00 to 19:00 tomorrow
for routine maintenance.
Remember, monthly users meeting
this Weds at 5 pm.
% date
Weds July   5   11:08:17 EDT 1980
% who
   td        tty10      Jul 5       7:03
   kc        tty18      Jul 5       8:18
   alvy      tty11      Jul 5      11:03
   karl      tty03      Jul 5      11:03
% echo hello
hello
%
```

Figure 3.1. The first few commands in a UNIX System dialogue. In this picture of a UNIX System dialogue, the characters that are typed by the user (kc) are underlined and the computer's responses are not underlined. Remember that there is a carriage return at the end of each line.

names of files and directories are surrounded by single quotes as in '/usa/kc'. All other quoted items in this book are surrounded by double quotes. The file system is discussed in detail in Chapter 6.

One of the reasons for the login process is to establish your initial environment. One of the elements of your environment is the name of your current directory. When you first login the system makes the current directory your home directory. Each user usually has a different home directory. If your account has just been created for you, then your home directory is probably empty except for a few administrative files.

The pwd (print working directory) command will print the name of the current directory. Since different files are available in different directories, you should always be aware of the name of the current directory. Type the command

    pwd

to learn the name of the current directory. On my system the pathname '/usa/kc' is displayed on my terminal when I run the pwd command just after login. On your system the name of your own home directory will be displayed. The organization of the UNIX file system and the use of pathnames (e.g., '/usa/kc') are discussed in the next chapter. The remainder of this chapter only requires you to understand that files are grouped into units called directories.

Besides knowing the name of the current directory, you often want to know what files are in the current directory. The ls (list) command is used to list the files in a directory. Enter the command

　ls

A list of the files in the current directory will be printed. If your account has just been created, it will contain only a few (none on some systems) administrative files.

There are certain standard directories on most the UNIX Systems. The directory '/bin' usually contains many of the programs that you use. The command

　ls /bin

will display a list of the files in the '/bin' directory. Whenever you supply the name of a directory as an argument to the ls command then all of the files in that directory are listed.

The UNIX System allows you to change your context so that any accessible directory becomes the current directory. Enter the change directory command

　cd /bin

to make the directory '/bin' the current directory. (On older systems the change directory command is often called "chdir".) Now you can enter the command

　pwd

to verify that you are in a new directory.

Now that you are in the '/bin' directory you can use the command

　ls

to list all of the files in '/bin'. Remember that when you were in your home directory you had to use the argument '/bin' with the ls command in order to get this same list of files.

As you can see, the operation of some commands varies according to what directory you are in. Many people are very confused by the rather changeable UNIX System environment. Operations that work in one directory often don't work in another. You should always be aware of the name of the current directory. Once you understand the UNIX System directory structure you will see that it is an asset, not an impediment.

3.4 UNIX System Dialogues

Users engage in dialogues with the UNIX System. Typically the user enters a command and then the UNIX System replies. For simple commands the reply usually occurs in a second or so. Complicated commands can take much longer, and even simple commands can take forever when a UNIX System is seriously overloaded. We discuss the dialogue rules in some detail because the dialogue is central to working effectively with the UNIX System.

Entering a UNIX System command is analogous to submitting a job on certain other computer systems. When you enter a UNIX System command you get the computer to do something for you. For now you can imagine that the phrase "entering a command" means that the computer runs a program for you. As you learn more about the UNIX System you will realize that entering a command often involves more than just running a program, and you will begin to understand how the UNIX System environment makes the whole greater than the sum of its parts.

As a beginner you should enter just one command on a line. Later chapters will show you how to enter several commands on one line, or to run several commands at once. You enter a line of input by typing a string of characters and then hitting the carriage return key or the newline key. The carriage return (newline) specifies the end of a line of input and when you are entering commands it usually specifies the end of a command entry and tells the UNIX System to execute the command.

One difference between the computer and human listeners is that the computer virtually ignores your sentence (command) until you hit return. It is easier to talk to human listeners because they give you feedback as you talk. Another difference between computers and human listeners is that the computer is extremely picky about what you say (type). People will usually understand what you are saying even if your grammar or pronunciation is poor, but the dumb computer is stopped cold by the simplest typo. You have to be careful as you type your commands or you will spend most of your time reentering them.

Once you hit the return key the UNIX System suddenly becomes interested in what you have typed. The UNIX System immediately attempts to figure out what you want. The first word of the command is always the command name and a program called the shell attempts to locate that particular command. Let's suppose that you want to run the ls program but by mistake you enter the command

    lx

Since there is no command named "lx" you will get an error message similar to

    lx: not found

or perhaps

    sh: lx: not found

In either case the program named "sh" (the shell) is telling you that it is unable to find a command called "lx".

If the command is located, then it takes over and each particular command has its own format for telling you about errors in your input. If you wanted to list the files in the '/bin' directory but by mistake you entered the command

    ls /bum

then the ls command would tell you something like

    /bum: not found

When you make a mistake in entering the argument to a command it is the command itself that prints an error message. Although an attempt has been made to make all the UNIX System error messages uniform, you will certainly encounter some misleading messages. Your only consolation is the fact that the UNIX System is much better than most systems at flagging your erroneous input.

The characters that you type are not sent directly from the keyboard to the screen (or printing element if you use a printing terminal). Instead, the characters are sent first to the UNIX System and then back to your screen (or printhead). This rather complicated arrangement is for flexibility. The UNIX System gets each character before it is printed on your screen so that it can perform any necessary transformations. As an example the UNIX System might translate a tab character into an appropriate number of space characters. Or the UNIX System might refrain from returning characters to you at certain times such as when you are entering a private password.

As you type in your line of input, the UNIX System is spending most of its time attending to other matters. However, two special characters are attended to immediately: the erase character and the kill character. The erase character will erase the already entered characters one at a time and the kill character will erase the whole line so you can start over.

You can specify which key on your keyboard should be used for the erase character and which should be used for the kill character. On many UNIX Systems the erase character initially is assigned to the sharp key (#) and the kill character is initially the commercial at sign (@). The sharp and the at are used because they are present on most terminals and they are seldom used otherwise. If your terminal has more suitable characters, the erase and kill should be reassigned. On many terminals the Control-H key or the rubout key is used instead of the sharp as the erase character and the Control-U key is often used in place of the commercial at sign as the kill character. (A control character is formed by holding down the CTRL button and then hitting the specified character.)

On most systems the only way to correct errors during the entry of your login name and password is to use the sharp and the at because the reassignment can't occur until near the end of the internal login procedure.

Here is an example of using the erase character (assigned in this case to the default sharp):

    qgi###wgo##ho

If you follow the character sequence shown, you will see that the user actually specified the who command.

Here is an example of using the kill character (assigned in this example to the commercial at sign) to erase a mangled input line so that it can be completely retyped:

    echohello@
    echo hello

The exact appearance of a line following the entry of the kill character varies from system to system. On some systems the kill character erases the input line if you are using a display terminal. This is very hard to show in a book. On other systems the kill character automatically advances you to the next line (as shown in the example above), while on some older systems the kill character logically erases the line but there is no acknowledgment on the screen.

While you are typing a line you can use the erase character to erase portions of the line or the kill character to erase the whole line and start over. However, once you strike the return key your input cannot be altered. It is impossible to erase characters on the previous line. Make sure that your lines are typed correctly before you hit return.

Many commands perform one function and then stop. For example, a program to type a file will type the file and then be finished. Other commands work interactively. One example of an interactive command is the UNIX System text editor. The text editor interactively accepts commands from the user to form a dialogue similar to the UNIX System command dialogue that we are describing in this chapter.

While you are executing an interactive program only the commands of that program are directly available. When the interactive program terminates you return to command level and a prompt is printed to tell you that the UNIX System is ready to accept your commands. You always have to remember the context while using a computer. Once you become familiar with the system this context switching will become a reflex. When things don't work as you expect you should explicitly think about the context of the situation. Perhaps you are entering editor commands while you are in the UNIX System command mode or perhaps you are entering UNIX System commands while you are in the editor.

Occasionally you will run a program that you want to stop. In the UNIX System you stop a running program by striking the interrupt character. The interrupt character is similar to the erase and kill characters because it leads to immediate action by the system. On most newer systems the interrupt character is the delete (often labeled "DEL" on terminals), whereas the interrupt character is the Control-C on older systems. The interrupt character can be assigned to any key on your terminal.

Because certain programs must not be halted during critical sections of their operation, the UNIX System allows programs to disable the interrupt function. If a program has disabled the interrupt function, then the interrupt key will have no effect. For example, the text editor disables interrupts during most of its operation because you don't want to lose the file that you are working on by accidentally striking the interrupt key. (Those of you who understand the internal working of computer hardware should be careful not to confuse the UNIX System interrupt function with hardware interrupts.)

3.5 Logging Off

It is much easier to log off than to log on. When you are finished using the UNIX System you should log off. Logging out informs the system that you are not going to place any further demands upon the system. In a system where you are billed by the minute it is very important to log off as soon as you finish your work. In a system where computer time is "free" logging off is simply a courtesy to the other computer users.

You can log off by typing a Control-D. The Control-D is the UNIX System's end of file character. Typing an end of file character tells the UNIX System that there are no further commands to process. If you are using a dial-up terminal, the Control-D will not hang up the line. The system will print the "login:" message to indicate that it is ready to accept a new login. If you are connected to the system by a dial-up line an alternate way to log off is to hang up the phone.

3.6 The UNIX System Manual

One of the major reference documents for anyone who is using the UNIX System is the UNIX Programmer's Manual (UPM). (Some editions use the title the UNIX User's Manual.) The UPM contains information about most of the commands that are available on your system. Make sure that you have the manual that is appropriate for the version of the UNIX System that you are using. Obsolete manuals frequently are more readily available than the latest manuals.

This book is not a replacement for the UPM. The UPM contains specific information for your system and it contains specific information for many obscure commands and features that aren't discussed in this book. The strength and the weakness of the UPM is the fact that it is specific. In contrast, this book attempts to present general information that pertains to all UNIX Systems. Another function of this book is distinguish the common and useful programs from the obscure. Naturally the UPM gives equal treatment to all programs.

The UNIX System manual is designed by and for people who are familiar with the basic operation and services of the UNIX System. If you are a novice user, you will probably find that most of the descriptions in the manual are too terse to be very helpful. As you become a more advanced user, you might find that the terse style of the manual makes it more useful than a verbose manual.

Most simple commands are described adequately in the manual. For example, the reference for the pwd command in my manual states clearly:

Pwd prints the pathname of the working (current) directory.

However, the manual entries for many of the more complicated commands are much less useful for a novice. Some of the more complicated commands are described in separate documents, often in papers published in academic journals. These accounts usually are adequate descriptions for computer scientists, but often they are indecipherable for casual users.

The UPM is divided into eight sections. The first section describes most of the commands that are available on the system. Sections 2 through 8 describe aspects of the system that programmers are interested in. For the nonprogrammer Sections 2 through 8 are mere curiosities (except for Section 6 — Games).

Section 1 of the manual contains an alphabetized list of citations for the

UNIX System commands. There should be a citation in Section 1 for most commands that are available at your installation. Commands that are unique to your installation, such as graphics commands at a graphics laboratory, are often described in a locally distributed addendum to the manual. Some UNIX Systems are created by acquiring programs from a variety of sources. The manual for these systems probably is inadequate.

Closely related commands are occasionally discussed in a single citation. In my UPM, the mv (move), cp (copy), and ln (link) commands are all discussed in a single citation because they all shuffle files. If you can't remember the exact name of a command, you should try looking up any related word in the permuted index. For example, you could look up the word "move" in the permuted index in order to discover that the cp citation describes how to copy, link, or move files. The permuted index in the UPM is similar to the keyword in context index used by some abstracting services and scholarly journals.

Each citation in Section 1 of the UPM follows a fairly uniform format. The top of the citation shows the name and a brief description followed by a synopsis of the command. For the ls command the top of the citation looks like

NAME
       ls - list contents o f directories
SYNOPSIS
       ls [-ltasdriu] names

The synopsis gives you an indication of how you would enter the command. The synopsis for ls indicates that you enter the word "ls" optionally followed by a list of options (one or more of the characters "ltasdriu") followed by a list of names of directories or files. Square brackets in the synopsis indicate that the bracketed quantity is optional.

The description of the command usually follows the synopsis. For the ls command, the description is a little more than a page long. The description of a command usually describes the basic operation of the command and how you can alter the basic operation by using various options. For example, the ls command has options that allow you to display additional information along with the list of file names.

After the description are several brief paragraphs: the FILES paragraph names any files that are used by the program, the SEE ALSO paragraph lists related commands whose citations might contain useful information, the BUGS paragraph might contain some useful caveats, and the DIAGNOSTICS paragraph might help you to decipher error messages. Any or all of these four paragraphs may be omitted. The entire citation for most commands is about a page long.

The citations in Sections 2 through 8 follow a similar format that should be understandable by anyone who needs to use these sections. They will not be discussed here. Remember that as a novice you should use only Section 1 of the manual. The description of the system calls in Section 2 will not help you use the similarly named commands described in Section 1.

CHAPTER

4

The UNIX System Shell

Computers are very good at performing operations at great speed, but they have no sense of value. The computer cannot distinguish between useful work and idle cycling. Since computers have no initiative they must be told exactly what they should do. Occasionally someone writes a program that makes it appear that a computer has initiative but in reality the computer is a sloth.

People have developed command languages to make it easier to control a computer. Most command languages are designed so that there are easy commands to specify common operations. Commands specify exactly what programs the computer should execute.

Computers do not have an innate ability to decipher the commands that you type at the terminal. Most operating systems provide a command interpreter to perform this function. The standard command interpreter in the UNIX System is called the shell. To use the UNIX System effectively you have to know how to enter commands. The shell provides a wealth of features that make it possible to specify very powerful commands. It is possible to use the UNIX System with only a slight knowledge of the shell. However, using the UNIX System will be much more rewarding if you learn about the shell. For those of you who want to learn a lot about the shell there are several more chapters which discuss shell programming and other advanced features. This chapter presents the shell at a level that can benefit all users.

4.1 Simple Shell Commands

A simple command is a sequence of (one or more) words separated by blanks or tabs. The first word of the command specifies the command's name. Subsequent words specify the command's arguments. (You should remember from Chapter 3 that arguments are used to pass additional information to a command.) The simplest simple command is a single word. The ps (process status) command will print a list of the programs that you are currently running.

Enter the command

>   ps

and observe the output. Unless you have done something unusual the output on your system will be similar to the output on my system:

PID	TTY	TIME	CMD
136	53	0:18	-sh
15390	53	0:04	ps

The first column shows you the process identification number, the second column shows the identification number of your terminal, the third column shows the cumulative execution time of the command, and the final column shows the command name. The ps command output shown above reveals two current processes, -sh and ps. The UNIX System shell program -sh was automatically started for you at the end of the login procedure and the ps program was explicitly started by you when you entered the ps command.

You can enter several commands on one line by separating the commands with semicolons. This feature is useful when you know in advance the sequence of programs that you are going to run. If you wanted to know the name of the current directory and what files are in the current directory, you might run the pwd program followed by the ls program:

>   pwd ; ls

When you enter two commands on a single line the shell runs the programs in quick succession, first pwd and then ls. An equivalent form of the command is

>   pwd;ls

since you don't have to put spaces around the shell's special characters.

4.2 Command Arguments

In Chapter 3 we mentioned arguments to commands. Arguments are used to pass additional information to a program. It would be silly to write a program that performed some function (e.g., displaying a file on your terminal) for only one particular file. Instead programs are written to provide general services.

The ps command that we used in the first example in this chapter didn't require any arguments since we wanted to use the standard function of ps. You can modify the operation of ps by supplying an argument specifying a long listing. A long listing prints more information about each process. Arguments that alter the operation of a command are often called flags or options. On some other operating systems the options are called switches or controls. You can get a long listing of your processes by using the option argument "-l" with ps:

>   ps -l

The name of the command and the argument must be separated by one or more spaces or tabs. (If you omit the separator then you will get an error message stating "ps-l: not found".)

You should still see two processes but more information will be printed for each process. In the UNIX System it is customary to insert a hyphen in front of option arguments. (A few commands ignore the custom.)

Arguments to commands often specify file names. The UNIX System cat program (cat is derived from the word concatenate, which means to combine) can be used to display a file on your terminal. You specify which file by using an argument or arguments . (Other uses of cat are discussed in Section 8.2.) The simplest use of cat is to print a single file on the terminal. The command

```
cat /etc/motd
```

will type the message-of-the-day file on your terminal.

When you enter the command "cat /etc/motd" the shell performs a variety of functions. The command consists of two words, "cat" and "/etc/motd". First the shell makes sure that there is a command named "cat". Then the shell performs a series of interpretations on the words following the command name. Following the interpretations (more on that in Section 4.8) the total list of words in the command is passed to the program and the program is started.

The first word of a command is called the command name. The following words of a command are the arguments. (Some people prefer to call the command name the zeroeth argument because it sits in front of the numbered arguments 1, 2, 3, etc.) Words in a command are separated by spaces or tabs. A quoted word can contain spaces or tabs. For example " "the end" " is a single word consisting of the seven characters "t" through "d" (including one space). Quoting is discussed in Section 13.5.

The shell knows nothing about the particular arguments that specific programs need. In the example given above, the shell doesn't make sure that the word "/etc/motd" references a file. However, the cat program expects that its arguments do in fact reference files and it is an error to supply an argument to cat that doesn't reference a file. The shell is responsible for passing the argument list to the program, but the program is responsible for making sure that the arguments are reasonable.

4.3 Background Processes

Sometimes you need to run programs that take a long time to finish. If the program doesn't require input from the terminal, then you can run it unattended. The shell has a special feature that enables you to start a program and then let it run unattended while you continue to enter shell commands. The program that is running unattended is said to be running in the background while the subsequent commands that you enter are running in the foreground. The background processes and the foreground process are running simultaneously. Normally the shell executes your commands sequentially. However, if you place an ampersand after a command then the shell will start the program in the background and immediately prompt you to enter another command.

Suppose you want to run a time-consuming program called acctxx. Presumably the acctxx program takes a long time to run, so you might prefer to do something else while it is working. The exact function of acctxx is not important for this example. If you enter the command

    acctxx &

the shell will start the acctxx program running in the background, print the process identification number of actxx, and then immediately return to you for another command. If acctxx produces output that is sent to the terminal, then there will be ample evidence that acctxx is really running. However, if acctxx places its output in a file, then you might prefer to see some evidence that actxx is actually running. If you enter the command

    ps

you will get a list of your processes on your terminal. On my system the following was output:

PID	TTY	TIME	CMD
136	53	0:39	-sh
15388	53	0:14	acctxx
15390	53	0:04	ps

Notice that three programs are running instead of the two that were shown in the previous example. Here the acctxx program and the ps program are running simultaneously. From the ordinary output of the ps command there is no way to distinguish the background process from the foreground process. (The long format output of ps allows you to deduce which processes are in the foreground and which are in the background.)

You shouldn't run a program in the background if it requires input from the terminal because both the background program and the shell will be fighting for access to the terminal. It is possible to run a background process that sends voluminous output to the terminal, but it is very awkward because the output is interspersed with the normal foreground output messages.

This brings up a very interesting point. While you are entering a command the shell is clearly running in the foreground. What happens to the shell while your command is running? In the UNIX System it is possible for a program to go to sleep while waiting for a certain event. When you enter a normal foreground command the shell sleeps during the execution of the command. When the command completes the shell wakes up and prompts you for another command. The sleeping shell and the executing command are both foreground tasks, but they don't fight over the terminal because the shell sleeps while the command executes. (Incidentally, the terms sleep, wait, and wakeup are all UNIX System terms. The UNIX System jargon is usually quite descriptive.)

Another way to start the acctxx program in the background and then run the ps command in the foreground is to enter the command

    acctxx & ps

After ps finishes the shell will prompt you for a command. Acctxx will still be running in the background. There is usually a limit to the number (often 20) of background processes that you can have running simultaneously.

4.4 The Standard Output and the Standard Input

The computer terminal is the basic communication device between the computer and the users. The UNIX System makes it very easy to access the computer terminal because most utility programs produce output on the terminal and many read input from the terminal. When a program types something on your terminal, the program is (usually) performing output operations to what is called the standard output. When you type at your terminal a program is (usually) reading your typed characters from what is called the standard input. The standard input and the standard output are UNIX System conventions that simplify programs. (The qualifier "usually" is used in definitions of the standard input and output because it is possible to access the terminal without using the standard input and output. However, the great majority of programs do use the standard input and output.)

For example, programs such as ps, ls, who, date, pwd, and echo use the standard output to deliver their information to you. Interactive programs (e.g., the shell and the editor) read your commands from the standard input and write their responses on the standard output. Standardization in the UNIX System and elsewhere is a key to increased convenience and productivity.

4.5 Output Redirection

The standard input and output are normally attached to the computer terminal. However, since the standard input and output are established by the shell it is

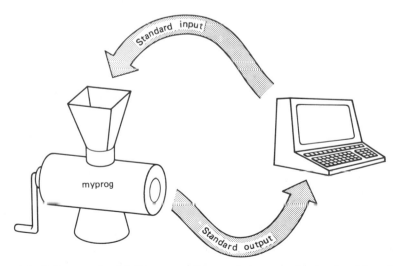

Figure 4.1. The standard I/O connections. A program's standard input and output usually are assigned to the terminal.

possible for the standard input and output to be reassigned by the shell. The shell's ability to reassign the standard input and output is one of the UNIX System's most important features.

Let's suppose that you want to save the output of the ps command in a file. If you enter the command

   ps

the process status program will write its information on the standard output – your terminal. However, if you enter the command

   ps > posterity

the results will be a little different because the standard output is redirected. The process status program will still write its information to the standard output, but because of the special notation ">posterity" the shell will connect the standard output to the ordinary file named 'posterity'. You won't see the output on your screen. The ">" is a special shell character specifying that the standard output of the command should be directed to the file indicated by the next word in the command. The command could also have been entered

   ps>posterity

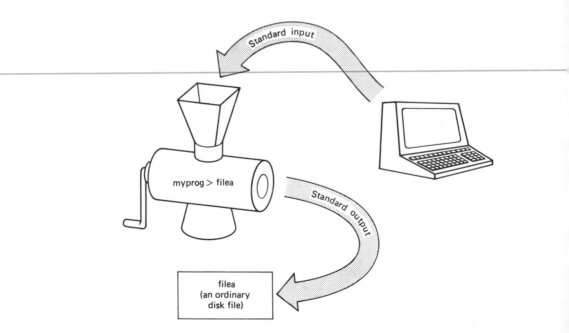

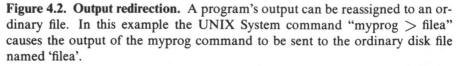

Figure 4.2. Output redirection. A program's output can be reassigned to an ordinary file. In this example the UNIX System command "myprog > filea" causes the output of the myprog command to be sent to the ordinary disk file named 'filea'.

because you don't have to surround the shell's special characters with spaces or tabs. In either case the file 'posterity' will contain the text that normally would have been typed on your terminal. You can verify this by typing the command

  cat posterity

Normal output redirection completely overwrites the output file. In the example given above the file 'posterity' would be overwritten and any previous contents would be lost. Occasionally you want to direct output to a file, but you want the output to be added to the end of the file. The command

  ps>>ps.logfile

will append the output of the ps command to the end of the file 'ps.logfile'. You could achieve the same results with a series of commands (ps>temp1;cat ps.logfile temp1>temp2;mv temp2 ps.logfile;rm temp1), but it is much simpler to enter the command as shown.

4.6 Input Redirection

The standard input can also be redirected. Thus far, the only program we have encountered that reads information from the standard input is the shell. The other programs we have used (ls, who, ps and pwd) all produce output without reading from the standard input. The shell normally reads commands from the standard input, that is, the shell reads commands that you type at the terminal. Since the standard input can be redirected, it is possible to have the shell acquire its commands from an ordinary file.

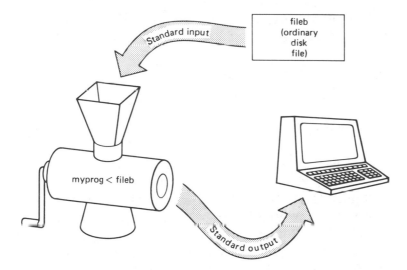

Figure 4.3. Input redirection. A program's input can be reassigned by the shell. In this example the UNIX System command "myprog < fileb" causes the myprog command to acquire input from the file named 'fileb'.

Suppose the file 'shellcommands' contains the following three lines:

```
ps
who
ls
```

(The file 'shellcommands' can be created using a text editor; see Chapter 5.) The file 'shellcommands' contains three familiar shell commands that you could enter at the terminal. If you often need to run these three commands, rather than typing the commands each time it might be easier to put the commands in a file and let the shell read the commands from the file. The shell is just an ordinary program that reads commands from its standard input. If we type the command sh we will execute another copy of the shell that reads commands from the standard input. However, if we redirect the input of the new shell we can force it to read commands from the file rather than from the terminal. The following command would create a new copy of the shell with input redirected from the file 'shellcommands':

```
sh < shellcommands
```

The output of this new shell, and the output of all of the commands that it runs, is directed to the terminal. When the shell reaches the end of the file 'shellcommands' it will exit and return control to your interactive shell. (Other methods for executing a shell command file are discussed in Section 13.1.)

When I entered the preceding command on my system, the output of the ps, the output of the who command, and the output of the ls command were displayed on my terminal. Then my interactive shell prompted me to enter another command. We've already seen the output of who and ls so there is no reason to discuss them further here. However, the output of the ps command is quite interesting. On my system the following information was displayed:

PID	TTY	TIME	CMD
136	53	0:39	-sh
14248	53	0:02	sh
14250	53	0:04	ps

Let's discuss each of the information lines that was output by ps.

1. The first line of the ps output details the information for a process called "-sh". The hyphen in front of "sh" is a clue that the shell was started as part of the login procedure. This is the interactive shell that I was using during my session with the UNIX System.

2. The second line of the ps output details the information for a process called "sh". This is the shell that we started in order to execute the commands from the file 'shellcommands'.

3. The third line of the ps output consists of a process identification number followed by the name "ps". Since the process status program is running at

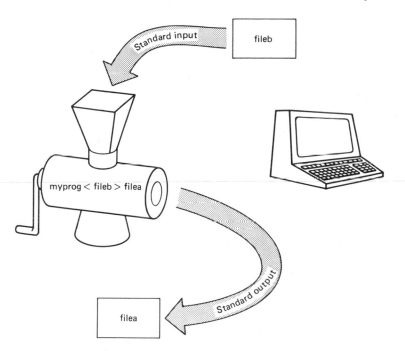

Figure 4.4. Input and output redirection. Both the input and the output can be reassigned simultaneously, as in this example where the command "myprog < fileb > filea" causes the output to be assigned to 'filea' and the input to be assigned to 'fileb'.

the time it determines the process status, it is one of the entries in the process list. In our case, the parent of ps is the shell that we explicitly initiated and the parent of the explicit shell is the login initiated shell.

The commands who and ls aren't mentioned in the output of ps because they haven't started to execute.

The procedure mentioned above is not the only way for the shell to process commands that are stored in a file. However, the other methods reflect specific capabilities that are built into the shell rather than the general ability to redirect input and output. The alternate methods are discussed in Section 13.1.

4.7 Pipes

A pipe connects the standard output of one program to the standard input of another program. A pipe is different from I/O redirection. Output redirection writes the output of a program onto a file and input redirection causes a file to contain the input for a program, whereas a pipe directly connects the output of one program with the input of another program.

Let's suppose we want to know how many files are in my home directory ('/usa/kc'). Perhaps the most obvious method would be to run the ls command

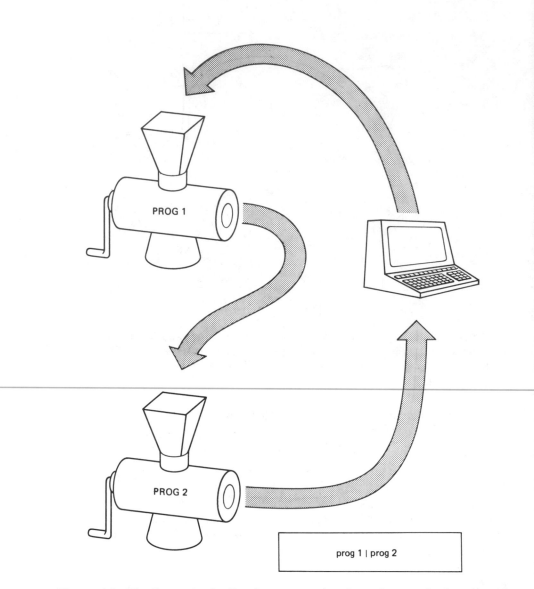

prog 1 | prog 2

Figure 4.5. Pipelines. A pipeline is a connection from the standard output of one command to the standard output of another command. In this example the command "prog1 | prog2" causes the output of the command prog1 to be sent as input to the command prog2. Pipelines can involve more than two stages, although only two stages are seen in this example.

and count the number of files that are listed on the terminal. For a directory with only a handful of files this might work but for a crowded directory the simple method is unattractive. Fortunately, the UNIX System contains a command for counting words (and lines and chararacters) called wc (see Section 8.5). Using ls we can generate a list of files in the '/usa/kc' directory, and using wc we can count the number of words in a list. It seems we have the basic tools for discovering how many files are in my home directory, but how can we combine these tools to work together? As with most work in the UNIX System, there are at least two reasonable methods. Let's explore both methods.

The first method will use the I/O redirection technique of the previous section and the second method will use a special UNIX System facility called a pipeline.

1. I/O Redirection Technique
   Method: Redirect the output of the ls program so that the list of files is saved in a temporary file. Then use wc to count the number of lines in the temporary file. (The -l option makes wc count lines.) Finally remove the temporary file. These actions are performed by the following three commands.

   ```
   ls /usa/kc > tempfile
   wc -l tempfile
   rm tempfile
   ```

2. Pipelines
   Method: Pipe the output of ls to wc. The special shell notation for a pipeline connection is a vertical bar ("|") or a caret ("^"). The following command pipes the output of ls to the input of wc:

   ```
   ls /usa/kc | wc -l
   ```

As you see, the pipeline method is simpler. Although the I/O redirection method works, it has some unpleasant side effects. If you don't have permission to create files in the current directory you won't be able to execute the "ls /usa/kc > tempfile" command because the command creates and writes to 'tempfile'. (Since the shell has to create tempfile and redirect the standard output to it before the ls program can run, the tempfile will be one of the files in the list of files if the current directory is '/usa/kc'. Therefore the count of files may be one too large.)

A pipeline is a connection between the standard output of one program and the standard input of another program. In the pipeline example shown above the ls program creates a list of files in the '/usa/kc' directory and that list is then passed to the wc program. The wc program counts the number of words in the list and then outputs the count to the standard output, the terminal. All that you see is the final count, not the intermediate list generated by ls.

Figure 4.6. I/O redirection and pipelines. It is possible to combine input and output redirection with pipelines. In this example the command "prog1 < file1 | prog2 > file2" assigns the input of prog1 to 'file1', and the output of prog2 to 'file2' and connects the output of prog1 to the input of prog2.

Pipelines make many procedures conceptually easier. Since each program in a pipeline can concentrate on one aspect of a task, it is possible to write coherent, unified programs. It would be very awkward to write the ls program so that it could perform all conceivable operations on its output. The ls program concentrates on listing files and the wc program concentrates on counting. In the UNIX System you can create a new function that counts the number of files in a directory by connecting ls to wc by using a pipe.

Many of the text file utilities (Chapter 8) can be used in a pipeline with ls in order to augment the capabilities of the ls command. It would not be reasonable to build all of these capabilities into the ls program, but all of these capabilities are built into the UNIX System via the pipe mechanism. You should note that if ls is part of a pipeline, then it is always the first element. Since ls does not acquire information from the standard input, there is no way to deliver information to ls via a pipe.

Wc is a typical example of a text manipulation program that can perform processing on files named as arguments (the command "wc -l tempfile" in the previous example) or on text supplied via the standard input (the command "ls | wc -l" in the previous example). This flexibility is one of the most powerful features of the UNIX System.

4.8 Metacharacters and File Name Generation

Most of the command line arguments that you supply to programs are file names. It is very common to name files so that related files have related names. For example, all C-language program names end with the suffix ".c". All of the chapters of a book might be stored in a series of files named 'chap1', 'chap2', and so on. If you wanted to perform some operation on all of the C-language files in a directory, it would be very tedious to type in all of the names as arguments on a command line.

In order to avoid tedium, the UNIX System allows you to specify sets of file names automatically. When you enter the arguments to a command, the shell examines your arguments to see if you are using the file name generation shorthand. You control file name generation by specifying a model for the file names. The shell compares your model to all of the file names in the current directory. If any of the file names match the model, then the alphabetized list of matching file names is delivered to the program. If none of the file names in the directory matches the model, then the unchanged model is delivered to the program.

A model consists of ordinary characters and metacharacters. The ordinary characters stand for themselves while the metacharacters have special meanings. A model that consists entirely of ordinary characters (e.g., "myfile") doesn't invoke file name generation.

You need to learn about the file name generation process because it can occur every time you enter a command. The least that you can safely know is the fact that file name generation occurs and that you should not use the metacharacters "*", "?", and the square braces in your file names. As a next step you should master the metacharacters "*" and "?" because they are really quite simple to use and you should know how to turn off the special meanings of the metacharacters. If you really want to use the UNIX System as a master, then learn about character classes.

Most of the UNIX System documents use the phrase regular expression to refer to what I am calling a model. I prefer the term model because it lends a nice intuitive perception to the confusing topic of file name generation. In some other operating systems the phrase wild card is used to refer to the special characters that control the file name generation process.

The following metacharacters are used to control file name generation on most UNIX Systems:

```
*    Matches any character string
?    Matches any single character
[    Introduces a character group
]    Terminates a character group
-    Indicates a character range
```

The asterisk and question mark metacharacters are very easy to use. An asterisk will match any string of characters, including the null string. Thus the model "*.c" will match the file name '.c' or 'a.c' or 'aaaaaaaa.c' but not the file name 'a.ca'.

A question mark will match any single character. Thus the model "??.c" will match the file name 'ab.c' or '77.c' but not 'a.c' or 'abc.c' or 'bc.cc'.

Square brackets and hyphens are used to form models for groups of characters. The characters in the group are enclosed by the brackets. The model "abc[aeiou]" will match any file name that starts with the string "abc" and ends with a single vowel. The hyphen can be used inside a pair of square brackets to indicate a range of characters. The model "def[0-9]" will match any file name whose first three characters are "def" and whose fourth and final character is a numeral. The range is inclusive (both zero and nine are included in the example above) and is defined by the numerical sequence of the ASCII character set.

The hyphen loses its role as a metacharacter when it is used outside of the square brackets. The asterisk and the question mark lose their power as metacharacters when they are used within the square brackets. In the model "-[*?]abc" only the square brackets are active metacharacters. Thus the model "-[*?]abc" would match exactly two file names: '-*abc' and '-?abc'.

Sometimes the power of the shell is a valuable asset and you want to use its special features such as metacharacters, I/O redirection, pipelines, and background execution. However, at other times the special shell characters used to control these functions are needed for more mundane operations. If you explicitly want any one of the special shell character to lose its power you can precede it with a backslash character. Thus the command

    ls **

will output a list of all of the files in the current directory whose names end with an asterisk.

Another way to remove the power from special shell characters is quoting. The model "answers\?" matches the file named 'answers?' but not the file named 'answers1'. Of course the model "answers?" would match both 'answers?' and 'answers1'. If both 'answers1' and 'answers?' are text files in the current directory, then the command

    ls answers?

will list both files while the command

    ls "answers?"

will only list the file 'answers?'. You can also use the command

    ls answers\?

to list only the file 'answers?'. When there is only one special character that needs to be escaped it is easier to escape it with a backslash, but when there are several then quoting is usually easier. Quoting is discussed more thoroughly in Section 13.5.

The role of metacharacters is not the only thing you should understand about the shell's file name generation procedure. When the shell compares the model strings to the file names, any leading period in a file name must be matched explicitly. So if you have a file named '.invisible', the model "*visible" will not match. The model name ".*visible" will match the file name '.invisible'. The model name ".*" will match all of the file names that begin with a period.

Another aspect of file name generation that many people find confusing is the fact that slash characters in a pathname must be matched explicitly. A pathname is a path from directory to directory that leads to a file. The name '/etc/motd' mentioned earlier is a simple pathname which leads from the '/etc' directory to the file 'motd'. Pathnames will be discussed in detail in Section 6.4.

The metacharacters are used only to generate file names within a directory. The model "/etc*.c" would not match the files with the ".c" suffix in the '/etc' directory. However, the model "/etc/*.c" would match those files. This restriction on explicitly matching the slash characters in a pathname is basically sensible because the current directory is the default environment unless you explicitly state otherwise.

Let's suppose that the current directory contains the following files:

ch1	ch2	ch3	ch4
33.doc	abc	ab.c	ch3.a

The command

    ls ch*

will list the following files: 'ch1', 'ch2', 'ch3', 'ch3.a', and 'ch4'. Notice that the list is alphabetized because file name generation occurs alphabetically.

The command

    ls *3*

will list the following files: '33.doc', 'ch3', and 'ch3.a'. Notice that the asterisk can stand for a sequence of zero or more characters.

The command

   ls ch?

will list the following files: 'ch1', 'ch2', 'ch3', and 'ch4'. Since a question mark always matches exactly one character 'ch3.a' is omitted.

The command

   ls ch[2-9]

will list the following files: 'ch2', 'ch3', and 'ch4'. The file 'ch1' is omitted because "1" isn't in the range "2-9" and 'ch3.a' is omitted because of the trailing ".a".

Here's one for the masters. The command

   ls ch[0-15]

will list the file 'ch1'. Although the character class appears to include the numerals zero to fifteen, it actually contains just three characters: "0", "1", and "5". You should remember that a character class is formed from a group of characters. The sequence "15" looks like the number fifteen but in a character class it is simply two characters.

4.9 Conclusions

Using the UNIX System effectively is equivalent to understanding the basic operation of the shell. You should know how to run a normal foreground process and how to run a background process. You should also understand the idea of command line arguments and you should understand the search procedure that the shell follows in order to locate your commands. I/O redirection and pipelines are essential for everyone — why use the UNIX System without using its strongest features? Everyone should at least be aware of file name generation. Learn to use file name generation if you want to get the most out of the UNIX System.

These few topics are just a small fraction of the power of the shell. However, for people who use the shell as an interactive command interpreter the topics presented in this chapter are enough to use the UNIX System productively. The shell is one of the most impressive features of the UNIX System so for those of you that want to know more there are several more chapters on the shell.

CHAPTER

5

The UNIX System Editor

In order to do anything useful computers need information. In general you (or somebody) enters information and then the computer performs some mystifying feat and then information is handed back to you. The first step — information entry — is often the most painful.

Computers acquire information from many sources. Sometimes computers acquire information from other computers. This is ideal for distributing information, but no new information ever emerges. In many applications information is collected automatically, as in the cash registers that remember each item of each sale and the banking machines that keep track of transactions as they accept and disburse funds. Computers in laboratories often are attached directly to experimental apparatus, and these computers acquire their information automatically as experiments progress.

When you can't get your information into a computer automatically you have to enter it by hand. The easiest and most general way to store information in a computer is to place it in a text file. A text editor is a program that you use to enter and examine information in text files. Text editing is extremely important because it is the primary method of information entry for most UNIX System users. If you use the UNIX System for a single specific function, you might avoid text editing, but for most users text editing is central.

We can imagine a text editor program that acts just like a typewriter, no more features, no less. Let's use the name "ugh" for our hypothetical text editor program. Ugh accepts text as you type it and places it in a file. The ugh program cannot modify previous text, and it does not allow you to move text or delete text or acquire text from other documents. The main advantage of ugh is simplicity; it does not contain a large repertoire of commands that you have to master.

Virtually all text editing programs do a lot more than our hypothetical ugh text editor. However, as text editing programs acquire more features they become harder to use. Most UNIX System text editing programs allow you to move text, add text, delete text, and acquire text from other text files. You can replace one word (or part of a word) with another in one location or throughout a section of a file or throughout an entire file. You can also browse through a text file, printing all of the lines in one section of the file, printing all of the lines that contain a particular word, and so on. However, in order to use a powerful text editor you have to devote some time to understanding the editor.

The text editor is an interactive program. You direct the editor by entering commands. Editor commands allow you to add text to the file or change text that has already been entered. Like the shell dialogue, the editor dialogue consists of your commands followed by the editing program's responses.

Unfortunately there is no standard UNIX System editor. (Throughout this chapter an "editor" is a program for editing text.) Every different UNIX System that I have used has had a unique set of text editors. Yes, a different set. Most UNIX Systems have several text editors available. For the purpose of this book let's divide the editors into two categories, those that are related to or similar to the UNIX System editor and those that mimic some other family of text editing programs. This chapter describes the UNIX System editor and its relatives and imitators; the other editors are ignored here.

One reason for the variety of editors is that many universities have implemented changes to the UNIX System including changes to the editors. The major improvement offered by some of these editors is visual editing, which will be discussed at the end of Chapter 10.

This chapter introduces the basic commands that you should master in order to use a text editor. If you are going to do a lot of text editing, it would probably be valuable to learn to use all of the features of your text editor. Chapter 10 presents some advanced features that apply to most editors, and the reference manual for your system describes any unique features of your editor. The hardest part is learning the basics. Once you understand a few commands the rest is easy.

The first few sections of this chapter introduce some of the general concepts that you need in order to use a text editor. If you have used text editors previously, then skip to Section 5.3.

5.1 Text Files

A byte is a binary number which can contain one of 256 different values. In the UNIX System a file is a sequence of bytes. When the bytes in a file contain all of the 256 possible values we say that the file is a binary file. ASCII (American Standard Code for Information Interchange) is standard method of coding text using about 100 different values. Files whose bytes contain only the ASCII codes are called text files.

Text files are used to store many types of information. The following three general categories include most of the common uses of text files:

1. Documents

   Documents such as letters, manuals, manuscripts, and books can be stored in ordinary text files. Computer-assisted document preparation is advantageous because the text has to be entered only once; changes can be made in the document without reentering the whole document. In addition, the computer can be used to check spelling and grammar, to generate indexes, and to catalog versions and revisions. The file 'letter-to-john' is an example of a document stored in a text file:

   Dear John,

      Feel free to come over
   and use the system any
   time after 5 pm next week.

      Susan

2. Program Source Code

   Computer programs are written in languages that are designed to allow people to express logical solutions. Programs are created as text files that contain the program's instructions. The file 'me.c' contains the C-language source code instructions for a program which prints the message "I am a C-language program".

   ```
   main()
   { printf("I  am  a  C-language  program \ n");  }
   ```

3. Text Data

   Simple lists of data are often stored in ordinary text files. Here is a text file named 'groceries', which contains a short list of grocery items:

   ```
   yams
   eggs  (half  dozen)
   half  pound  of  gruyere
   Alpo
   ```

   The grocery list is stored in a text file because it is just a short list of items and the easiest way to store it in a computer is in a text file. The grocery list for the United States Army is probably not stored in a text file because it is too big and complicated.

This list of uses of text files is just intended to give you a feeling for the types of things that are stored in text files. Of course the grocery list could be part of a document describing the eating habits of modern Americans, and the C-language program could be (and is) part of a book on the UNIX System. There are no firm distinctions between documents, program sources, and lists of data.

There are many situations where information is not stored in a text file. Text files waste space because only about 100 of the 256 possible values for each byte in the file are used. In situations where you know a lot about the format of the information (e.g., a check processing system, an accounting system, an airline reservation system, or a data-base retrieval system) you often use more efficient coding techniques. When information must be stored compactly or retrieved quickly it is usually stored in a binary file.

5.2 Line Editing

A text file is divided into elements called lines. The lines in a text file correspond exactly to your intuitive understanding of a line. To put it simply, a line of a text file is the amount of a text file that usually appears across one row of a computer terminal. Occasionally a text file contains a line that is too long to fit on your terminal. Some terminals fail to display the end of overly long lines while other terminals wrap-around and display the end of the line on the next row of the screen. Although there is no firm rule, lines are almost never longer than 256 characters .

Most UNIX System text editors are called "line editors" because they operate on lines of text. If you were editing some text using paper and pencil techniques, you would always be focusing your attention on some particular part of the text. The same idea is true for editing text with a computer. When you are editing a text file, there is always a "current line." The current line is the area of the text that will usually be affected by the editing commands.

In a line editor it is possible to change a single character of the file, but only by specifying the line of the file that contains the character and then specifying the change. Although this seems to be a lot of effort for a small result, you will see that it is easy and natural to work with the constraints built into line editing.

The other types of interactive editing are character editing and visual editing. In a character editor you move a character pointer through the file character by character. All changes are made relative to the current position of the character pointer. Character editors are very powerful but often hard to use. TECO (Text Editor and Corrector) is probably the best known character editor.

Visual editors can be used only with video display terminals. A visual editor provides a window into a text file. The screen constantly contains an up-to-date picture of the text in the window. A cursor is a small (often blinking) underline or box on a video terminal which indicates the current screen position. A visual editor is simple to use because the video terminal's cursor can be positioned on the screen with easy cursor positioning commands and then changes can be made relative to the cursor's position on the screen.

A visual editor requires a lot of communication from the computer to the terminal. A simple change can cause the entire screen to be updated. If simple changes lead to long delays while you wait for the screen to be redrawn, then the editor becomes unpleasant to use. Visual editors aren't very useful for terminals that are connected to the computer over telephone lines because of the low rate of data transmission over a telephone line. However, when terminals are connected directly to the computer by a high bandwidth (high data transmission rate) system visual editing is wonderful.

Besides the requirement of communication bandwidth, visual editors consume a lot of computer power. When an editing change leads to a complicated display change the processor must do a lot of work. Many UNIX System installations discourage or prohibit visual editing because of the heavy demands it places upon the system. However, the heavy demands a visual editor places on the computer are balanced by the minimal demands that a visual editor puts on the human operator. Visual editors are very pleasant because they are easy to use.

5.3 Starting the Editor

In order to start the UNIX System text editor you must be logged onto a UNIX system. The editor is started by typing its name followed by the name of a file that you want to edit. For example, the shell command

    ed firstsession

directs the shell to invoke the text editor named ed to edit the file named 'firstsession'. If you have never worked with the file 'firstsession', then the editor will create the file for you. Once you have entered the command the contents of the file are immediately available for editing. The current line is set to the last line in the file and the editor is ready to accept your commands.

When the editor is running you should enter only editor commands. During your session using the editor the shell commands are not directly available. Your last editor command (unless you hang up the phone or the computer crashes) will be to stop the editor and return to the shell. When the editor finishes executing the shell will prompt you to enter another shell command. You have to remember to enter editor commands while the editor is running and shell commands during your dialogue with the shell.

After a little practice you will be able to switch from shell command mode to editor mode with little trouble. Changing modes is natural; don't most of us behave one way at home and another way at work and another way on vacation?

While you are using the editing program you are working with a copy of the file, not the file itself. If you make a major mistake, the original file is still available. However, since you are working with a copy of the file you have to remember to update the original file at the end of the editing session. If you forget to update the original file, the editor will remind you as you attempt to exit from the editor.

The editor has two modes of operation, command mode and text-entry mode. In command mode the editor is waiting for you to enter commands. Anything that you type in command mode will be interpreted as an editor command. Editor commands can change lines, print lines, read or write disk files, or initiate text-entry mode. In text-entry mode the editor is waiting for you to enter lines of text. Anything that you type in text-entry mode will be added to the file. You can leave text-entry mode and reenter command mode by entering a line of text that consists of single period.

When you are in command mode all of the lines that you type are interpreted as editor commands; when you are in text-entry mode all of the lines that you type are added to the file. You should always be very careful to remember which mode you are in. The most common problem for beginners using the editor is entering commands in the text-entry mode or entering text in the command mode.

5.4 Basic Editing Commands

The following sections in this chapter introduce the basic editing commands. (See Figure 5.1.) A mastery of these commands will enable you to use the editor; serious users of the editor should also know the commands in Chapter 10, "Advanced Editing." You should also examine the local documents for your editor to find out about any commands that are unique to your installation.

All of the editor commands are invoked by entering a single character mnemonic. Most commands refer to either a specific line or range of lines in the file. For example the "p" command can print one or more lines in the file. If you enter the command

    20p

you will print the twentieth line in the file. Lines 20 through 30 can be printed by using the command

    20,30p

The period is a special editor symbol denoting the current line. If you enter the command

    .p

you will print the current line of text. The same effect will occur if you enter the command

    p

because the default line for the print command is the current line.

5.5 Adding Text to the Working File

The append command ("a") is used to change the editor from command mode to input mode. When you are in command mode every line that you type is assumed to be an editor command. When you enter the append command the

Commands That Don't Use Addresses

q   Quit the editor. The working file is NOT automatically written out to the permanent disk file.

w   Write the working file out to the permanent disk file.

Commands That Use One Address †

.a   Enter input mode; the new text is placed after the addressed line. Once you are in input mode everything that you type will be added to the working file. You can leave input mode by typing a period alone on a line.

.i   The insert command causes you to enter input mode; the added text is placed before the current line.

$=   Print the line number of the addressed line.

Commands That Use Two Addresses † †

.,.c   The change command deletes the addressed lines and then the editor is placed in input mode; the input text is put in the file in place of the deleted text.

.,.d   The addressed lines are deleted from the working file.

.,.l   The list command prints the addressed lines unambiguously. All of the control characters are printed using escape codes.

.,.m a   The move commands moves the addressed lines after the line addressed by a.

.,.t a   The transfer command places a copy of the addressed lines after the line addressed by a.

.,.p   The addressed lines are printed.

.,.s/regexp/replacement/
     The substitute command replaces the text pattern that matches the regular expression with the replacement text on the addressed lines.

1,$w   The addressed lines are written to the permanent file.

---

† The default line address is shown: 1 is the first line in the text buffer, "." is the current line, and "$" is the last line.

† † The default addresses are shown.

Figure 5.1. The Basic Editing Commands.

assumption changes: every line is assumed to be text which is added to the working file. The command

    a

will put the editor in input mode. All subsequent lines that are typed will be added to the text file until a line containing a lone period is entered:

The append command is difficult because it causes the editor to change mode. Suddenly everything you type is interpreted differently. One of the most common errors is entering editor commands in input mode or entering text in command mode. If things seem funny, you should try entering a period alone on a line. If you are in input mode, the period will return you to command mode; if you are already in command mode, the period will simply print the current line.

The following example shows a few lines of text being added after line 10

    10a
    The UNIX System is a general purpose operating
    system for small to large computers.
    The UNIX System is renowned for
    its simple construction, portability,
    and powerful command language.

5.6 Printing Lines of the File

The "p" command is used to print lines of the working file on the terminal. The print command can be used to print one line or a group of lines. For example, the editor commands

    p
    1p
    1,$p

will print the current line of the file, the first line of the file, and all of the lines of the file.

The list ("l") command is a variant of the print command. The list command is used to show all of the special characters that are stored in the line. By special characters we mean characters (e.g., the tab or the backspace) that are not directly visible when you print the line. Consider a line of text that contains the following eight characters:

    a,b,c,<backspace>,d,<tab>,e,f

If you use the print command to display the line, it will appear as follows:

    abd   ef

The c is not visible because the backspace character that follows it essentially erases it and the tab character is expanded into the appropriate number of spaces. However, the backspace and the tab are visible if you display the line using the list command:

abc\bd\tef

The " \b" and the " \t" conventions indicate a backspace and a tab character.

5.7 Updating the Original File

Whenever you have made any substantial changes or additions to the file you should use the write command to update the permanent copy of the file. Remember that while you are editing you are working with a temporary copy of the file. It is necessary to update the permanent copy in order to save your changes.

The write command is used to write a line (or more usually a group of lines) to a disk file. The general form of the write command is

n1,n2w filename

where "n1" and "n2" are line specifiers and "filename" is the name of a disk file. If no lines are specified, all of the lines in the file are written; if no filename is specified, the default file is the original file being edited. Therefore the editor command

w

will write all of the lines of the working file to the original file.

Occasionally you want to save only a group of lines, or to save lines in a file other than the original file. The editor command

10,20w safety

will write lines 10 through 20 to a file named 'safety'. This might be a good safety precaution before making a major change to the lines.

5.8 Ending the Editing Session

After you have completed your changes and updated the original file you use the quit ("q") command to leave the editor. There are no options or line numbers for the quit command.

q

You must be very careful to save any changes in the permanent file if you want to retain the changes. The editor does not automatically write the text buffer to the permanent file when you enter the quit command.

```
% ed firstsession                [ shell command to edit 'firstsession' ]
a                                [ editor command to append text ]
This is line 1.                  [ the first line of appended text ]
This is line 2.                  [ the second line of appended text ]
This is the last line            [ the third line of appended text ]
.                                [ a period to reenter command mode ]
1,3p                             [ editor command to print lines 1 through 3 ]
This is line 1.                  [ these three        ]
This is line 2.                  [    lines are printed ]
This is the last line            [        by the editor ]
w                                [ editor command to write contents to disk ]
54                               [ editor prints the number of bytes written ]
q                                [ editor command to quit the editing session ]
%                                [ the UNIX System shell prompt printed by the shell ]
```

Figure 5.2. A short editing session. During this short editing session, the editor is called upon to edit the file 'firstsession', a few lines of text are appended to the working file, and then the working file is written back to the permanent disk file ('firstsession') and the session is ended. The commands and text for the session are shown on the left half of the page, and comments enclosed in square brackets are shown on the right half of the page.

Most editors have a feature that will remind you (perhaps a cryptic reminder such as a question mark) if you have made changes to the working file without updating the original file. If you enter the command

    q

and the editor replies with a "?" or with a message similar to "No write since last change", then you know that you haven't updated the permanent file. To let you update the permanent file the editor will have ignored the quit command. At this point you can enter a write command to save the temporary file or you can repeat the quit command to actually quit the editor.

Usually the command

    Q

can be used to quit the editor without checking to see if changes have been made to the buffer since the last write.

5.9 Lines and Line Numbers

Most editor commands operate on lines or groups of lines. For example, the print command can print a given line or a given group of lines. The append command appends text after a certain line, the write command writes a group of lines to the output file.

Since lines are so important to the UNIX System text editors, you might expect a lot of ways to identify lines of text. Naturally you can identify a line by mentioning its line number. The first line of text in a file is line 1, the second line is 2, and so on. The command

    2p

tells the editor to print line number 2 (not two lines).

In a small file it is easy to identify lines by line numbers because there are just a few lines. However, it is pretty cumbersome to use line numbers in a file with several dozen lines, and it becomes even harder in a file with thousands of lines.

One way to identify lines in a large file is by using relative line numbers. If you use the number "-1", you are referring to the line in front of the current line. Whenever a number is preceded by a plus "+" or a minus "-" sign the editor interprets it as a relative line number. A relative line number specifies a line relative to the current line. For example, if the current line is line number 3, then "-1" refers to line number 2 and "+2" refers to line number 5.

The command

    -5, + 5p

will print the five lines before the current line, the current line, and then the five lines after the current line. At the conclusion of the command the current line will have increased by five.

Usually when you are modifying a text file you are concentrating on a small portion of the whole document and relative line numbers let you specify lines in the current neighborhood.

Another way to identify lines is by context. Context identification is a very powerful technique. The first line following the current line that contains the text pattern "hello" is referenced by typing

    /hello/

in place of a line number. You can use a context pattern anywhere that you can use a line number. If you want to type the first line following the current line that contains the text pattern "program" you would type the editor command

    /program/p

If you wanted to type all the lines from the first one containing "program" to the first one after that containing "PASCAL", you would enter the editor command

    /program/,/PASCAL/p

When you enter a context pattern in place of a line number the editor searches for that pattern starting at the line after the current line. If the pattern is not found before the end of the file, the editor jumps to the top of the file and searches down through the file up to the current line. The first line where the pattern is found is used as the line number. If the text pattern is not found, the editor prints a question mark or a short error message.

Besides the forward search that we have already mentioned, you can direct the editor to perform a reverse context search by surrounding the text pattern with question marks. The editor command

    ?world?p

will search backward from the current line to print the first line encountered that contains the pattern "world". If the editor reaches the beginning of the file without a successful match, the editor jumps to the end of the file and searches backward to the current line.

The term "wraparound" is used to describe the process of jumping from the beginning to end (or end to beginning) during a search. Conceptually you should imagine the file as a list of lines linked into a circle. The last line in the file is just the line before the first line in the circular analogy. The best physical analogy is the "Rollodex" used by secretaries to store telephone numbers. Of course the file is not really stored in a circle, but the way that text searches work makes it useful to remember the circular analogy.

You can combine context addresses with relative addresses as in

    ?world?-3,.p

which will search backwards to find the line containing the pattern "world", then move three lines in back of that, and then print from there to the current line.

The editor also allows you to add trailing plus and minus signs to a line specifier. The command

    ?world?---,.p

is the same as the previous command. You can also back up a few lines in the file by entering the command

    ----

or forward a few lines with

    + + +

Using trailing pluses and minuses is useful for browsing through a file.

Occasionally you need to convert a context line number into an absolute line number. The editor command

    . =

will display the absolute line number of the current line. You can also use a context pattern like

    /PASCAL/ =

to discover which line contains the word "PASCAL".

You can use absolute, relative, and context line specifiers interchangeably in the editor. The choice depends on what you are doing. Absolute line numbers are the safest in that there is no ambiguity; relative line numbers are pretty safe if you really are where you think you are in the file; and context line specifiers are very convenient but rather hazardous.

5.10 Deleting Lines of Text

The editor delete command ("d") removes one or several lines from the text. If no line numbers are specified; then the delete command deletes the current line. If one line number (or one context pattern) is specified, then the delete command deletes the specified line. If two lines are specified, then the delete command deletes that entire range of lines. As examples, consider the following editor commands:

    10d
    + 10d
    d
    10,15d
    20,/there/d

The first command deletes line number 10, the second command deletes the tenth line after the current line, the third command deletes the current line, the fourth deletes lines 10 through 15, and the fifth command deletes from line 20 to the line containing the pattern "there".

You should be very careful with the delete command because it is easy to delete lines by mistake. In some editors the undo command ("u") can be used to undo the action of the previous command. However, many editors don't contain the undo command and it is possible that you won't be aware of the damage until it is too late to use the undo command.

To avoid disastrous deletions, it is good practice to print lines before you delete them. If you want to delete lines 10 through 20, you should enter the command

    10,20p

to make sure that you are referencing the correct lines before entering the command

    10,20d

to actually delete the lines. Remember that the print command usually changes the current line, so you could delete the tenth line after the current line by entering the command

    +10p

to make sure that it's the correct line and then entering the command

    d

to delete the line.

Another good practice in deleting lines is to use absolute line numbers until you become an expert at using the editor. If you wanted to delete the group of lines from the pattern "here" to the pattern "there", you might attempt to use the brash command

    /here/,/there/d

It would be more prudent to first enter the command

    /here/p

to find and print the first line in the deletion. If the line that is printed is correct then enter the command

    .=

to print the number of the current line (the first line in the deletion). For this example let's suppose that the number 20 is printed. Then enter the command

    /there/

to find and print the last line of the deletion. Again use the command

    .=

to print the number of the current line (the last line of the deletion). Suppose that the number 30 is printed. As a final precaution use the command

    20,30p

to make absolutely sure that lines 20 to 30 are ready to be discarded. Finally enter the command

    20,30d

to actually delete the lines. The approach shown here is extremely cautious, but it is usually easier to be cautious than to reconstruct 10 (or a 100) missing lines.

Context line numbers are great for finding text, but because of the number of occurrences of a text pattern such as "there" in a piece of text it is unwise to use context line numbers when you are altering text.

5.11 Inserting and Changing Lines of Text

The editor insert command ("i") is used to insert text before the specified line. Inserting is similar to appending ("a") except that text is added before the specified line rather than after the specified line. If no line is specified, then the insertion is made before the current line.

The insert command causes the editor to enter text-entry mode. After entering the insert command everything that you type will be interpreted as text and it will be added to the file. You can stop inserting text by typing a line consisting of a single period.

The editor change command ("c") first removes one or several lines from the text, and then text is appended interactively in place of the deleted lines. Like the insert and append commands, the change command causes the editor to enter text-entry mode.

Figure 5.3 shows a fragment of an editing session using the change and the insert commands.

5.12 Moving and Transferring Lines of Text

The editor move command ("m") is used to move text from one place in a file to another. If no source lines are specified, then the current line is moved after the destination line. If one source line is specified, then the specified line is moved after the destination. If two source lines are specified, then the group of specified lines is moved after the destination.

The following commands show all three forms of the move command:

    m50
    30m31
    /hi/,50m0

The first command moves the current line after line 30, the second command moves line 30 after line 31, and the third command moves a group of lines after line 0. The third command is interesting because the addressed text is moved after line 0. In the UNIX System editors, the first line of text is always line 1, but line 0 exists conceptually so that text can be moved to the beginning of a file. Any text placed after line 0 will always be at the beginning of the file.

3p	[command to print line 3]
Thursday	[the editor prints line 3]
3i	[command to insert before line 3]
Tuesday	[the first inserted line]
Wednesday	[the second inserted line]
.	[exit text-entry mode]
2,5p	[editor command to print lines 2 to 5]
Monday	[the editor prints line 2]
Tuesday	[the editor prints line 3]
Wednesday	[the editor prints line 4]
Thursday	[the editor prints line 5]
3,4c	[change lines 3 to 4]
Tuesday,Wednesday	[the new text]
.	[exit text-entry mode]
2,4p	[editor command to print lines 2 to 4]
Monday	[line 2]
Tuesday,Wednesday	[line 3]
Thursday	[line 4]

Figure 5.3. Inserting and changing lines of text. This figure shows a fragment of an editing session demonstrating the insert command and then the change command. The actual edit session dialogue is shown on the left and comments are shown on the right in square brackets. Items that were typed by the user are underlined. Keep in mind that this dialogue is just part of an editing session.

The transfer command is almost the same as the move command; the only difference is that the addressed text is not disturbed during a transfer. The move command takes the addressed text and removes it from one place and puts it back somewhere else; the transfer command makes a copy of the addressed lines of text and places them in the destination. The move command has no effect on the size of the file, the transfer command increases the size of the file. Figure 5.4 shows a fragment of an editing session using the move command and the transfer command.

5.13 Substituting Text

The substitute command is used to change one pattern of text on a line to another pattern. The general format of the substitute command is

    n1,n2s/pat1/pat2/

where n1 and n2 are line specifiers and pat1 and pat2 are text patterns. The

45,47p	[print lines 45 to 47]
The goat	[line 45]
of the goatherder.	[line 46]
got the goat	[line 47]
47m45	[move 47 after line 45]
45,47p	[print lines 45 to 47]
The goat	[line 45]
got the goat	[line 46]
of the goatherder.	[line 47]
45,47t47	[transfer lines 45 through 47 after 47]
45,50p	[print lines 45 through 50]
The goat	[line 45]
got the goat	[line 46]
of the goatherder.	[line 47]
The goat	[line 48]
got the goat	[line 49]
of the goatherder.	[line 50]

Figure 5.4. Moving and transferring lines of text. This figure contains a fragment of an editing session that demonstrates the move and the transfer editing commands. The left column shows the actual editing session, the right contains comments, and the characters that were entered by the user are underlined.

command causes pat1 to be replaced by pat2 in the group of specified lines. The simplest form of the substitute command is

    s/pat1//

which removes the text represented by pat1 from the current line.

If line 20 in the workfile is "The URIX Operating System", then the command

    20s/URIX/UNIX/

will change the typo "URIX" to "UNIX". If you are in the habit of typing "URIX" instead of "UNIX", then the command

    1,$s/URIX/UNIX/

will change the first occurrence of "URIX" on every line in the file to "UNIX."

If the current line in the workfile is "Who'ss on first?" then the command

    s/s//

will remove the extra "s" from the first word.

```
1,3p                              [ editor command to print lines 1 to 3 ]
Jack be nimble                    [ line 1 ]
Jack be quick.                    [ line 2 ]
Jack jump over the candlestick.   [ line 3 ]
1,3s/Jack/Jill/                   [ Change "Jack" to "Jill" ]
1,3s/be/is/                       [ Change "be" to "is" ]
3s/jump/jumps/                    [ Change "jump" to "jumps" ]
1,3p                              [ Print lines 1 through 3 ]
Jill is nimble.                   [ line 1 ]
Jill is quick.                    [ line 2 ]
Jill jumps over the candlestick.  [ line 3 ]
s/candle/broom/p                  [ Change "candle" to "broom" and print the result ]
Jill jumps over the broomstick.   [ The changed line ]
```

Figure 5.5. The substitute command. This fragment of an editing session shows several examples of using the substitute command. Notice that the command to substitute "is" for "be" on lines 1 through 3 fails to perform a substitution on line 3. If a substitution is made on any of the lines in the group, then no error occurs. However, when you specify that a substitution should occur throughout a group of lines, it is an error if the substitution fails on all lines. Notice that the editor does not automatically print the changed line (or lines). However, if you want the editor to print the changed line, you can enter "p" for print at the end of the command as in the last substitute command in this figure. Notice tha t the changed line is printed. If you are making a substitution throughout, a group of lines then the trailing "p" will only cause the last substitution to be printed.

If the current line of the workfile is "Don'tread on me." then the command

```
s/Don'tread/Don't tread/
```

will change the line to "Don't tread on me." You need to supply only enough context to enable the editor to recognize the part of the text that must be changed. Therefore, any of the following commands would have performed the same repair as the preceding command:

```
s/n'tr/n't tr/
s/'t/'t t/
s/'/'t /
s/t/t t/
```

Be careful when you supply minimal context because you can easily get into trouble. Consider the following line of text.

```
The rain in Spain falls mainly on the plain.
```

The text pattern "he" occurs twice, the pattern "ain" occurs three times, and the pattern "in" occurs four times, and the patterns "a" and "i" each occur five times.

Suppose that the previous line had been mistyped as "The rain in Spain falls mainly on the plainly." Clearly the goal is to remove the extra "ly" in "plain." You can't enter the command

```
s/ly//
```

because the "ly" in "mainly" will be removed instead of the "ly" in "plainly." The solution is to specify a text pattern that clearly specifies the errant "ly." The command

```
s/plainly/plain/
```

will repair the line, but you have to remember to include a lot of surrounding context to correctly specify the correct "ly" because there are two One of the reasons for the popularity of visual editors is that visual editors allow you to alter text on a line without using the substitute command. Figure 5.5 shows a fragment of an editing session using the substitute command.

CHAPTER

6

The UNIX File System

Files are named collections of information stored on a mass storage device such as a computer disk or tape. The file system is the organizational framework for the group of files. On many computer systems files are "organized" by lumping them together into one big heap. As long as there are only a few dozen files in the system this works fine. Unfortunately, a simple file system is inappropriate for a multiuser computer system with large modern disks that can store several hundred thousand files.

Several ideas contributed to the development of the UNIX file system. The most important idea was convenience. The UNIX System needed a file system that encouraged users to group their files logically. A group of files is called a directory and in the UNIX System you are encouraged to create directories as necessary.

Organizing files into more manageable groups is a good first step but it doesn't solve the problem. If you have several hundred users with several directories each plus dozens of directories for system information, then you are right back in an unmanageable situation. The key idea of the UNIX file system is that it is hierarchical. Some other hierarchical systems are the Prussian Army, the corporate ladder, and the Catholic Church.

File access restrictions are an essential part of a file system on a multiuser computer. Without an access validation system nobody would be willing to put private information in a computer and nobody could vouch for the safety of the system's files and tables. Access modes are a necessary evil of shared computer systems.

One of the novel features of the UNIX System is the association of all of the I/O hardware with special files. Access to I/O hardware itself mimics access to ordinary disk files. Each I/O device (printer, terminal, disk, etc.) has at least one special file. A program can access a special file in order to actually access the I/O hardware. Although this sounds complicated it is actually a great simplification compared to most other computer systems.

All of these aspects of the UNIX file system are discussed in the remainder of this chapter. You should have a working knowledge of these ideas in order to use the UNIX System effectively. A few advanced file system topics are presented in Sections 18.11 through 18.13. These sections are not required reading for most users. Some of the data structures that the UNIX System uses to maintain the file system are discussed in Section 19.6.

6.1 Ordinary Files

An ordinary file is used to store information. An ordinary file might contain a program that you can execute, the text of a document, the records of a company, or any other type of information that a computer can process. During a session with the UNIX System you will encounter dozens of ordinary files.

Ordinary files are a vital part of a computer system because they allow information to be stored permanently. Without long term information storage the information processing ability of computers would not be very useful. Besides ordinary files, UNIX Systems contain directory files, special files, and some systems contain named pipes. (Named pipes are also called fifo files; see Section 18.11.) Ordinary files are the only file type that is used for long term storage of general information.

The names of files can be up to 14 characters long and no two files in the same directory may share the same name. However, it is possible for one file to have several names. (See ln command; Section 9.2.) You can use whatever characters you want for file names, although file names that contain unprintable characters, space characters, tabs, and shell metacharacters are very difficult to use. Since every UNIX System directory always has the file names '.' and '..' built in, you cannot ever use these names for your own files.

The UNIX System does not impose any naming conventions on files. However, certain UNIX System programs expect files to be named with certain suffixes. For example, files with the suffix ".sh" (such as 'bakup.sh') are usually shell programs, files with the suffix ".bas" (such as 'aster.bas') are usually BASIC programs, and files with the suffix ".c" (such as 'xrefer.c') are usually C-language source files. Files that contain executable programs (such as 'who') customarily have no suffixes.

There are two types of ordinary file: text files and binary files. Text files contain only ASCII (American Standard Code for Information Interchange) characters, whereas binary files contain all 256 possible values for each byte. Let's first discuss text files.

About 100 ASCII characters are recognized by common terminals and printers. Most terminals can display the following printing characters:

```
ABCDEFGHIJKLMNOPQRSTUVWXYZ
abcdefghijklmnopqrstuvwxyz
0123456789
!@ # $ % ^ & * ( )  _ - + = ~ ` { }
[ ] : ; " < > , . ? / \ |
```

In addition to the printable characters shown above the ASCII character set defines codes for the space character, the horizontal and vertical tab characters, the newline character, the form-feed character, and a whole host of control characters.

One example of an ordinary text file is the message-of-the-day file ('/etc/motd') that is printed at your terminal each time you log onto the system You can have the message-of-the-day file typed on your terminal anytime by entering the command

```
cat  /etc/motd
```

The UNIX System utility cat is often used to display text files on your terminal. (See Section 8.2.)

Files that contain codes that are not part of the ASCII character set are called binary files. Since binary files use the full range of possible values for the bytes in the file, binary files are a slightly more efficient way to store information. A binary file cannot be directly typed on your terminal because most of the 256 possible values for each byte are not printable ASCII characters.

You can inspect the contents of a binary file by using the octal dump (od) program. (See Section 7.17.) Od takes the values in a file and converts them into printable characters. If you use the command

```
od  /unix
```

you will dump the file '/unix'. On most systems the file '/unix' contains a copy of the UNIX System kernel that is currently operating the computer.

Virtually every command that you enter references ordinary files. Four commands are especially important for controlling your collection of ordinary files: mv (move), cp (copy), ln (link), and rm (remove). These four commands are discussed in Chapter 9.

6.2 Directory files

Directories are files that contain lists of files. The UNIX Operating System maintains the directory system. Executing programs can read the directory files but the operating system prevents programs from changing directory files in order to guarantee the integrity of the directory system.

Executing programs can have entries added to directories by asking the system to create a file. Entries can be removed from directories by asking the system to delete the file. The system is always responsible for making the changes to directory files.

The files listed in a directory can be ordinary files, directory files, special files, or (in some systems) fifo files.

Each user has a special directory called the home directory. When you log onto the system you are placed in your home directory. During the course of your session with the UNIX System you are free to move from one directory to another. If you want to move to the directory named '/bin', then you would enter the command

    cd /bin

The directory that you are in is called the current directory or the working directory.

In Version 7 the UNIX System remembers your home directory so that you can return to it at any time by typing the command

    cd

(On older systems the cd command is usually named chdir and you usually have to specify the name of your home directory in order to return to it.) The name of the current directory will be printed if you enter the pwd command. Cd and pwd are discussed in Section 7.1.

The mkdir (make directory) command is used to create a directory and the rmdir command is used to remove a directory. Directories are created empty except for the standard files '.' and '..'. (The standard entries '.' and '..' are discussed below.) You can only remove a directory that is empty (except for the files '.' and '..'). Mkdir and rmdir are discussed in Section 9.5.

6.3 The Hierarchical File System

Files in the UNIX System are grouped into directories and the directories are organized into a hierarchy. The top of the hierarchy is a special directory called the root directory. The root directory contains a variety of system-related files and it usually contains some standard directories such as '/bin', '/usr', '/dev', '/etc', and '/lib'. A typical, but very simplified view of a file system hierarchy is shown in Figure 6.1.

The advantage of a hierarchical file system is organization. Let's use the corporate analogy. In a corporation you could allow every worker to report directly to the president. This type of organization works well for a small Ma and Pa grocery but it would be disastrous for a huge organization such as General Motors. Similarly, in the UNIX System it is a great advantage to organize the system by loosening the connection between files and the root directory.

The UNIX file system is often called tree-structured because diagrams of it resemble a tree. The current subtree is that part of the file system that is at a lower level in the hierarchy than the current directory. If the '/usr' directory were the current directory, then all of the user's directories, and all of their subdirectories, and so forth, would be the current subtree − Figure 6.2. Most UNIX System commands work with files in the current directory unless you specify another directory. A few UNIX System commands work with the current subtree.

6.4 Pathnames

The files in the current directory are directly accessible; they can be referenced by simply entering their name. Files that are not in the current directory must

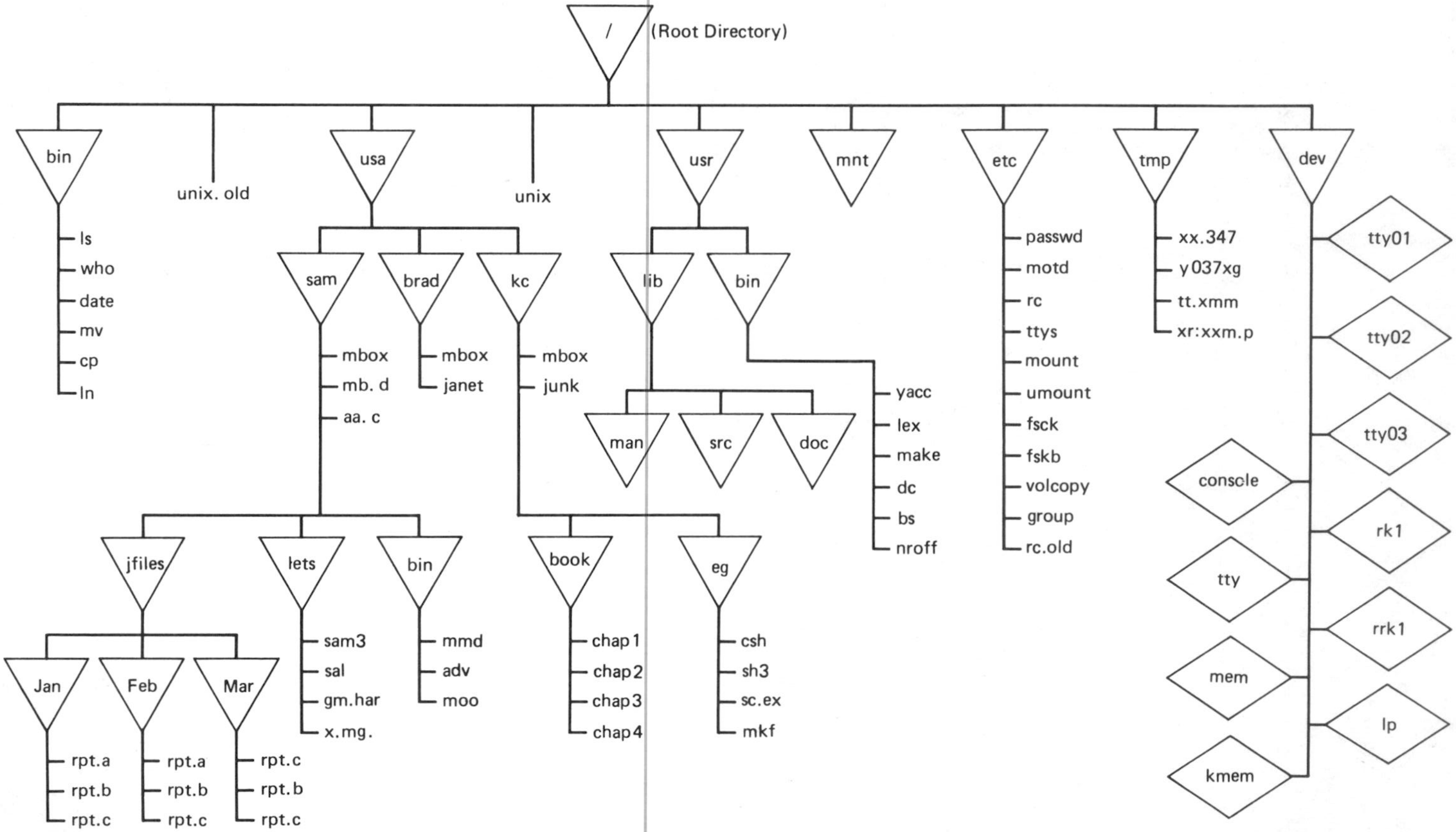

Figure 6.1. Diagram of a typical UNIX file system. In this diagram, directory files are shown in triangles, special files are shown in diamonds. Ordinary files are shown without borders.

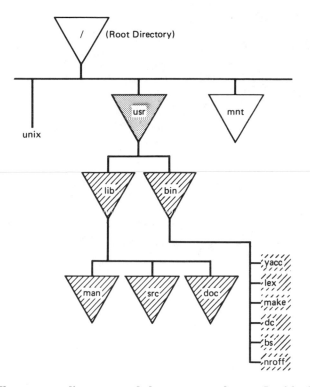

Figure 6.2. The current directory and the current subtree. In this diagram the current directory is '/usr' (shown shaded). The current subtree consists of all of the directories and files below '/usr' in the file system hierarchy (shown hatched).

be referenced by using a pathname. A pathname specifies a path through the file system that leads to the desired file. Paths through the file system can only start in one of two places: your current directory or the root directory. Pathnames that start with the "/" (slash) character are absolute pathnames, specifying a path starting in the root directory. All other pathnames are relative pathnames and they specify a path starting in your current directory.

Every directory (except the root directory) contains entries for the names '.' and '..'. These two entries are the glue that holds the file system together. The entry '.' is a pseudonym for the name of the current directory. Programs that want to read the current directory file can use the name '.' rather than scrounge around to determine the name that was given to the directory when it was created.

The name '..' is another name for the parent directory of the current directory. The entry '..' in each directory allows you to specify a pathname that ascends the file system. Notice that all of the other entries in a directory specify files that are at a lower level in the file system hierarchy. You should be comfortable with the ideas behind the names '.' and '..' because you will use these names very often in your interactions with the UNIX System.

A few simple rules apply to all pathnames.

1. If the pathname starts with a slash, then the path starts in the root directory. All other paths start in the current directory.

2. A pathname is either a list of names separated by slashes or a single name. The initial names in the list (if there are any) are directories. The final name in the list is the target file, which may be a file of any type.

3. You can ascend the file system hierarchy by specifying the name '..' in a pathname. All other names in a pathname descend the hierarchy.

4. No spaces are allowed in a pathname.

Let's show a few examples of pathnames. The pathname '/usa/kc' is an absolute pathname specifying the file 'kc'. Since the pathname starts with a

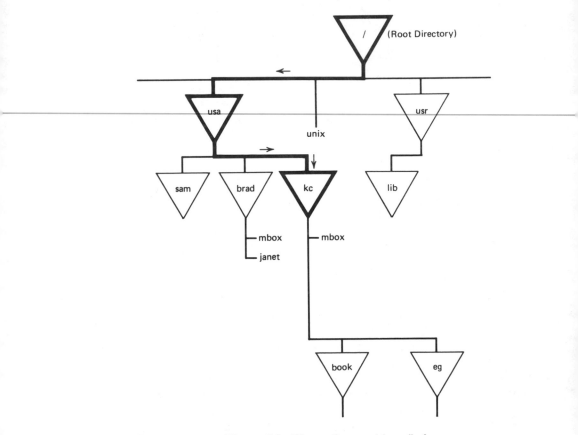

Figure 6.3. The pathname '/usa/kc'.

slash it is an absolute pathname that starts in the root directory. Obviously the directory 'usa' is a subdirectory of the root directory (Figure 6.3).

The pathname 'jfiles/Jan/rpt.a' is a relative pathname because it doesn't start with a slash. Hence the path starts from the current directory, which is '/usa/sam' for this example (Figure 6.4). The directory 'jfiles' is a subdirectory of the current directory, 'Jan' is a subdirectory of 'jfiles', and 'rpt.a' is a file in 'Jan'.

The pathname '../../brad/janet' is harder to understand. The path starts in the current directory, which is '/usa/kc/eg' for this example (Figure 6.5). The

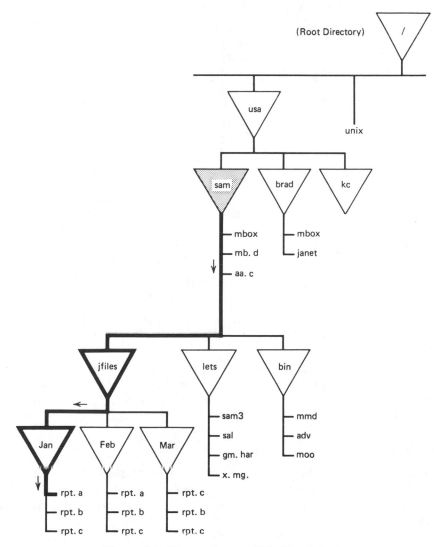

Figure 6.4. The pathname 'jfils/Jan/rpt.a'.

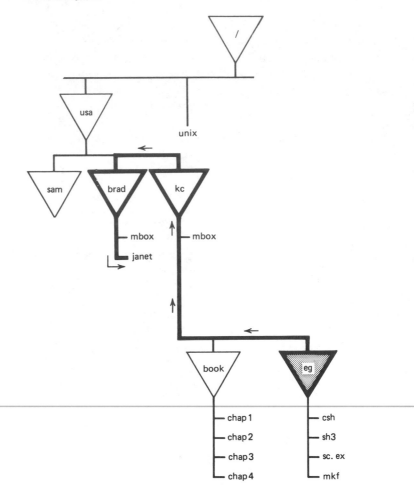

Figure 6.5. The pathname '../../brad/janet'.

path leads to the parent of '/usa/kc/eg', which is '/usa/kc'. The path then
ascends further to '/usa', and then descends to the directory 'brad'. The target
file is 'janet' in the 'brad' directory. Long pathnames are very hard to use. It is
usually better to change directory to the scene of the action.

6.5 File Types and Modes

We have already said that a file is a collection of information. This is correct as
far as it goes, but there is more to a file than the information it contains. The
UNIX System maintains a variety of information that describes each file. The
information that describes a file includes access privileges, the file type, the
important dates for the file, the size of the file, and the exact location of the file
on the disk.

The implications of file types and modes resound throughout the UNIX System. Many operations assume a file of one type or another. For example, you should not use the command

```
cd /usa/kc/mbox
```

because '/usa/kc/mbox' is not a directory but an ordinary file containing electronic mail. Similarly, the command

```
cat /usa/kc
```

will produce gibberish because '/usa/kc' is a directory, not a text file.

Each time you access a file the system checks your right to perform that access. The privileges normally are set so that you have fairly free reign over your own files and much more limited access to your neighbor's files. Some of the more cryptic UNIX System error messages are simply trying to tell you that you are unable to access a certain file because of the file access protection system.

First of all the UNIX System has to remember the type of each file. Files come in several types: directory, ordinary, special, and fifo files on some systems. Directories are files that the system manipulates in order to maintain the hierarchical file system and ordinary files are files that users use to store information. Users are allowed to read information in directory files but only the system is allowed to write in directory files.

Special files are used to provide linkages to I/O hardware. There are two basic types, character special files and block special files. The differences between these two types are discussed in the next section. Special files frequently are used to provide an interface to a disk or tape storage unit. However, no information is actually stored in a special file; the information is stored on the disk or tape. When a program reads information from a special file the information actually comes from the associated I/O device, and when a program writes information to a special file the information is actually sent to the associated I/O device. Each special file is associated with two numbers, the major and minor device numbers. The device numbers are used by the kernel when special files are accessed in order to figure out what I/O hardware is logically connected to each special file.

From a programmer's point of view special files are a great simplification, but most users don't need to know very much about special files. For example, at some installations you must redirect output to the special files for printers in order to get printed output, but most installations have programs to handle the printers. The programs work through the special files, but it is transparent to the user.

In the UNIX System there are three operations that can be performed on a file: reading, writing, and executing. Reading a file means the contents of the file are made available. Writing a file means the contents of the file are changed. Executing a file either means loading the file into main memory and performing the machine instructions that are stored in the file, or it means reading shell commands from the file and executing those commands. (Execute permission for a directory file means that you can search the directory in the course of resolving a pathname.)

Each UNIX System file is owned by a particular user and each file is always associated with a particular group. (In the UNIX System a group is a set of users who have something in common — typically groups are users from one department, people working together on a project, etc.) The UNIX System file access protection scheme depends on the type of access that is requested (read, write, or execute) and who is doing the access. There is a set of privileges for the file owner, another set for members of the file's group, and a third set for everyone else. The privileges for a file can be displayed using the ls command. Several examples are shown in Figure 7.2.

The owner of a file is able to control the permissions of that file by using the chmod (change mode) command (discussed in Section 9.3). The ownership and the group association can also be changed by using the chown (change owner) and chgrp (change group) commands (also discussed in Section 9.3). The superuser (the system manager uses the superuser privilege to perform operations that are denied to ordinary users) is also able to change the modes of your files, although in an ethically managed system this is not likely to happen unless you request some help.

Many UNIX System files are known by several names. The number of names that a file has is also called the number of links because each pseudonym is a link from a directory entry to the system's internal bookkeeping system for the files. Directory entries always contain at least two links because each directory entry contains the pseudonym '.' for itself. Directories that contain subdirectories contain more than two links because each subdirectory references the parent directory using the pseudonym '..'. It is also possible to explicitly create several names for a given file by using the ln (link) command, as discussed in Section 9.2.

6.6 Special Files

Ordinary files are conceptually easy because they contain information, just like a file in a file cabinet. Special files are harder to understand because they don't contain information. Special files are used to provide a convenient channel for accessing Input/Output mechanisms. For each I/O mechanism (card reader, terminal, disk, tape, etc.) that is connected to a computer there is at least one special file. Most of the special files are stored in the directory '/dev'. The names of the special files usually indicate what type of device they are associated with. For example, '/dev/pt' is a paper tape reader/punch, '/dev/tty4' is a terminal (teletype), '/dev/rp0' is a type RP06 disk, and '/dev/lp' is a lineprinter.

When a program writes data to a file such as '/dev/pt' the operating system intercepts the data and sends them to the paper tape punch. When a program reads data from a file such as '/dev/pt' the operating system is actually acquiring the data from the paper tape reader mechanism.

A program does not have to know anything about the details of the paper tape I/O mechanism to read or write the '/dev/pt' special file. Special files are an interface between general purpose application programs that need to ignore hardware details and the UNIX System kernel's internal routines, which exist only to revel in the details of the computer hardware.

Some I/O devices handle one character at a time. A good example of a character- oriented I/O device is your terminal. The computer sends characters to the terminal one at a time. The special files that provide links to character I/O devices are called character special files.

Some I/O devices work most efficiently when large groups of data are transferred together. Most disks require transfers of 512 characters; 512 bytes is called a block of data and devices which work most efficiently with blocks are called block I/O devices. The special files that provide links to block I/O devices are called block special files.

Most block I/O devices also have a character special interface. The character special interface to block I/O devices is also called the raw interface and it is mostly used by programs that perform operating system maintenance functions. The character special interface to block I/O devices will be discussed more fully in the chapters on the UNIX System internals.

Since there are no characters stored in a special file, the length field in a long listing does not contain the length of the file. Instead, the major and minor device numbers are shown. The major device number identifies the type of I/O device that the file references. A computer often is connected to several of each type of I/O device. For instance, a UNIX System computer is usually connected to several (or several dozen) terminals. There is a special file for each of the terminals and the minor device number of each special file specifies which terminal.

The UNIX System uses special files to access I/O hardware rather than some other mechanism because the UNIX System wants to make the interface to I/O hardware similar to the interface to ordinary files. Therefore, special files appear as entries in directories, they are part of the file system, and access to them is controlled by the usual three-tiered protection system.

The special files for terminals are usually owned by the system when they are not being used. During the login process the ownership of the special file for your terminal is transferred to you. Since you own the special file that links programs to your terminal, you can control its access modes. When you log off the ownership of your terminal's special file is transferred back to the system.

Special files that provide linkages to the disks and tapes are usually owned by the system and access to them by ordinary users is often restricted. Special files that provide linkages to printers, paper tape readers, video displays, laboratory peripherals, and the like, etc. are usually owned by the system and their access modes are often set so that anyone can use them. It is up to you to coordinate your use of these resources with other users so that two people aren't using one resource at one time.

6.7 Directory Access Modes

Directories have the standard read, write, and execute permissions for owner, group, and other. However, in a directory these permissions are interpreted differently from ordinary files.

The read permission for a directory means that standard utility programs are allowed to open and read the information in the directory. For example, the ls program reads directories to discover their contents. If the read privilege is denied, then it is impossible to discover (until the read privilege is restored) what files are contained in the directory.

It is possible to operate in directories where you are denied read permission. As an example, on one of the UNIX Systems that I often use all of the directories containing the operating system source code have the read permission denied. However, since I am very familiar with the organization of these directories I had no problem examining the source files during the research for this book. Restricting read privileges of directories keeps the uninformed away but it isn't real protection — it is an annoyance.

The write privilege for a directory means that you are allowed to create or remove files in that directory. You do not have to have the read privilege to create files or remove files in a directory. Making the write privilege control the creation and deletion rights makes a lot of intuitive sense when you consider that creating a file in a given directory means that the system has written the name of the created file into the directory file. Similarly, in deleting a file the system must erase the entry for the vanishing file from the directory file.

Denying write privilege for a certain directory does not mean that files in that directory cannot be modified. The write privilege on each individual file controls your ability to modify that file.

The execute permission for a directory means that the system will search the directory in the course of resolving a file name. When you specify a pathname in place of a simple file name, each of the directories in the pathname is searched for the name of the next directory in the sequence. If you ask the system to

    cat /usr/bin/source/README

then you must have execute (search) permission for the directories 'usr', 'bin', and 'source'. Denying a directory's search permission is real protection against people using files in that directory. You cannot change directory to a directory where execute permission is denied.

CHAPTER

7

What's Going On Utilities

One of the strengths of the UNIX Operating System is its large set of utility programs. Different installations will have different sets of utility programs; therefore, there is no way that this book can be a complete guide to all of the utilities on all of the systems. Instead we attempt to discuss and show examples of the most useful utilities.

This chapter focuses on the utilities that allow you to observe and control your interactions with the UNIX System. Utilities for text files are covered in the next chapter and the utilities for general files are covered in a later chapter. Utilities for programmers are covered in Chapter 16 and utilities for the system manager are covered in Chapter 18.

The idea of these chapters is to describe a set of programs which form a useful and powerful nucleus of UNIX System knowledge. Anyone who seriously uses the UNIX System will be very familiar with most of these programs; less serious users will probably use at least half of them. Large, complicated programs (e.g., the shell, the editor, and the advanced word processing and programming aids) are discussed individually elsewhere in this book (shell — Chapters 4, 12, 13; editor — Chapters 5, 10; Word Processing — Chapter 11). For specific information on the operation of a particular program you should consult the UNIX System manual.

One of the things that novices often find confusing is the fact that the UNIX System environment is variable. As an example, consider the fact that two different users would usually have different home directories and different access rights to files. They might have different types of terminals, and they might need to use very different sets of programs. One of the strengths of the UNIX System is its ability to support many environments. The utilities in the "What's Going On" category help you understand the current environment.

7.1 Pwd and Cd — The Current Directory

The name of the current directory is probably the most basic piece of information about your current environment. The pwd (print working directory) command reveals the name of the current (working) directory.

The UNIX System is divided into directories (see Chapter 6). At any given time just one of these directories is your current directory. When you log onto the system the current directory is your home directory. You can move from directory to directory using the cd command (see next section). After each move it is a good idea to make sure that you landed in the desired directory. The command

```
pwd
```

will print the name of the current directory. Immediately after logging in you are in your home directory, the directory assigned to you by the system manager. My home directory is '/usa/kc'. If I execute the pwd command immediately after logging in, then "/usa/kc" is printed on my terminal. If expected files are not present, or if things are not working as you expect, use pwd to make sure you are where you think you are.

The remedy for being in the wrong directory is to change directory to the correct directory. The change directory (cd) command will change the current working directory to the named directory. If no directory is named, the new directory will be the home directory. For example, the command

```
cd /usr/ron/source
```

will move you to the directory '/usr/ron/source'.

If no directory is named when you enter the cd command, the new directory will be the home directory. Either of the following two commands can be used to move back to my home directory ('/usa/kc') from anywhere in the file system:

```
cd
cd /usa/kc
```

The pathname argument to the cd command may either be an absolute pathname as in the second command above or a relative pathname as in the following two commands:

```
cd ../../source
cd junk/programs
```

The first of these makes the current directory the child directory named 'source' of the parent of the current directory's parent. The second makes the current directory the child directory named 'programs' of the child directory named 'junk.'

7.2 Ls — List Files

The ls command is used to list the contents of directories and to print information about files. The ls command accepts many arguments and options, most of which are not discussed here.

Each argument to the ls command is either the name of an ordinary (or special) file, the name of a directory, or an option (option list). The options are used to control the order of the list of files and the information that is printed for each file. For each ordinary (or special) file argument the requested information is printed. For each directory argument the requested information is printed for all of the files in the directory (unless the "d" option is used).

The following four options seem to be used very frequently. More options are mentioned in the abridged manual at the end of this book and you should also examine the information distributed with your system.

1. The "l" Option.
   The long list option is used to print a lot of information about each listed file. Without the "l" option only the file names are typed.

2. The "t" Option.
   The time sort option sorts the list of files according to each file's modification date. The most recently modified files are printed first. The time sort option is used to show which files have been active recently.

3. The "d" Option.
   The directory option is used to force ls to simply print the requested information for each directory in the argument list. Normally all of the directories named in the argument list are searched and the requested information is printed for all of the files in those directories.

4. The "a" Option.
   Normally when you use the ls command to print a list of the files in a directory the files whose names begin with a period are omitted from the list. However, when the "a" option is used even files whose names begin with a period (such as the standard entries '.' and '..') are printed.

For ordinary files in the argument list only the file name and the requested information is printed. For each directory named in the argument list the files contained in that directory are listed. If there are no files or directories named in the arguments, then the contents of the current directory are listed.

The command

   ls

will print an alphabetized list of the files in the current directory. You can also use ls to print lists of groups of files. The command

   ls *.c

will list (in alphabetical order) all of the files in the current directory whose names end in ".c". The "-t" option can be used to order the files according to modification dates rather than alphabetic ordering. The command

    ls -t *.c

will print a list of all of the files in the current directory whose names end in ".c", sorted according to the modification dates of the files.

One thing that confuses many UNIX System users is the difference between the command

    ls

and the command

    ls *

The first command has no arguments so by default a list of the files in the current directory is produced. The second command uses the metacharacter "*", which matches the names of all of the files in the current directory. Therefore, the shell provides the second command with one argument for every file in the current directory. For ordinary files the two commands produce the same output, but for subdirectories of the current directory the first command lists only the subdirectory name, whereas the second command lists the subdirectory's contents because the subdirectories are explicitly mentioned in the argument list. (See Figure 7.1.)

When you need to know a lot of information about a file you use the "l" option to ls. Using the long option allows you to see the mode of the file, the number of links to the file, the owner of the file, the group of the file, the size of the file, and the modification time of the file. For special files the major and minor device numbers are printed in place of the file size. Figure 7.2 shows some typical outputs of the ls command using the "l" option.

Understanding the output of the long format output of the ls command is very important because interacting with the UNIX System involves accessing files. The long format output of ls is the only way to discover the key information for each file (file type, mode, ownership, and size). The output of the ls command on your system might be somewhat different from the output shown in Figure 7.2 because the format of the long listing varies slightly from system to system.

The first field in the long format listing is the mode field. It usually consists of ten characters, the first character indicates the file type and the next nine characters indicate the file access privileges. The coding for the file type (the first character in the mode field) is given in the following table:

Code	Meaning
-	Ordinary file
d	Directory file
c	Character special file
b	Block special file
p	Fifo (named pipe) file

```
% ls
book
eg
junk
mbox
% ls *
junk
mbox
book:
chap1
chap2
chap3
chap4
eg:
csh
mkf
sc.ex
sh3
%
```

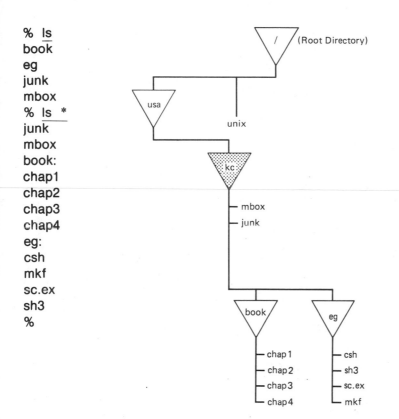

Figure 7.1. Examples of the use of ls. The command "ls" and the command "ls
*" act very differently when the current directory contains subdirectories
('book' and 'eg' in this example). Without arguments the ls command will print
a list of the files in the current directory (the first command shown above).
When the ls command receives the name of a directory as an argument the requested information is printed for each file in that directory. In this case the
command "ls *" is equivalent to the command "ls book eg junk mbox" because
of the shell's expansion of the metacharacter "*" into a list of all of the files in
the current directory. Therefore, the files in the directories 'book' and 'eg' appear in the list (the second command shown above).

ls -l /etc/rc

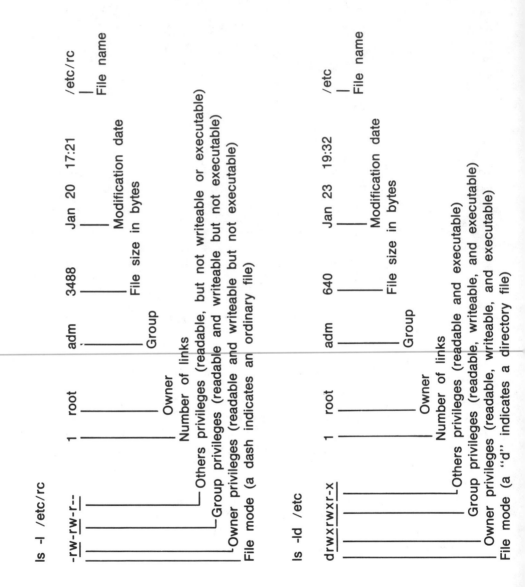

```
-rw-rw-r--  1  root  adm  3488  Jan 20  17:21  /etc/rc
```

File mode (a dash indicates an ordinary file)
Owner privileges (readable and writeable but not executable)
Group privileges (readable and writeable but not executable)
Others privileges (readable, but not writeable or executable)
Number of links
Owner
Group
File size in bytes
Modification date
File name

ls -ld /etc

```
drwxrwxr-x  1  root  adm  640  Jan 23  19:32  /etc
```

File mode (a "d" indicates a directory file)
Owner privileges (readable, writeable, and executable)
Group privileges (readable, writeable, and executable)
Others privileges (readable and executable)
Number of links
Owner
Group
File size in bytes
Modification date
File name

80

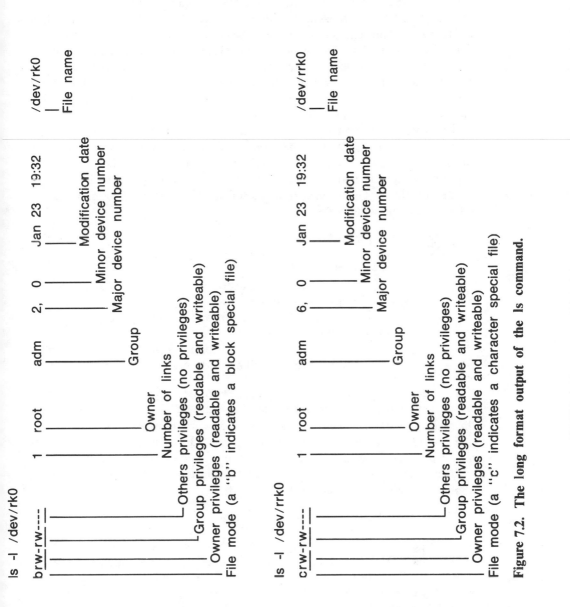

Figure 7.2. The long format output of the ls command.

81

The file type is the most basic information about a file. After a short while you will automatically interpret the first character in a long listing.

In Section 6.5 we discussed the three operations that can be performed on a UNIX System file: reading, writing, and executing. We also discussed the three tiers of access privilege, the owner's privileges, the group's privileges, and the other's privileges. Since there are three access operations (read, write, and execute) and there are three tiers of protection (owner, group, and others) there are nine (three times three) access permissions associated with each file. The first three characters of the permissions show the read, write, and execute privileges of the owner, the second set of three characters shows the read, write, and execute privileges of members of the group, and the third set of three characters shows the read, write, and execute privileges of all others. If a privilege is allowed, the appropriate letter (r, w, or x) is shown. If the privilege is denied, a hyphen is shown. The access privileges for the first example in Figure 7.2 are shown in the following table:

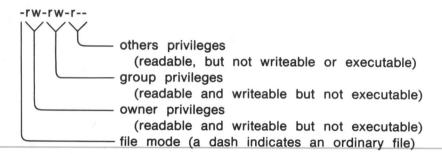

If a privilege is denied and you attempt to exercise the privilege, your attempt will be thwarted by the operating system. In many UNIX System environments the read and write privileges associated with files are immaterial because everyone customarily allows everyone else free access. In some other UNIX System installations file access modes are carefully controlled to ensure system integrity.

Occasionally you need to know the access modes or some other information about a directory. If you enter the command

    ls -l /usa/kc

you will get a long format listing of all of the files in the '/usa/kc' directory. When ls receives the name of a directory as an argument the standard behavior is to list all of the files in that directory. The "d" option is used to suppress this normal behavior and force ls to simply list the required information for the named directory. The command

    ls -ld /usa/kc

will print a long format listing of the file for the '/usa/kc' directory. These two commands are shown in Figure 7.3.

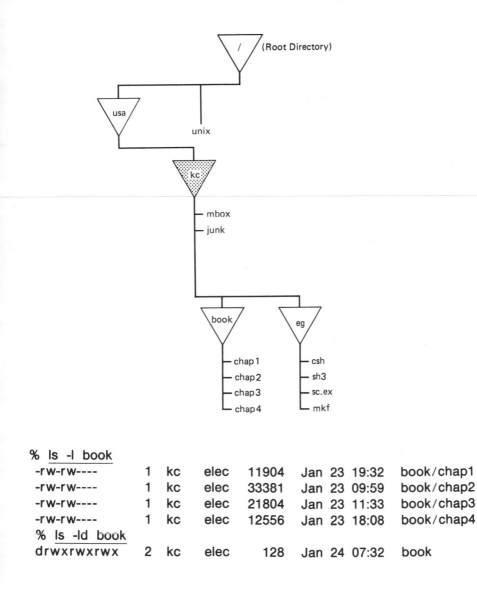

```
% ls -l book
-rw-rw----      1  kc   elec   11904   Jan 23 19:32   book/chap1
-rw-rw----      1  kc   elec   33381   Jan 23 09:59   book/chap2
-rw-rw----      1  kc   elec   21804   Jan 23 11:33   book/chap3
-rw-rw----      1  kc   elec   12556   Jan 23 18:08   book/chap4
% ls -ld book
drwxrwxrwx      2  kc   elec     128   Jan 24 07:32   book
```

Figure 7.3. Listing directory contents. When ls is passed the name of a directory its usual response is to list the requested information for every file in that directory. The first command above shows ls listing in long format all of the files in the directory 'book'. The "d" option to ls can prevent ls from descending into the named directories to list their contents. In the second command shown above ls lists in long format the information for the directory 'book' rather than the information for the files contained in 'book' because of the presence of the "d" option.

7.3 File — Deduce File Types

The file command attempts to determine what type of information is stored in the files named as arguments. Whereas the ls command prints hard facts about files, the file command makes an educated guess concerning the files' contents. The most important use of the file command is probably to determine whether the file contains text or binary information. Text files can be typed on your terminal; binary files cannot. (Attempting to type a binary file on your terminal may lead to disaster because some of the binary values in the file are probably interpreted as control codes by either your terminal or modem.)

If a file contains binary information, the file program will attempt to determine whether the information is an executable program or binary data. If the file contains text, the file program will attempt to discern the language. On most systems the file program knows about languages such as the shell, C, Yacc, and FORTRAN as well as English, French, and Spanish. Naturally the classification determined for each argument may be wrong. The command

```
file  *
```

will list the file types of all of the files in the current directory.

7.4 Date and Who

The date command prints the current date and time. You can use the date command to print the date by entering the command

```
date
```

In addition, the superuser can invoke the date command to set the date.

The who command prints a list of the people who are currently using the system. Enter the command

```
who
```

for a list of the users of the system, their terminal identification, and the time that they logged on. Your login name should be in the list. Some of the older systems were adept at difficult philosophical questions such as "who are you", "who am i" ("whoami" on some systems), and "who is god". Perhaps your system still knows the answers.

7.5 Ps — List Processes

The process status (ps) command prints a list of all of your processes. The ps command often is used by the system programmer (and occasionally by nosy administrators) to determine what is happening on an entire system. You are most likely to need the ps program to determine the process identification numbers of errant processes so that you can kill them. For a real surprise, try the ps program during a bout with the learn program. You may be surprised by the number of processes that you are running. For a list of all of your processes simply enter the command

ps

The command name, process identification number, controlling tty name, and the cumulative execution time of all of your processes will be printed. (The controlling tty name is the UNIX System's name for the terminal that is associated with the process, e.g. '/dev/tty34'.) You should expect to see the process for the ps command, the process for your interactive shell, and any background processes that are running for you.

If you are executing a process in the background, you can use the ps command to monitor that process. If the process identification number of the background process is 2150, then the command

ps 2150

will print the information for process 2150. As process 2150 progresses you can repeatedly use the ps command to watch the cumulative execution time increase. At some point process 2150 will complete and then the command

ps 2150

will print a message similar to "2150: no such process".

7.6 Kill — Abort Background Processes

When a program is running in the foreground you can usually stop it by striking the interrupt character (usually Control-D or DEL). However you cannot stop a background process by striking the interrupt character. Instead the UNIX System has a special command called kill for killing your own background processes. Only the superuser can kill other people's processes.

When you run a command in the background the shell automatically prints its process identification number. If your background process is number 1234, you can kill it by entering the command

kill 1234

If you have forgotten the process ID number use the ps command. Process 1234 will be killed only if it exists and if it is your process and if it does not catch or ignore the kill. If the process that you are trying to kill is a fairly ordinary command, such as a text processing job, then the kill will probably work. Unproven machine dependent background processes are often impossible to kill.

Processes that catch or ignore the ordinary kill signal can definitely be killed by sending signal number nine. The command

kill -9 1234

will send signal nine to process 1234. Using the "-9" option with kill is the surest way to stop a command.

Since processes kill themselves while running (the system doesn't kill them either directly or immediately), a process that is sleeping or waiting for some event will not die immediately. Processes that are waiting for events that will never happen can never die. Processes can arrange to catch the kill signal and either ignore it or respond in some unique fashion. The point of this discussion is that the kill program only kills reasonable processes; really aberrant processes live on.

When you log off the system, any processes that are still running in the background will be stopped unless you have used the nohup command or unless the process has arranged to ignore the signal. When things get very weird or uncontrollable hang up and start from the beginning.

7.7 Nohup — Run Programs While Logged Off

The nohup command allows you to run a command that will continue to run after you hang up or log off the system. This is very useful for large jobs, such as big text processing commands, sorts of very large files, and major program recompilations. Usually you use nohup on a background job.

If you had a shell command file called 'nroffbook' that performed the text processing on a book manuscript you could use the command

```
nohup sh nroffbook &
```

to invoke a shell that was immune to hangups to process the commands in the file 'nroffbook'. You can log off the system immediately after entering the command and the work will proceed in your absence. If you don't use nohup, the processing will cease when you log off. Any output of the command that nohup executes will be sent to the file 'nohup.out' unless you make other arrangements.

7.8 Nice — Run Processes at Low Priority

The nice command is usually used to reduce the priority of a command. You should use nice whenever you are doing major processing and you want to reduce the demands on the system. Programs run using nice usually take significantly longer than programs run at the usual priority. Nice often is used in conjunction with background tasks, especially with tasks that are run using nohup.

Nice essentially reduces the size of the time slice allocated to a process, but the process is bound to consume some CPU time under all conditions. Unfortunately, there is no method in the UNIX System for running a job that only executes when the system has absolutely nothing else to do. Very demanding jobs that can wait till the wee hours of the morning or the weekend should be run at those times in order to completely minimize interference with the normal processing on the system.

The command

```
nice sh nroffbook &
```

will invoke a shell to execute the commands in the command file 'nroffbook' in the background. If you want to log off while the processing is proceeding then the command

  nice nohup sh nroffbook &

will perform the chore at low priority, in the background, immune to hangups.

7.9 Time — Time Processes

The time command is used to time processes. You might want to time a process in order to compare two different methods or you might just want to know how long something takes. For example, you might want to time the ps command. The command

  time ps

would time the ps command. After the ps command completes the time command will print three key timing statistics. The first statistic is the total elapsed time for executing the command, the second statistic is the time spent executing the command, and the third statistic is the time spent by the system on behalf of the command. The elapsed time is accurate to a second, whereas the execution time and the system time are accurate to a sixtieth of a second. This discrepancy can occasionally lead to peculiar results on very lightly loaded systems.

The reported times can vary depending on load conditions and other random influences. Timing a command several times in quick succession is likely to generate consistent data; timing a command at several different times of the day is likely to generate less consistent data. The ratio of system time to execution time indicates the relative importance of system calls during the execution of the process. (See Section 15.6.)

7.10 Man — Print Manual Entries

The man command is used to print entries from the UNIX System manual. For example, to reproduce the UNIX System manual entry that explains the use of the ls command enter the command

  man ls

The manual entry will appear on your terminal. The man command is seldom used if you have a current UNIX System manual at your side.

On older systems the man command goes through a lot of work to reproduce the manual entry. If you will need to see the output again in the near future, you should save the output in a file.

  man ls > ls.man

On some systems the output of man is designed to be printed on a photo-typesetter. Use the option "-n" or the option "-Tterm" (see your UNIX System manual) so that the output will look OK on your terminal.

7.11 Passwd — Change Login Password

The passwd command is used to change your login password. Some people change their passwords periodically (some system managers insist) to maintain security. When you enter the command

        passwd

the system will prompt you to enter your current password. This prevents some-one from changing your password without your permission. When you have entered your password the system will ask you to enter your new password. A good password contains both upper case and lower case letters, does not appear in the dictionary, and is longer than five or six letters. If your password is too skimpy, the system might ask you to choose another. When the system is happy with your choice it will ask you to enter it again to make sure that you typed it correctly. A typo during this procedure means beginning again, so type care-fully. Note that echoing is turned off while you are entering your passwords. If you forget your password, the system administrator can remove your old pass-word and give you another one.

7.12 Echo — Repeat Command Line Arguments

The echo command repeats its arguments. When the arguments are simple words the echo command is useful for printing messages on the terminal, espe-cially when it is used in shell program files. The command

        echo Load second reel and THEN strike return.

will print the message "Load second reel and THEN strike return."

   The echo command is also used to investigate the shell's argument processing capabilities. Arguments that you supply to programs are scanned by the shell to discover whether you have used any of the shell's special characters. The spe-cial characters are used to control various substitutions that the shell performs. For example, the shell maintains a system of variables. The word "$PATH" is a reference to a shell variable named "PATH" which codes the current search string. (Shell variables are discussed in Section 13.2 and the search string is dis-cussed in Section 13.4.) You can discover the current value of the $PATH vari-able by entering the command

        echo $PATH

On many systems the output will be ": /bin: /usr/bin".

   File name generation is another form of argument substitution that the shell performs. The shell metacharacters "?", "*", and "[" provide mechanisms for generating lists of files. You can use the echo command to discover what argu-ment lists are passed to programs when you specify arguments containing the shell metacharacters. The commands

        echo c*
        echo c?
        echo [cde]*xyz

will reveal the argument lists. The first command will display a list of all of the files in the current directory that start with the letter "c", the second will list all of the files with two character names beginning with the letter "c", and the third will list of all of the files in the current directory that begin with "c", "d", or "e" and end in the text sequence "xyz". File name generation is a powerful technique for focusing the attention of certain commands on certain groups of appropriately named files — use the echo command when you want to know exactly what argument lists are being generated.

7.13 Find — Search for a File

The find command is an aid for locating misplaced files. Find examines a file system subtree looking for files that match a set of criteria. For example, the command

    find . -name checklist -print

will search the file system tree starting in the current directory (named '.') for a file named (the -name option) checklist. If the file is found, the pathname will be printed (the -print option). Numerous examples of the find command are in the Abridged Manual and several uses of find in shell programs are shown in Section 14.5.

System administrators often use find to search the file system for dangerous or wasteful uses of the file system. Find takes a long time to search through a large subtree; it is best to make the subtree as small as possible. You should probably run find during the wee hours of the morning if you are going to search through an entire large file system.

7.14 Mail and Write - Communicating with Other Users

The mail program is used to read mail that is sent to you or to send mail to other users or to groups of users at your computer installation. When you login the system will print the message "You have mail." if someone has sent mail to you. You can read your mail by entering the command

    mail

The system will print your mail, one message at a time. At the conclusion of each message the mail program pauses and prints a "?". You should respond with a command that indicates what you want to do with the mail. (See your manual for details.) The most common actions are saving the message in a file, deleting the message, or forwarding the message to other users.

If you want to send mail to somebody, the first thing you have to do is find the person's login name. Login names can be found in the '/etc/passwd' file, and you can also use the who command to see the login names of the people who are logged on. If you want to send mail to "td" and "alvy", use the command

    mail td alvy

After you enter the command, type in your message interactively. The mail command swallows your lines of input as you type — you cannot go back a few lines and correct your previous input. When you have completed your message simply strike the EOF key (Control-D) to indicate the end of the message.

Using the mail program to send mail is demonstrated below. Note that the parts entered by the user are underlined and the Control-D character is indicated using the notation "^d".

```
% mail e mike
Meeting tomorrow on documentation standards,
3pm in O'Flanagans Bar. (Bring Quarters)
^d
%
```

Entering your message interactively as shown above is good only for short messages, because it is impossible to back up a few lines to fix mistakes. If you have a long message, you should first place the message in a file using the text editor. The text editor allows you to polish and refine your message. You can mail a message that you have stored in a file called 'message.fil' by using input redirection:

```
mail tom alicia < message.fil
```

If the mail program cannot locate one of the recipients, then your message will be saved in a file called 'dead.letter' so that you can find the correct user name and resend the message without reentering the text.

The write command is used to establish typed communication between two UNIX System users. Using a telephone, or an intercom, or two tin cans and a string is usually a better way to communicate. Since someone may unexpectedly write to you someday, you should prepare by learning how to use the write command.

When someone writes to you, the message "Message from harry on tty33" (or similar) will appear on your terminal. You should respond by stopping whatever task you ar engaged in and running the command

```
write harry
```

Once both parties have executed the write command anything that either person types will appear on both terminals. Therefore, it is best if only one person type at a time. The person who initiates the conversation usually types a few lines and then types a line containing a single "o" which stands for over. The other person is now free to respond with a few lines and then type The conversation continues until someone types a line containing "oo" for over and out. You can terminate the conversation by striking the EOF (Control-D) character. If two people type simultaneously, the outputs are intermixed and it is almost impossible to sort it all out.

7.15 Stty and Tty — Your Terminal Handler

The tty command is used to print the special file name of the terminal that is attached to the standard input. A message is printed if the standard input is not attached to a terminal. Sometimes the communication lines between terminals and the computer become intermittent. To log a complaint you need to know the name of your special file so that the repairman can locate the hardware for your communication line. The command

tty

will print a message such as "tty30" indicating that your terminal corresponds to the special file '/dev/tty30'.

The tty command is also used in shell programs to determine whether the standard input is a terminal. The exit status of tty is true if the standard input is a terminal and false otherwise. (See Section 13.7)

The set terminal options command (stty) allows you to control the way the system treats your terminal. Stty is very important because there are many different types of terminals. On some systems there is a program that automatically adapts the system to your terminal based on the value of the TERM parameter. On other systems you should include the appropriate stty command in the file '.profile' in order to set the modes appropriately at the beginning of each session.

The part of the UNIX System that performs the conversions to adapt to a particular type of terminal is called the terminal handler (also called the tty handler). This section discusses some of the options that can be enabled in the tty handler using the stty command. A complete discussion of all of the possibilities is beyond the scope of this book.

If you enter the command

stty

then the settings of a few key modes will be printed. On my system the following is displayed:

```
speed 300 baud; tabs
erase = #, kill = @, intr = ^?
```

This message indicates that the communication speed is 300 baud, that the tabs option is set, the erase character is the sharp, the kill character is the at sign, and the interrupt character is the DEL (indicated cryptically by the "^?" notation). The tabs option indicates that the system believes that I have a terminal capable of handling tabs (more on that in a few paragraphs). The erase, kill, and interrupt characters are discussed in Section 3.4.

The erase character is used to erase the previously entered character and the kill character is used to erase the entire line. Because the standard UNIX System erase and kill characters are awkward, many people reassign them. Frequently the Control-H character is used for erase and the Control-U character is used for kill. You can reassign erase and kill by using the command

stty erase \^h kill \^u

The notation of a caret followed by a letter indicates a control character to stty; the backslash is used to escape the caret because the caret has a special meaning to the shell. We can verify that the assignments have actually changed by using the command

stty

On my system the new output looks like

speed 300 baud; tabs
erase = ^h, kill = ^u, intr = ^?

Striking the interrupt character sends an interrupt signal to the currently executing foreground processes. Some programs such as the shell and the editor choose to ignore the interrupt but most other programs, such as cat and grep, are halted when they receive the interrupt. Many people prefer to use Control-c as the interrupt key rather than the default DEL key. The command

stty intr \^c

will assign the interrupt function to the Control-c key. You could use the stty command to verify the reassignment.

The handling of tabs varies from one terminal to another. Some terminals recognize and expand the tab character, other terminals ignore it. The command

stty -tabs

informs the system that you are using a terminal that doesn't know how to expand tabs. The UNIX System terminal handler will expand the tabs into spaces so that output appears correct on your terminal. The command

stty tabs

informs the system that your terminal expands tabs, thus tabs will pass directly through the terminal handler. You should use this setting on terminals that expand tabs because it slightly increases the output speed when a tab is encountered.

It is possible, although very difficult, to use the UNIX System with a terminal that doesn't produce lower case letters. The command

stty lcase

informs the system that you are using a terminal that only supports upper case. When you are using an upper case terminal all input is automatically translated from upper to lower case and all output is automatically translated from lower to upper case. In the upper case mode if you enter backslash followed by a letter, then an upper case letter is generated. For example, the input " \JOHN \ DOE" is translated to "John Doe" when you are in upper case mode. The command

stty -lcase

will return you to the normal mode where upper case and lower case letters are acceptable. You may inadvertently get into the upper case only mode if the terminal's shift lock key is depressed during login. During the login process the system attempts to determine the type of terminal and make the proper settings. If you enter your login name in all upper case letters then the system assumes that you are using an upper case terminal and you have to use the stty command to revert to normal mode.

You can also use stty to change the baud rate for communication between the terminal and the computer. (The baud rate is a measure of the speed at which characters are passed between a terminal and a computer. As a rough estimate, the baud rate divided by 10 is the number of characters that can transferred in a second.) Once you tell the UNIX System about a new baud rate you must be able to change your terminal's rate to match. You can use the command

   stty 1200

to set the communication rate to 1200 baud.

The stty command adjusts the settings of the terminal that is the current standard input. You can exploit this feature to change the settings of a terminal other than the one you are using interactively. For instance, if you want a display of the settings of tty33, you can use the command

   stty < /dev/tty33

(You need superuser privilege in order to open /dev/tty33 for reading in most systems.) Similarly, you can use the command

   stty 9600 < /dev/tty33

to set the baud rate to 9600 on tty33. This method for setting the baud rate is useful for controlling communication channels for special devices such as receive-only printers. You will seldom have a reason to interfere with communication channels that are being managed by the login process (channels where it is possible to log in).

Stty contains many other options you can use to adapt the system to individual terminals. You really have to know a lot about terminals, computers, and serial communication to use most of the options of the stty command. You should find out what options you need to use and place the appropriate stty command in your '.profile' file.

7.16 Du — Disk Usage

Occasionally you want to see how much disk storage your files are occupying. If you enter the command

   du

you will get a summary of the number of blocks of disk storage used in every directory in the current subtree. (The current subtree consists of all of the files in the current directory, all of the files in any subdirectories, etc.) You can also specify which subtree should be examined. The command

        du /usr/sys/src

will print a summary of disk usage in the subtree attached to the '/usr/sys/src' directory.

One of the maxims of the UNIX System is "users' disk storage requirements expand to fill the available space." Periodic removal of old files is necessary to keep your storage charges down and to keep free space on the system. People often use du when they are cleaning their directories in order to concentrate on the directories that consume the most space.

The df (disk free) command can be used to see how much free space exists on a particular storage volume. (See Section 18.6.) System managers often run df periodically to keep track of free space. When the free space diminishes to a certain point most administrators ask the users to prune their directories.

7.17 Od – Dump Files

Occasionally you want to know exactly what binary codes are contained in a file. The octal dump (od) program is used to produce octal, decimal, ASCII, and hexadecimal format dumps of a file. The various formats can be produced together or separately.

The term "dump" originated many years ago when program debugging was usually performed by producing a printout of all of the values in memory following a program failure. Since the quantity of information was large and the programmer's deciphering job was unpleasant, the printout was called a dump. Today much debugging is done more intelligently, although "dumps" are still used. Most program failure "dumps" are examined today with the help of programs that make interpreting the information much easier. Whenever a UNIX System program fails inexplicably a dump is performed into the file named 'core' in the working directory of the program and the mysterious message "core dumped" is produced.

The octal dump program is often used to search for control characters embedded in text files. For example, suppose you wanted to know whether a certain file contained tab characters. If you were to cat the file onto your screen, the terminal handler or your terminal would automatically expand the tabs into the correct number of spaces. However, if you used the od program to dump the file, you could examine the output for the notation " \t" which indicates a tab. During a dump in ascii format, printable characters are displayed normally, unprintable control characters are printed in octal except for a few very standard characters which are represented as follows:

        Backspace   \ b
        Tab   \ t
        New Line   \ n
        Carriage Ret \ r
        Null   \ 0
        Form Feed   \ f

The command

    od -c chapt

would dump the file 'chapt' in ASCII character (the option "-c") format.

Od can dump special or directory files as well as ordinary files. The superuser could use od to examine (in the octal radix) the information stored on a disk by entering the command

    od /dev/rp0

Od also allows you to examine a file starting in the middle by specifying an offset. The disk could be examined starting at byte 1024 by using the command

    od /dev/rp0 + 1024

The argument "+ 1024" indicates that you should start dumping 1024 bytes past the start of the file. The same offset could be specified in terms of blocks (a block is 512 bytes) by entering the command

    od /dev/rp0 + 2b

CHAPTER

8

Text File Utilities

Many UNIX System users use the system because of its excellent text processing facilities. It is not surprising that many programmers love the UNIX System because much of the work of programming is manipulating text. Secretaries, scientists, and businessmen as well have found that the UNIX System's text facilities can increase their productivity.

Naturally the UNIX System contains programs to type files on the terminal or to print files on a printer. The UNIX System also contains programs to sort files, to search through files for text patterns, to count lines, words, and characters in files, and to check for spelling errors in document files. These programs are described in this chapter.

The UNIX System also contains a variety of much more sophisticated programs for working with text files. The first section of this chapter is a guide to the UNIX System's sophisticated text manipulation programs. All of these programs are covered elsewhere in this book.

8.1 Text Utilities

Text files are often created by using a text editing program. A text editor allows a user to enter and change text in a file. Many UNIX Systems have several text editors, most of which resemble the standard UNIX System text editor described in Chapter 5. Some of the advanced features of the standard editor are described in Chapter 10.

The UNIX System contains programs that can format a file of text. Formatting smooths out the margins, inserts titles and footnotes, adjusts the spacing, aligns columns of tabular data, and handles all of the special characters in mathematical equations. The UNIX System programs nroff, troff, eqn, and tbl are described in Chapter 11.

The UNIX System also contains programs that can help you write programs that recognize command languages and grammers. These recognizers are useful if you are writing a text formatter or a programming language translator or a variety of other programs that perform various actions based upon text. The UNIX System programs to assist you in writing recognizers, named Lex and Yacc, are described in Chapter 17.

Text files often are derived from other text files, and there may be several versions of a text file. To help you maintain systems of text files the UNIX System contains the make program, which keeps track of dependencies in a group of files, and the Source Code Control System (SCCS), which keeps track of different versions of a file. Make and SCCS are described in Chapter 12.

8.2 Cat — Type Files

The concatenate program (cat) is one of the most versatile text manipulation programs. The standard use of the cat program is to type files on your terminal. The command

    cat /etc/motd

will type the file '/etc/motd' on your terminal. Since cat is an abbreviation for concatenate it is reasonable to expect cat to concatenate files. If you enter the command

    cat /etc/greeting /etc/motd

the greeting file and the message-of-the-day file will be combined (concatenated) and typed on your terminal. The ability of cat to concatenate files is also useful in the following way:

    cat chapt1 chapt2 chapt3 chapt4 chapt5 > book

The command concatenates five chapters of a book into a single file called 'book' using output redirection. The command could have been entered more elegantly as

    cat chapt[12345] > book

because file name generation occurs alphabetically. (Numbers are alphabetized as you would expect, "1," "2," etc.) If there were only five numbered chapters in the directory the command could also have been entered as

    cat chapt? > book

or it could have been entered as

    cat chapt* > book

However, you should note that the command

    cat chapt3 chapt1 > newchapters

is not equivalent to the command

    cat chapt[31] > newchapters

The second case relies on the shell's file name generation process to generate the argument list for the cat program. File name generation always produces an alphabetized list, so if you are relying upon file name generation when you are concatenating files, remember the alphabetization. You can use the echo command to see the difference. The command

    echo chapt3 chapt1

will produce the output "chapt3 chapt1", whereas the command

    echo chapt[31]

will produce the output "chapt1 chapt3".

Another use of the cat command is to create empty files. Use the command

    cat /dev/null > empty

to create an empty file named 'empty'. The UNIX System "bit bucket" is a special file named '/dev/null'. If you direct output to the null device, it is discarded. If you read input from the null device, you immediately encounter an end of file. Therefore, performing a cat of the null device will produce a zero length output (which was directed above to the file named 'empty').

Another way to create an empty file is to use the command

    > naught

to create the empty file name 'naught'. When you enter a command that consists solely of an output redirection the shell creates the named file.

Another use of the cat program is to place a few lines of text in a file without the bother of using a text editor. If you execute cat without arguments, it reads from the standard input until an end of file is encountered. Thus the command

    cat > quick

will cause cat to read whatever you type at your terminal and place it in the file 'quick'. Since cat is not an editor you cannot back-up a few lines and fix errors, but for simple one or two line inputs this command is useful. When you strike Control-D cat will receive the end of file indication and close the output file and exit. Then the shell will prompt you to enter another command.

Many UNIX System text processing programs read their input from the standard input if you don't explicitly mention input files in the command line. When used intentionally this is a powerful technique, but when you accidentally fail to mention input files the programs are very willing to sit there all day waiting for input from the terminal while you sit there all day waiting for them to complete their chores.

8.3 Pr − Title and Format Files

The pr command is used to paginate and title text files. If you use pr to type a file, the file will be sectioned into pages, each page will be numbered and titled, and there will be blank lines at the top and bottom of each page. The most common use of the pr command is to prepare a text file for printing on a lineprinter.

Pr is also used to produce several columns of output, compress files by replacing spaces with tabs, expand tabs into spaces, number the lines in a file, or perform other simple reformatting tasks. The command

ls | pr -5 -t

will pipe the output of the ls command into the pr command. Pr will then produce five-column output (the -5 argument) without titles or pagination (the -t argument). Columnating the output of ls will allow more files to be displayed on one screen.

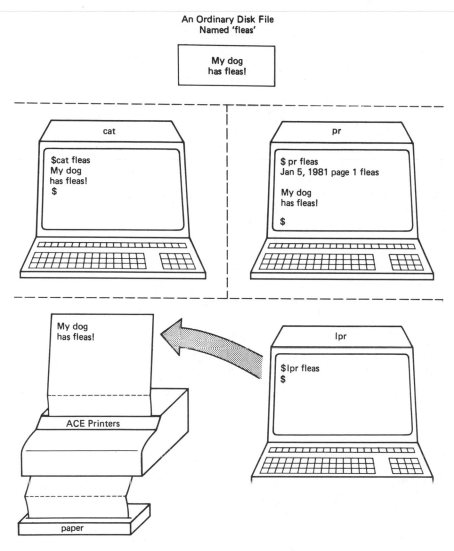

Figure 8.1. Cat, pr, and lpr.

A standard use of pr is to paginate and title a file as in the following command:

```
pr chapt1 > chapt1.pr
```

8.4 Lpr – Print Files

The lpr command prints files on the system lineprinter. Systems with several lineprinters usually offer several versions of the lpr command. On my system the lpr is for the main lineprinter, and vpr, dpr, and npr are for the other printers.

It isn't possible to share a printer among several users simultaneously. Instead the printer is assigned to a single user for the duration of a print request. The main role of the lpr command is to synchronize requests for the line printer. If the lineprinter is busy when you enter the lpr command, your files will be placed in a queue and then printed when the printer is free. Lpr will return control to you as soon as the print files are placed in the queue.

The lpr command normally prints a banner page before and after the file, but the file contents are not changed. Lpr does not insert blank lines at the top and bottom of pages or number pages or perform any of the other actions of the pr command. If you want to paginate or title the contents of the file, you should use the pr command first.

Suppose you want a printed listing of the contents of several directories. One method would be to enter the following four commands:

```
ls -l /bin /usr/bin > dirfile
pr dirfile > dirfile.pr
lpr dirfile.pr
rm dirfile dirfile.pr
```

A simpler method using pipes would be the command

```
ls -l /bin /usr/bin | pr | lpr
```

Of course the most common use of the lpr command is to print a file or group of files as in this example:

```
lpr chapt1.pr chapt2.pr chapt3.pr
```

8.5 Wc – Count Lines, Words, and Characters

The word count (wc) program will tally a count of characters, words, and lines in a text file. The command

```
wc chapt?
```

would print the number of characters, words, and lines in each of the chapt files stored in the current directory, and a cumulative total for all of the mentioned files. Flag arguments can be used to direct word count to count only characters, words, or lines.

8.6 Diff — Compare Files

The diff program is used to show which lines are different in two text files. The output of diff consists of a line that resembles an editor command followed by the affected lines from the two files. Lines from the first file are preceded by a "<" and lines from the second file are preceded with a ">".

The diff command produces three types of editor pseudo-command lines:

```
n1  a  n3, n4
n1, n2  c  n3, n4
n1, n2  d  n3
```

Line numbers n1 and n2 refer to lines in the first file and line numbers n3 and n4 refer to lines in the second file. The first of these editor pseudo-commands indicates that the second file contains lines (n3 through n4) that are absent from the first file after n1, the second indicates that the lines n1 through n2 in the first file are different from the lines n3 through n4 in the second file, and the third indicates that the first file contains lines (n1 through n2) which are missing from the second file after n3.

For example, if the file's 'arlinote' and 'arlinote2' are identical except that 'arlinote2' contains the line "Susan - 586-1234" after line 10, then the command

```
diff  arlinote  arlinote2
```

will produce the following output:

```
10a11
>Susan - 586-1234
```

The output indicates that the two files will be identical if the line "Susan - 586-1234" (line 11 in 'arlinote2') is appended after line 10 of 'arlinote'.

8.7 Sort — Rearrange Files

The sort command is used to sort and/or merge text files. Sort rearranges the lines in a file according to your command line specifications. The specifications are complex so they will not be discussed in detail. Unless you make other arrangements, the sorted output will appear on the terminal. Naturally you can redirect the output to a file if you want a permanent copy of the sorted output.

Each line of the input can contain several fields. The fields are delimited by a field separator, which is usually a tab or space but may be assigned to some other character. The portion of the input line that the sort program examines in order to determine an ordering for the file is called the sort key. The sort key can be one or more fields, or parts of fields, or the entire line.

As an example, let's sort a file containing a list of people's telephone numbers and initials. To sort a file, you must have a file with a regular structure and you must know the details of that structure. In our example, let's suppose that each line of the file contains a person's initials, a tab character, and that person's telephone number, in that order. For simplicity let's consider a hypothetical file named 'telnos' containing the following three lines:

```
kc      362-4993
gmk     245-3209
arm     333-3903
```

The command

```
sort +0 -1 telnos > namesorted
```

would sort the 'telnos' file according to the people's initials. The arguments "+0" and "-1" inform the sort program that we want to restrict the sort key to the first field; the "+0" indicates that the sort key starts at the beginning of the line, and the "-1" indicates that the sort key stops at the end of the first field. If we wanted the file sorted according to the telephone numbers, we could use the command

```
sort +1 telnos > numbersorted
```

The "+1" argument informs the sort program that we want to restrict the sort key to start after the first field. After the sorts, the file called 'namesorted' (in our example) would contain the following arrangement:

```
arm     333-3903
gmk     245-3209
kc      362-4993
```

and the file called 'numbersorted' would contain

```
gmk     245-3209
arm     333-3903
kc      363-4993
```

Of course much more sophisticated sorting can be accomplished (see the examples in the Abridged Manual).

8.8 Grep – Search for Text Patterns in Files

The grep program (and its relatives fgrep and egrep) searches for text patterns in files. Whenever the text pattern is recognized on a line, that line of the file is typed on the standard output. You can think of the grep program as performing a horizontal slice through a file based on a text matching criterion. The word grep is derived from the phrase "global regular expression print."

The first argument to the grep command is the text pattern and the following arguments specify the files that should be examined. The text pattern for grep can use most of the regular expression syntax of the standard the UNIX System text editor. The text patterns for egrep can be more complicated, while the text patterns for fgrep are limited to fixed strings. As you might expect, fgrep (fast grep) is faster than grep which is faster than egrep (extended grep). Grep is powerful and fast enough for most casual use.

Suppose you want a long format list of the subdirectories of the root directory. If you enter the command

ls -l /

you will produce the desired list intertwined with a list of all of the ordinary files
contained in the root directory. The grep command can be used to filter out all
of the unwanted information. If no files are supplied as arguments to grep, then
it reads from the standard input. Thus grep can be used in a pipeline as follows:

ls -l / | grep '^d'

This command pipes the output of the ls command into the grep command. The
text pattern for grep is quoted because it contains a caret, a meaningful character to the shell. The editor regular expression "^d" matches all lines that begin
with the letter "d." Thus only directories will be listed, since directory lines in a
long listing start with a "d" while ordinary file lines start with a "-". When I ran
this command on my system the following lines were printed:

```
drwxrwxr-x      4   bin    3136   Sep 17 11:28      bin
drwxr-xr-x      9   root   3648   Sep 16 17:24      dev
drwxrwx--x      4   root   2496   Sep 17 18:40      etc
drwxrwxr-x      5   bin     752   Jul  1 11:24      lib
drwxrwxr-x      6   root    160   Aug 26 13:37      mnt
drwxr-x--x     12   mel     528   Sep  2 15:48      source
drwxrwxrwx      2   root    896   Sep 17 19:27      tmp
drwxrwx--x     26   root    416   Jul 27 12:57      usr
```

Notice that all of the lines begin with the letter "d."
    The standard use of the grep command is to find all of the occurrences of
some word in a document. I have a bad habit of typing "teh" when I mean
"the". The command

grep teh chapt*

will search all of the chapt files in the current directory for the text pattern "teh".
Of course I could do the search using the editor, but it is easier to use grep to
identify those files that contain the error before using the editor to fix the error.

8.9 Cut and Paste — Rearrange Columns of Files

The cut and paste programs are used to take vertical sections of files. Cut and
paste are most useful for files that contain tabular data. The cut program is used
to cut a vertical section from a file, whereas the paste program merges several
vertical sections into one file. Both cut and paste manipulate input files and produce their output on the standard output (the terminal). Usually you will want
to redirect their output to a file. (Note that cut and paste are not as widely available as the other programs discussed in this chapter.)
    To use cut and paste you have to understand the way the columns (fields) of
the files are constructed. The easiest field separator is a tab, although other
characters can be used.

Let's suppose that we need to separate the initials from the telephone numbers in the 'telnos' file described above. As you remember, the 'telnos' file contained the following three lines:

```
kc        362-4993
gmk       245-3209
arm       333-3903
```

The command

```
cut -f1 telnos > initials
```

would place the first field (the initials) in a file named 'initials' while the command

```
cut -f2 telnos > numbers
```

would place the second field (the numbers) into a file named 'numbers'. The initials file would contain

```
kc
gmk
arm
```

while the 'numbers' file would contain

```
362-4993
245-3209
333-3903
```

We can use the paste command to recombine the 'initials' file and the 'numbers' file into a new telephone numbers file which we will call 'newtelnos'. In 'newtelnos' the numbers will come before the initials on each line. Paste will automatically separate the two columns with a tab character.

```
paste numbers initials > newtelnos
```

The file 'newtelnos' contains the following three lines:

```
362-4993     kc
245-3209     gmk
333-3903     arm
```

8.10 Spell – Find Spelling Errors

The UNIX System spell program checks a text file for possible spelling errors. Spell uses a dictionary of common words. Each word in the input text is looked up in the dictionary. Spell is rarely fooled by prefixes, suffixes, and inflections, and spell is able to ignore nroff/troff formatting commands (see Chapter 11).

If "frequent" is in the dictionary, then spell will accept "frequents", "frequently", "frequenting", and other variants. Because some words don't follow the normal rules for prefixes and suffixes there is a separate dictionary listing all of the exceptions. Words from this dictionary (called the stop list) must be matched exactly.

There are many many possible spelling errors in a document which spell is incapable of finding. Spell also complains about a large number of correct words because its dictionary can't possibly contain every word, especially in technical subjects. Spell also is likely to object to proper names, places, and the like. Spell is a valuable proofreading aid but it is not a substitute for careful proofreading.

The normal use of spell is

```
spell  chapt1.doc
```

to check the spelling in the file 'chapt1.doc'. The questionable words will be printed on the standard output. Spell will find hundreds of problems in a moderately large document, so you should usually collect the words in a file:

```
spell  chapt1.doc  >  chapt1.errwds
```

If no files are mentioned, then spell reads from the standard input. This is useful for checking spellings interactively or for using spell in a pipeline.

8.11 Crypt — Encode Files

The crypt program reads the standard input, encodes it, and writes to the standard output. You can encrypt your files if you want to make sure that they are absolutely private. Encryption is more secure than using the file protection mechanism because the superuser can access any file, but the superuser cannot decrypt files. An encrypted file can be decoded only if you know the password or if you are very good at cryptanalysis and you have substantial computer time to devote to the decoding.

The command

```
crypt xyZZy321  <  chaptn.doc  >  chaptn.cry
```

will encode the file 'chaptn.doc' using the password "xyZZy321". The result will be placed in the file 'chaptn.cry'. Somewhat equivalently you could enter the command

```
crypt  <  chaptn.doc  >  chaptn.cry
```

In this case crypt would print a message on your terminal asking you to enter the password. Echoing would be turned off during your response. This is one of the relatively rare cases where a program needs to read input from the controlling terminal, not from the standard input.

The original file can be recovered using the same password:

```
crypt xyZZy321  <  chaptn.cry  >  chaptn.new
```

The file 'chaptn.new' should be identical to the file 'chaptn.doc'.

8.12 Tee — Duplicate Output

The tee program reads the standard input and diverts it to the standard output and to one or more named files. It is analogous to the tee pipefitting that plumbers use to split one pipe into two pipes. Tee is usually used when you want to divert a program's output to a file and also see it on your terminal. The command

```
spell mybook.n | tee errwords
```

will collect the suspicious words from the file 'mybook.n' in the file 'errwords' and display the list on the terminal.

Tee can also be used to collect intermediate results in a pipeline. If you want to print a five-column titled document showing the contents of a directory, you might use the command

```
ls | pr -5 | lpr
```

You could save the two intermediate files by inserting the tee command in the the pipeline:

```
ls | tee lsfile | pr -5 | tee lsprfile | lpr
```

The file 'lsfile' will contain the original output of the ls command and the file 'lsprfile' will contain the five column titled version of the the ls output.

8.13 Tail — Print the End of a File

The tail program is used to print the end of a file. This allows you to see the end of a large file without sitting through a tedious display of the entire file. The command

```
tail book.new
```

will print the last few lines of the file 'book.new'. Various options to tail allow you to control just how much of the end of the file is printed. The command

```
tail -132 book.new
```

will print the final 132 lines of the file 'book.new' and the command

```
tail +66 chapt.1
```

will print all but the first 66 lines of 'chapt.1'. A number preceded by a plus indicates an offset in lines from the beginning of the file, whereas a number preceded by a hyphen indicates an offset in lines from the end of the file.

Tail can also be used in pipelines. The command

```
ls /usr/bin | tail -20
```

will display the last 20 (in an alphabetic list) files in the '/usr/bin' directory.

CHAPTER

9

Managing Your Files

The UNIX Operating System is a tool for managing information. This chapter describes the UNIX System utilities that allow you to manage your files. All of these programs perform very simple functions, usually functions that are analogous to the functions that you perform during spring cleaning. Periodically during your interactions with the UNIX System you have to remove old information, make room for new information, adjust the file access privilege system for certain files, and occasionally acquire files from other users.

While there are some areas where information management occurs automatically, in most cases you have to supply the management talent. The unit of information in the UNIX System is the ordinary file. Most operating systems, including the UNIX System, contain programs to create ordinary files, to move ordinary files from one location to another, to rename files, to make copies of files, and to remove files. You need to perform these functions as necessary on your collection of files.

In a multiuser operating system all files are owned by someone and it is necessary to have a privilege system so that owners can protect their files from unwanted access by others. Therefore, the UNIX System has programs to control the access rights of files and to change the ownership of files.

The UNIX file system is more than a big bunch of files. In the UNIX System files are grouped into directories and directories are arranged in a logical hierarchy. The hierarchy makes it easier to organize and arrange your collection. Because of this the UNIX System contains several programs to maintain the directory system. One of the major aspects of your information management task is to decide how you are going to organize your directories. A well-organized set of directories will make it much easier to use the UNIX System, especially if you use it for several different functions.

9.1 Rm — Remove Files

The remove (rm) command allows you to delete ordinary files. (The rmdir command is used to remove directories. See Section 9.5.) In order to remove a file
you must have write permission in the directory containing that file but you
need neither read nor write permission for the file itself. If the file is write protected, then the system will ask you if you really want to remove the file.

The command

    rm myfile

will remove the file 'myfile'. Be very careful when you use rm because removed
files really are gone. The only way to recover a removed file is to ask the system
administrator to recover a copy of the file from a recent backup. Whenever you
are in doubt, refrain from removing files. It is a good idea not to use lots of files
with very similar names because it is easy to remove the wrong file through typing error or momentary mental lapse.

The command

    rm *

will remove all of the ordinary files in the current directory. Don't use this command unless you want to entirely clean out a directory.

The remove command contains two very useful options. If the "-i" flag is
present, then the remove program will interactively ask you if you really want to
remove every mentioned file. The command

    rm -i chapt*

will ask you to retain or remove every file in the current directory whose name
begins with 'chapt'. The name of each file (files whose name begins with
"chapt" in this case) will be printed followed by a question mark. If you reply
with a "y" or "yes", then the file will be removed. Any other reply will cause the
file to be retained.

The interactive remove is especially useful if files with untypeable names
appear in your directory. Any name containing control characters is either
difficult or impossible to type. Weird, unnameable files are occasionally produced by errant programs or by other transient problems. If you want to
remove a file with an unprintable name, enter the command

    rm -i *

and then reply no for each file except for the one with the unprintable name.

Another very useful option is "-r", which is used to remove a directory, all of
its contents, and all of the files and directories in that directory's subtree. Enter
the command

    rm -r bookdir

to remove the directory 'bookdir' and all of its contents, subdirectories, etc. The
recursive option obliterates the whole tree below the mentioned point. Natur-

ally you should be very careful when using the "-r" option. As a general rule it is safer to remove ordinary files using rm and then remove directories using rmdir.

9.2 Mv, Cp, and Ln — Move and Copy

The commands move, copy, and link (mv, cp, and ln) allow you to move and copy files. The move command moves a file from one location to another. If both locations are on the same file system, then the movement is essentially a renaming operation since the data in the file don't have to be relocated. If the locations are on different file systems, then the data in the file must be relocated from one device to another. The command

    mv chapt3 chapt3.save

will rename an ordinary file. The old name is 'chapt3' and the new name is 'chapt3.save'. After the operation there will be no file named 'chapt3'. The first file ('chapt3') is called the source file and the second file ('chapt3.save') is called the target or destination.

In general you can't use mv to rename directories. The one exception is when the source and target directory have the same parent. If 'mydir' is a directory, then the command

    mv mydir mynewdir

is legal because the source directory file 'mydir' and the destination directory file 'mynewdir' both have the same parent directory. The command

    mv mydir ../mynewdir

is illegal because the source and target don't have the same parent.

If the source file is an ordinary file and the target file is a directory file, then mv will move the source file into the target directory. If 'wkfile' is an ordinary file and 'mydir' is a subdirectory of the current directory, then the command

    mv wkfile mydir

will move 'wkfile' into the 'mydir' directory. You can verify the operation by entering the command

    ls mydir/wkfile

As an extension this idea you can have several source files if (and only if) the target file is a directory. The command

    mv wkfilel wkfile2 wkfile3 mydir

will move all three source files into the 'mydir' directory.

The copy command makes a copy of a file. The difference between mv and cp is that mv obliterates the source file, whereas after a cp operation the source file and the target file both exist. The command

    cp chapt4 chapt4.archive

will make a copy of the file 'chapt4' in the file called 'chapt4.archive'. The file 'chapt4' will not be changed by the operation. It is not permissible for the source file to be a directory for a copy operation.

If the target of a cp operation is a directory, then the copy operation will copy the source file to that directory. The target directory must exist before the operation. I have a directory named 'bkpdir' where I keep copies of important files. The command

   cp chapt4 bkpdir

will place a copy of the file named 'chapt4' in the directory 'bkpdir'.

As before, you can also have several source files when the target file is an existing directory. The command

   cp chapt* bkpdir

will place copies of all of the chapters in the 'bkpdir' directory.

The link command is used to establish pseudonyms for files. In the UNIX System it is possible for a file to have several different names.

When you use the copy command two copies of the file are produced. Changes to one copy of the file will not affect the other copy. When you use the link command a new name is created which references the file. No new copies of the actual data in the file are produced by the link command.

The command

   ln chapt8 genfilchapt

will establish a second name for the file 'chapt8'. The new name is 'genfilchapt'. Both names are equally valid and either name can be used to reference the file. There are several reasons for wanting two names for a file. The reason in this case is that we want one naming system for a group of files that reflects the number of the chapter, 'chapt8', and one system that reflects the contents of the chapter, 'genfilchapt'.

You can discover the number of links that a file has by using the ls command. The command

   ls -l chapt8 genfilchapt

will reveal that both names have two links. You can tell that the two names are actually links to just one file by using the inode option ("-i") of the ls command. (An inode is a structure that the system uses to define the characteristics of a single file. See Section 19.6.) If two names reference the same file, then both names will be associated with the same inode number. The command

   ls -i chapt8 genfilchapt

will reveal the inode numbers of the two names. If the names are actually links to one file, as in this case, then the numbers will be identical. If the names refer to different files, then the inode numbers will be different.

Another place where pseudonyms (links) are important is in the directory hierarchy. The name '..' always references the parent directory. When a directory is created the system links the name '..' to the parent directory and it links the name '.' to the current directory. The whole directory hierarchy is maintained with links between directory files. You cannot use the ln command to change the linking that binds the file system together.

9.3 Chmod, Chown, and Chgrp — Change File Modes

The change mode (chmod), change owner (chown), and the change group (chgrp) commands are used to control the access rights to files. The ability to fine tune the file system for flexible and protected access to files is one of the strengths of the UNIX System. All of these commands are operable only by the owner of a file or by the superuser.

The three operations that can be performed on a file are reading, writing, and execution. There are three levels of privilege associated with each file, the owner's privileges, the group's privileges, and the other's privileges. For each level of privilege, each of the three basic operations may either be allowed or denied. (The set id modes and the sticky mode can also be allowed or denied, but they are not discussed here because they are system programming attributes.)

You are allowed to determine the modes of the files that you own. For example, if you want to make a file unreadable and unwriteable to anyone but yourself, you would enter the command

    chmod go-rw file

The word "go-rw" is the new mode for the file. The letters "g" and "o" indicate that you want to control the group and other's permissions, the character "-" indicates that you want to deny privileges, and the letters "r" and "w" indicate the privileges reading and writing.

A symbolic mode control word ("go-rw" in the example above) consists of three parts: who, operator, permission. In the example the who part was "go" to indicate group and others, the op was "-" to remove permission, and the permission part was "rw" to indicate read and write. The characters used in constructing the symbolic mode control word are summarized in the following tables:

	Who		Operators
u	user (owner)	-	remove permission
g	group	+	add permission
o	other	=	assign permission
a	all (ugo)		

Permissions

r	read
w	write
x	execute
s	set user (or group) id mode
t	the save text (sticky) mode
u	the user's present permission
g	the group's present permission
o	the other's present permission

The command

    chmod a = rw myfile

will make 'myfile' readable and writeable for the owner, members of the file's group, and everybody else. The command

    chmod g + x newdoo

will add the group execute permission for the file 'newdoo'. The command

    chmod o-rwx newdoo

will make 'newdoo' inaccessible to others.

The commands chown and chgrp change the owner and group associated with a file. These commands usually are used when one user inherits another user's files or when one user gets copies of files from another user. The command

    chown kc *

will transfer ownership of all of the files in the current directory to the user named "kc". The name of the new owner must be either a valid login name or a user identification number. The login names and the corresponding numbers are found in the '/etc/passwd' file.

The command

    chgrp staff corelist

will associate the group "staff" with the file named 'corelist'. The groups mentioned in the chgrp command can either be group names or numbers from the '/etc/group' file. Many systems make very little use of the UNIX System group feature.

9.4 Mkdir and Rmdir - Create and Remove Directories

The make directory (mkdir) command is used to create a directory. When the system creates a directory it automatically inserts the entries for the names '.' and '..'. The name '.' is a pseudonym for the directory and the name '..' is a pseudonym for the parent directory. All directories contain these entries and ordinary users are prohibited from removing these entries. A directory that contains only the entries for '.' and '..' is considered empty.

The command

> mkdir morestuff

will create a directory named 'morestuff', which will be a subdirectory of the current directory. If you enter the command

> ls morestuff

you will discover that 'morestuff' is empty. The command

> ls -a morestuff

will reveal that 'morestuff' contains two entries, '.' and '..'. The command

> ls -id . morestuff/..

will reveal that the '..' entry in 'morestuff' and the current directory reference the same inode. (See the description of ls in Section 7.2 and in the Abridged Manual for more information on the options a, i, and d.)

In the course of using the 'morestuff' directory it would naturally fill up with a lot of files. If you then wanted to remove the directory 'morestuff', you would have to remove all of its contents. If 'morestuff' contained just ordinary files, then the command

> rm morestuff/*

would empty it. If morestuff contained subdirectories, emptying it would require more work. Once morestuff is empty the command

> rmdir morestuff

will actually remove the directory.

CHAPTER
10

Advanced Editing

Chapter 5 presented the basic commands for entering and modifying text. The basic commands are sufficient for casual use of the editor, but for greater efficiency you should master the ideas presented in this chapter.

As before, I will attempt to present the UNIX System text editing concepts that are common to most of the available UNIX System text editing programs. The goal is hard to attain in this chapter on advanced editing features because it is in the realm of advanced editing that the various editing programs tend to diverge.

The end of this chapter focuses on two trends in UNIX System editing, open-line editing and visual editing. Both techniques simplify the editing process, although neither technique is standardized.

10.1 Reading Text into the Work File

In Chapter 5 we discussed the easiest way to get text from a permanent disk file into the editor's working file. (The working file is often called the editor's text buffer.) If your shell command to start the editor mentions a disk file, then the contents of that file are automatically read into the working file. If the permanent file doesn't exist, then it will be created when you enter your first write command. The shell command

```
ed mydoc
```

will start the editor and read the contents of the file 'mydoc' into the working file.

The same result is attained if you enter the shell command

```
ed
```

to start the editor and then you enter the editor command

```
e mydoc
```

The editor's edit command ("e") instructs the editor to clear the work space and then read the contents of the named file into the work space. Any previous contents of the work space are lost. The "e" command can be used at the beginning of an editing session as in this example or it can be used in the middle of a session to start work on a new file. The "e" command is just as dangerous as the "q" (quit) command; use it cautiously. Many editors will warn you if the old work space had been modified so that you can write it out to a permanent file before you start with a new file.

The editor does not require a file name in order to function. It is acceptable to start the editor without specifying an input file and then add text to the empty work space. The file name can be specified later either by using the filename command ("f") or by using the write ("w") command with an explicit file name.

Sometimes you need to combine the contents of a disk file with the current contents of the working file. The editor command

    Or headerfile

will place a copy of 'headerfile' after line zero in the work file. The editor read ("r") command reads in the named file and places its contents after the given line. If no line number is mentioned, the information is placed after the current line. The difference between the editor's read command and the editor's edit command is that the read command adds text to the current work space without clearing the contents of the work space.

The UNIX System editors do not allow you to read in part of a file. If you need to read in just a few lines of a file, you must make a copy of the file, then use the editor to prune the unwanted portion, and then finally edit the target file and read in the pruned version of the original.

10.2 The File Command

The editor remembers the name of the file that is being edited. The file command ("f") is used to either display or change the remembered file name. The editor command

    f

will cause the editor to print the remembered file name. The editor command

    f myaltdoc

will change the remembered name to 'myaltdoc'.

There are three commands that can change the remembered file name: "f", "o", and "w". The "r" (read) command has no effect on the remembered file name.

10.3 The Global Command

Most editor commands pertain to either a single line in a file or a local group of lines. The editor's global command ("g") is used to modify commands so that they pertain to all lines that contain a certain text pattern. Suppose you want to print all of the lines that contain the word "help". The editor command

```
g/help/p
```

will print all of the lines containing the word "help" (or "helping", or "help-less", etc.). The phrase "g/help/" modifies the print command ("p") so that the print command pertains to all of lines containing the text pattern "help". The "g" character introduces the global modifier phrase and the text pattern ("help" in this case) is enclosed in slashes.

The global command (and its variants discussed below) is extremely useful. The errors and problems in a text file often are very systematic. If you can identify a text pattern that is associated with a problem in a text file, you can probably devise a solution involving the global command.

The global command works in two phases. In the first phase the global command searches through the text and makes a list of all lines that contain the given text pattern. In the second phase the given command is performed on all lines in the list.

It is also possible to specify a range of addresses with the global command. If you want to print all of the lines containing the word "alpha" in lines 50 through 100, you can use the command

```
50,100g/alpha/p
```

Context addresses can also be used to specify the addresses for the global command:

```
/beta/,/dopa/g/zeta/d
```

This command deletes all lines containing the text pattern "zeta" from the first line (after the current line) containing "beta" to the first line after that containing "dopa". Lines containing "zeta" outside of this range are not deleted.

The "v" command is the negated version of the global command. The "v" command goes through the text and makes a list of all lines that don't contain the text pattern, and then the "v" command goes through the text again and performs the command on all lines in the list. For example, the command

```
v/-/s/330/340/p
```

would substitute "340" for "330" on all of the lines that contain no hyphens.

Besides modifying just one command, the global family of commands ("g" and "v") can be used to modify a command list. Suppose that you needed to change "hat" to "cap" and "sweater" to "coat" and "glove" to "mitten" on every line that contained the word "clothes". Of course you could use three separate global commands. However, it would be easier to enter the following imposing looking command:

```
g/clothing/s/hat/cap/ \
s/sweater/coat/ \
s/glove/mitten/
```

Commands That Don't Use Addresses

e [filename]
> The edit command is used to clear the text buffer and read in a permanent file, effectively starting a new editing session without leaving the editor. Any text in the buffer is lost. If a filename is mentioned, then the text is read from that file and the mentioned file becomes the remembered filename. However, if no filename is mentioned, then the text is read in from the remembered filename.

f [filename]
> The file command is used to change or display the remembered filename. When a filename is mentioned the file command changes the remembered filename; without a filename the file command causes the remembered name to be printed.

! command [arguments]
> The shell escape is used to execute an ordinary shell command without leaving the editor.

Commands That Use One Address †

.r filename
> The read command reads the contents of the named file and adds it to the editor's text buffer after the given line, or after the current line if no line is mentioned.

Commands That Use Two Addresses † †

1,$g/regexpr/edcmd
> The global command marks every line within the defined bounds that contains the pattern indicated by the regular expression. Then the editor command is performed on every marked line.

.,.+1j The join command combines two or more adjacent lines into one line.

1,$w [filename]
> If no filename is mentioned, the write command writes the addressed lines to the remembered filename. However, if a filename is mentioned, then the addressed lines are written to that file.

---

† The default line address is shown.

† † The default addresses are shown.

Figure 10.1. Some advanced editing commands.

This command will execute the three substitute commands on every line containing the word "clothing." Notice that every command in the command list (except the last) contains a backslash at the end of the line. The backslash is the clue that tells the editor that there are more editor commands in the command list.

10.4 The Join Command

The join command is used to glue two lines together. The editor command

    -,.j

combines the previous line with the current line. (The minus sign is a shorthand notation for the line in front of the current line.) A group of short lines can be joined as in

    10,20j

Be careful not to create lines that are too long (usually there is a 255-character limit).

The join command exists because it is too dangerous to allow people to combine lines by deleting newline characters. The editor cannot handle very long lines, so the editor checks to make sure that the created line is reasonable.

Although the editor will not join lines without using the special join command, it is possible to split lines using the general substitute command. Splitting lines is less troublesome than joining lines because the resulting line is never too long to edit. If you want to split a line into two parts, you can substitute a newline character at the appropriate point. The editor substitute command

    s/time /time \
    /

will split the line

    A stitch in time saves nine.

into the lines

    A stitch in time
    saves nine.

by placing a newline character after the word "time". In the above command, after typing the second "time" you type a backslash and then a return (or a newline character) and then a slash and then a return to complete the command. The backslash before the carriage return removes (escapes) the return's special meaning to the system: the "line" of input is therefore not complete until the second return. If you imagine the command on a single line, you should recognize the familiar command "s/pat1 /pat2/". When you strike the escaped carriage return you will advance to the next line on the terminal although you are still entering the same command.

10.5 Regular Expressions

Throughout these chapters on the editor we have been referring to text patterns. Text patterns are very important in the editor. Lines can be identified and changed using text patterns. A text pattern that is involved in pattern matching is called a regular expression. A regular expression matches one or more character strings.

Regular expressions are used in two situations in the editor: as a context address, and as the first part of a substitute command. When a regular expression is used as a context address it is surrounded by either a pair of slashes or a pair of question marks. When a regular expression is used in the first part of the substitute command any character other than space or newline may be used to delimit the expression, although slashes are very common delimiters.

The second text pattern in a substitute command (s/pat1/pat2) is called the replacement string. It is not a regular expression because it is not involved in pattern matching. The difference between a regular expression and a character string is that regular expressions are involved in text matching operations and they may contain special characters which indicate certain classes of matches. Characters that are special when included in regular expressions have no special meaning in replacement strings.

10.5.1 Special Characters in Regular Expressions

Up to this point we have been careful to use very simple regular expressions. In order to use the editor expertly you have to understand the rules of regular expressions. The following characters are special when used in a regular expression:

.	period
*	asterisk
[	left brace
\	backslash
^	caret
$	currency symbol

If you studiously avoid the characters listed above in forming regular expressions, then your regular expressions will always match themselves. If the following five text patterns are used as regular expressions, they will match themselves because none of the special characters are used:

```
hello
bye
This is a long regular expression!
abcdefghijklmnopqrstuvwxyz
01234
```

The backslash can be used to turn off the special meaning associated with the special characters. For example, the following text pattern matches the word "end" only when it is followed by a period:

```
end\ .
```

If the current line of text in the editor contained the sentence "This is the end of the end.", you could change the last word to "middle" by entering the following substitute command:

```
s/end\ ./middle./
```

In this example the regular expression is "end \." and the replacement string is "middle." Note that the period in the replacement string does not have to be escaped.

Suppose you were looking for a line of text containing the comic book expletive "!!&&*$$". The editor print command

```
/!!&&\*\$\$/p
```

would find and print the line. If you wanted to change the expletive to "heck" you could use the substitute command:

```
s/!!&&\*\$\$/heck/
```

Just knowing about the editor's special characters and knowing how to turn off their special meaning allows most people to use the editor without major surprises. However, mastery of the editor requires mastery of the syntax for regular expressions. The remainder of this section can be skipped if you plan to avoid (rather than master) regular expressions.

10.5.2 Single-Character Regular Expressions

Long, complicated regular expressions are built from single-character regular expressions. First we must learn the rules of single-character regular expressions. Here is the list of all of the single-character regular expressions that the editor accepts:

1. A single character other than the special characters. All of the characters other than the special characters form one-character regular expressions that stand for themselves. The character "a" stands for "a", the character "b" stands for "b", etc.

2. Escaped special characters. The special characters (period, asterisk, caret, currency symbol, left square brace, backslash) lose their meaning when they are preceded by a slash. Therefore, the following pairs of characters are actually one-character regular expressions that match the named character:

\	.	matches	period
\	*	matches	asterisk
\	^	matches	caret
\	$	matches	currency symbol
\	[	matches	square left brace
\	\	matches	backslash

In some editors some of the special characters can be permanently escaped by specifying the mode "nomagic". In the "nomagic" mode the special characters are special only when they are preceded by a backslash. Many editors do not have a "magic", "nomagic" selection.

3. The special character period. A period is a one-character regular expression that matches any single character except for a newline.

4. The special character left square brace. A left square brace introduces a character set. The end of the character set is indicated by a right square brace. The characters between the braces define a character set. The set of characters is a one-character regular expression that matches any one of the characters in the set.

Let's talk a little about character sets. The character set "[abcd]" matches any of the four first lower-case letters of the alphabet. A dash may be used to indicate an inclusive range of characters: for example, the character set "[a-d]" will match any of the first four lower-case letters of the alphabet. A dash at the end of the set loses its special meaning as in the set "[ab-]" which matches either "a", "b", or "-".

If there is a caret at the beginning of a set, then the one-character regular expression denoted by the set matches any character not in the set. The set "[^a-z]" matches any single character other than a lower-case letter. The caret loses its special meaning if it does not occur first in the set as in the set "[0-9^&]" which matches any numeral, a caret, or an ampersand.

The characters period, asterisk, left square brace, and backslash stand for themselves in a character set. The character set "[*.]" matches either a backslash or an asterisk or a period.

10.5.3 Combining One-Character Regular Expressions

Single-character regular expressions can be combined according to the following rules to form more elaborate regular expressions:

1. Catenation. A catenation of regular expressions matches the catenation of strings that the individual components match. Therefore, the regular expression "abc" matches only "abc", whereas the regular expression "a.c" matches any three-character sequence beginning with "a" and ending with "c".

2. The asterisk operator. A one-character regular expression followed by an asterisk matches zero or more occurrences of the one-character regular expression. Therefore, the regular expression "12*3" matches any of the following:

```
13
123
1223
12223
```

3. The currency symbol operator. When a currency symbol is placed at the end of a regular expression, then that regular expression is constrained to match the final segment of a line of text. It is not quite correct to say that a currency symbol placed at the end of a regular expression matches a new-line because the newline will not be involved in any text substitutions that occur. A currency symbol used in the beginning or middle of a line will match a currency symbol. The regular expression "123$" matches the character string "123" if it occurs at the end of a line. The regular expression "$123" matches the character string "$123" anywhere on a line.

4. The caret operator. The caret is a special character in two situations: when it is at the beginning of an entire regular expression and when it is the first character of a character set. In all other situations the caret matches itself. If a caret occurs at the beginning of an entire regular expression, then that regular expression is constrained to match the initial segment of the line. It is not quite correct to say that a caret matches the beginning of a line because the result of such a match is not involved in substitutions. We have already discussed the use of the caret at the beginning of a character set. The regular expression "^Hello" matches the character string "Hello" when it occurs at the beginning of a line. The regular expression "Hello^" matches the character string "Hello^" anywhere on a line.

Some editors allow segmentation of regular expressions. A segmented regular expression is divided into segments and the segments can be referred to using a special notation. The technique is not useful enough or universal enough to warrant further discussion here.

Note that one of the most unfortunate features of the UNIX System is the difference between the rules for regular expression matching in the editor and the rules for filename generation. An asterisk in the editor represents zero or more instances of the preceding single character regular expression, whereas the asterisk in the filename generation process matches any (possible null) sequence of characters. In the editor the period matches any single character, whereas in the filename generation process the question mark matches any single character.

10.6 More on the Substitute Command

The substitute command is probably the hardest editor command. Changing one word to another on a short line is easy, but changing the third asterisk on long line in a C-language program can require more skill than writing the program. One typical solution to the problem is deletion and then laborious manual reentry of the erroneous line. (Another difficult to correct typo often is the result.) This section is designed to demonstrate a few of the useful, but advanced, techniques for performing text substitutions.

The caret and the currency symbol frequently are used to simplify substitute expressions. Consider the following line from a table of binary numbers:

    1101 1101 1101 1101

If you had to change the last number (field) to "1011", you could use any of the following substitute commands:

```
s/1101 1101 1101 1101/1101 1101 1101 1011/
s/1101$/1011/
s/....$/1011/
```

The first of these amounts to retyping the line twice so it is obviously bad. The currency symbol in the last two commands forces the regular expression match to occur at the end of the line, thus less has to be typed. The second substitute command explicitly states that the last four characters should be "1101" and that they should be replaced by "1011". The third substitute command just replaces the last four characters on the line with "1011". The third substitute command will not work if there are trailing blanks or tabs.

The caret forces a match to occur at the beginning of a line. You can use the command

```
s/^/-/
```

to place a hyphen at the beginning of a line. In this example the regular expression consists of a lone caret. The replacement string is a hyphen.

The editor's "longest leftmost" rule determines what text is matched when several matches are possible.

1. Leftmost. The leftmost match is always preferred. The command "s/1/2/" applied to the line of text "111111" will produce the text "211111" because the leftmost match is preferred.

2. Longest. The longest match is preferred. The command "s/1*2/3/" applied to the line of text "1111124" will change the line to "34" because the whole string of ones followed by a two is matched. (Remember that the asterisk repeats the previous single character regular expression zero or more times.)

A harder problem is the application of the command "s/1*2/3/" to the line of text "2 1112". The leftmost rule here is in conflict with the longest rule. Clearly the longest match on the line would involve the "1112". However, the leftmost match on the line is the leading 2. (Remember that the regular expression "1*2" will match "2", "12", "112", etc.) Since the leftmost match is always preferred the text "3 112" is produced.

Occasionally you want to make more than one substitution on a line. For example, you might want to change all of the "jacks" to "janes" on some line. The letter "g" following a substitute command instructs the editor to make all possible substitutions. The editor command

```
s/jacks/janes/g
```

would change the line

```
jacks jacks and more jacks
```

to

```
janes janes and more janes
```

You need to understand the difference between the "g" option to the substitute command and the "g" global command. The "g" option specifies that the editor should perform every possible substitution on a line, whereas the global command specifies a list of lines on which a command should be performed. If you wanted to change all of the "teh" text strings to "the" throughout an entire file, you could use the command:

```
g/teh/s/teh/the/g
```

The leading "g" indicates the global command which makes a list of all of the lines containing a "teh", the substitute command is then performed on every line in the list, and "g" option specifies that every occurrence of "teh" should be changed to "the".

Naturally the "g" option modifies the "longest leftmost" rule. "Leftmost" no longer applies since all possible matches on a line are made. The "longest" rule does apply; each match is made as long as possible and the matches are performed starting on the left.

The other options that are commonly available when using the substitute command are "p" and "l" to print (or list) the changed line. For example, the command

```
s/jack/jill/p
```

will change the first "jack" to a "jill" and then print the result.

Occasionally your text files will acquire nonprinting characters. Weird characters usually creep in because of typing errors, but occasionally strange characters are caused by noise in dial-up circuits or inexplicable hardware problems. In any event the problem of strange visitors is twofold, identifying their presence and removing them.

One of the most common unprintable characters is the backspace. Unsuspecting novices (and occasional experts) sometimes type in backspace characters when they intend to type in the UNIX System erase character. Remember the erase character is the character (often a pound sign or a delete or a Control-H) that the system interprets as your command to erase the previous character. Typing backspaces often looks the same as typing erases, so it is easy to confuse the two operations. In any case if your text file becomes populated with backspaces, the lines you see on your terminal aren't the lines that are contained in the file.

If your lines of text are making noises when you print them or if your substitute commands aren't working or if unexplainable things are happening, use the "l" command to look for unprintable characters. The list command is similar to the "p" print command; the difference is the "l" graphically depicts all of the unprintables.

Once you have found undesirable unprintables in your file you can use the substitute command to remove them. (You should delete and reenter a really botched line.) The problem with using the substitute command is that typing unprintable characters usually is difficult. The easiest way to match an unprintable character is to use the period in a regular expression. If your text line contains a "1" followed by an an unwanted and unprintable character followed by a "2", the following command will remove the unprintable and then list the resulting line:

s/1.2/12/l

Remember that the period in a regular expression matches any single character including unprintables.

Perhaps you have noticed that the replacement string often contains text that is very similar to the regular expression. When you are adding characters to existing text the replacement string is often the original regular expression plus the added text. For example, if you are changing the word "awkward" to "awkwardly", you might use the following substitute command:

s/awkward/awkwardly/p

If you ever try to type the command, you will feel as awkward as the command looks. In order to reduce typing errors the UNIX System editor allows you to use an ampersand in the replacement string as a shorthand for the entire matched item that was matched by the regular expression. Using the ampersand, the command shown above could be entered as follows:

s/awkward/&ly/p

The ampersand in this case stands for the text string "awkward".

The ampersand notation even works when you are using complicated regular expressions such as in the following command which places a plus sign in front of the first number on a line and places ".00" after the number:

s/[0-9][0-9]*/ + &.00/p

The command above applied to the line

The year end balance is 550 dollars.

would produce the line

The year end balance is + 550.00 dollars.

This rather extended form is not very useful for making a change on a single line but it is a great advantage when you are changing many lines throughout a file.

Always be careful with the asterisk regular expression operator. The command

s/[0-9]*/ + &.00/p

applied to the original line above would produce the line

 + .00The year end balance is 550 dollars.

because the regular expression "[0-9]*" would match the leftmost null string.

In all of the examples of the substitute command given so far the regular expression and the replacement string have been delimited by slashes. In a substitute command (but not in a context pattern) any character other than space is allowed as a delimiter. The slashes are often used because they clearly delimit the expressions.

If you wanted to change the word "boy" to "adolescent" on the current line, you could use any of the following substitute commands:

```
s/boy/adolescent/
s,boy,adolescent,
szboyzadolescentz
saboya\adolescenta
```

In the four commands shown above the delimiters are slash, comma, "z", and "a". Whatever character is used as the delimiter becomes a special character in that command. In the last command shown above the "a" in "adolescent" has to be preceded by a backslash to escape its special meaning as a delimiter. Without the backslash the editor would interpret that "a" as the final delimiter in the expression, and the trailing characters "dolescent" would produce an error message. As a rule, it is easiest to choose expression delimiters that are visual (e.g., slash or comma) and not present in the expressions.

10.7 The Shell Escape

Occasionally while you are editing you will want to perform a standard UNIX System command. Of course you can write your file and quit the editor and then perform the command and then reenter the editor, but that's a lot of work. The editor's shell escape command allows you run standard UNIX System commands without leaving the editor. If you enter the command

```
!who
```

then the who command will be executed. At the conclusion of the command the editor prints an exclamation point to indicate that it is ready for more input.

The editing session is not affected by the shell escape. You do not have to write the text buffer to a permanent file before using a shell escape. If you want to enter several commands, you can semipermanently escape from the editor by entering the command

```
!sh
```

to create a new shell for you. This new shell will allow you to enter as many UNIX System commands as you like. You might try the UNIX System ps command to get a list of all the processes you are running. Your original shell, the editor, your new shell, and the ps command will all be in the list. You can terminate the new shell by striking Control-D.

The UNIX System is able to provide a shell escape because the shell is just an ordinary program that can be executed at any time. While you are executing a shell inside the editor the editor program is waiting patiently for the conclusion of the shell command, just as your original shell is waiting patiently for the editor to finish.

10.8 Open-Line Editing and Visual Editing

Because of the difficulty of using the substitute command a more graphic form of editing has been developed. Instead of specifying the change intellectually by creating and entering a substitute command, an open-line editor allows you to change a line by moving a cursor along a line and then changing the line near the cursor.

In an open-line editor only one line at a time is available for changes, and when you want to make a change throughout a file you have to resort to global substitutes. However, even if a typo occurs several places in a file, it is often easier and quicker for a nonprogrammer to change each instance manually rather than struggle with the substitute command.

To use the open-line feature a line must be explicitly opened using an open command. Once the line is open there are special control codes to move the cursor back and forth across the line. Although the control codes must be memorized, the actions are so simple that they are learned quickly. Once the cursor is positioned above the erroneous text special commands can be used to delete or add text to the line.

Visual editing is an extension of the idea behind open-line editing. In visual editing a portion of the file is displayed on your terminal. The terminal acts as a window into the file; any changes to the file are immediately displayed on the terminal.

As you move through the file, your window changes. Like open-line editing, most changes to the file during visual editing are made by positioning the cursor at the appropriate point and then entering the changes. If you need to change dozens of instances of an error, then you can still use a global substitute command.

Visual editing doesn't work on printing terminals or on some very dumb and inflexible CRT terminals. Visual editing is difficult over telephone lines because of the low data transmission speed, although reasonable results can be achieved by shrinking the window. Visual editing also imposes a heavy demand on the processor.

Open-line editing and visual editing are usually additional features to editors that otherwise function similarly to the standard UNIX System text editors. Visual editing and open-line editing are becoming more common.

CHAPTER

11

Text Formatting

UNIX System word processing is not a single program; it is a central concept applied to a broad spectrum of facilities. Text processing (also called word processing) is a central feature of the UNIX System. Of course the UNIX System has text editors, formatters, and utility programs for text files. But, more important, the UNIX System has a system of text processing programs that work together to increase productivity.

The UNIX System has a wealth of simple programs for working with text files. There are programs to count lines, words, and characters in files, programs to check the spelling in files, programs to print files, programs to sort files, programs to search files for text patterns, programs to compare files, and several programs to rearrange text files. All of these programs are discussed in Chapter 8. The UNIX System also has editors for creating and modifying text files. The standard UNIX System editor is discussed in Chapter 5 and the advanced features of the editor are discussed in Chapter 10.

This chapter focuses on the UNIX System's major text formatting programs: nroff, troff, eqn, and tbl. Nroff and troff are general purpose text formatting programs; nroff is used with printing terminals and troff is used with phototypesetters. Nroff and troff are almost identical; their slight differences are the result of the different capabilities of phototypesetters and computer printers. We use the term nroff/troff for statements that apply to both programs. You should always use nroff/troff in conjunction with a good macro package. Macro packages are discussed in Section 11.2. The eqn program is used with nroff/troff to format equations and the tbl program is used with nroff/troff to format tabular data.

There is no way for a chapter (or even an entire book) to describe all of the ways that the UNIX System text processing facilities can be used. Each text processing application presents a different set of requirements, and each individual or group of individuals working with text has a different set of preferences. The UNIX System has enough text processing options so that most operations

128

can be performed using any one of several distinct methods. For instance, if you wanted to replace the text string "Unix" with the text string "UNIX" throughout a group of files you could (1) use the text editor to perform the replacement manually, (2) use the text editor with an editing script stored in a file, (3) use the stream editor, or (4) use the lex program.

You should examine several criteria when you choose a method for performing a word processing operation. One criterion is familiarity. Unfamiliar tools are often harder to use than familiar ones. Another criterion is your anticipated amount of time performing an operation. If you are going to format a document containing a single short table of data, then ignore the tbl program and format the table manually using the familiar nroff/troff formatter. However, if you are going to use tables extensively, then you should take the time to learn about tbl. This chapter doesn't teach you enough to effectively use the formatting programs on your system; instead it is a guide to the text formatting capabilities that are usually found in the UNIX System and it is a general introduction to some of the terms and ideas that you will need to understand in order to use the reference materials and tutorials that are supplied for your system's formatting programs.

11.1 Nroff and Troff — Format Text

Nroff and troff are the UNIX System's general purpose text formatting programs. A text formatter takes an unformatted file of text and converts it to a formatted file of text. Unformatted text has rough margins and inappropriate spacing, whereas formatted text has adjusted margins, reasonable spacing, headings, footers, titles, and other niceties. Nroff is used to format text for printing on a printer while troff is used to format text for output to a phototypesetter. Since the great majority of UNIX Systems are not connected to a phototypesetter most people will use the nroff program. The two programs accept nearly identical input, but the output produced by troff is much fancier than the output produced by nroff because phototypesetters are more flexible than printers.

When you use an ordinary typewriter you specify the format of your document by the placement of the text on the paper. If you want two blank lines between paragraphs, then you hit return twice before each paragraph. If you want a large left margin, then you move the left margin in toward the center. Using the nroff/troff text formatting system is very different from using a typewriter because the format of the text that you enter has very little effect on the format of the final document. The format of the final document is specified by embedding format control lines in the text. We will show some examples of format control lines below and in the next section.

In the UNIX System text is almost always entered unformatted because it is very hard to type while worrying about the right margin and the spacing and the footnotes and the forthcoming (probably extensive) revisions. Since the text and the format are two separate items, a system has been developed for specifying the format within the text. Lines that begin with a period or a single quote are interpreted as formatting commands and all other lines are interpreted as text.

The system is really very simple. If you want to skip a line you merely enter the nroff/troff command

.sp

alone on a line in the textfile.

In the unformatted file the format control lines are just lines of text. However, when you run the formatter program the format control lines are removed and the corresponding action is performed. Format control lines are used to control spacing and to provide titles and headings and page numbering and indenting and lots of other features.

Files consisting of text interspersed with format control items are much easier to change than files containing formatted documents. If you change the length of a sentence in midpage in a formatted document, the entire page has to be adjusted. However, changing the text in the unformatted document file is painless. If you change the length of a sentence in an unformatted document, the whole page doesn't have to be adjusted because the page hasn't been assembled yet by the formatting program.

Nroff/troff has about 80 formatting commands built into it. Each of these commands usually performs one small specific function. An operation such as starting a new paragraph can be expressed as a short sequence of the basic built-in functions. For instance, the sequence of commands to start a new paragraph might consist of the skip line function and the indent a few spaces function. Would this work for paragraphs just at end of a page or at the top of a page? Obviously you don't want to skip a line if you are already at the top of a page and you don't want to start a paragraph on the last line of a page. Even relatively simple commands such as starting a new paragraph turn out to be complicated when you consider all the possibilities.

Nroff/troff allows sequences of basic operations to be packaged into bundles called macros. You can create a new operation by writing a macro that contains a sequence of native nroff/troff commands and previously defined macros. Macros can be invoked by entering their name in the unformatted text file or they can be invoked automatically when certain conditions occur, such as reaching a certain line on a page.

The commands that are built into nroff/troff are designed to control specific features of the output device. Nroff/troff has been compared to an assembly language because its native commands are more related to machine features than to human text processing requirements. In order to satisfy common text processing requirements several macro packages have been created. These macro packages perform common functions such as starting paragraphs, numbering pages, placing footnotes, creating tables of contents.

The most important thing to know about nroff/troff is that you shouldn't use its native commands directly. Instead you should use one of the macro packages that insulates you from the details of text formatting. Ms and mm are two of the most common general purpose macro packages. If your UNIX System is derived from a Bell Laboratories UNIX System, you will probably have one of the two packages. Other macro packages are available on many systems; consult some of the people who have used the packages for advice in choosing a macro package.

11.2 Using a Macro Package

The people who write macro packages are the only ones who should use most of nroff/troff directly. Everyone else should find out about the macro packages that are available on their system and ignore the nroff/troff documentation at least at the beginning. If you become a more demanding and more sophisticated text enthusiast with requirements that are not satisfied by the existing macro packages, then you should learn the nroff/troff system in order to expand your favorite macro package.

When you use a macro package in conjunction with nroff/troff you still use the nroff or troff program. The difference is that the native nroff/troff commands are supplemented by the high level macro commands.

To illustrate typical features of a macro package let's hypothesize a macro package called mh which contains the following three macros.

.P   Starts an indented paragraph.

.C   Centers the next line

.S   Skips a line.

A useful macro package contains more than three macros. We are just hypothesizing three macros to keep things very simple.

The following is a very simple example of some raw text that exercises the hypothetical macros:

```
.C
Starting a Paragraph in MH
.P
Some people use the .P macro command to start a
paragraph because they prefer indented
paragraphs.
This paragraph was started with a .P command.
.S
Other people use .S to start a paragraph because
they abhor indentation.
This paragraph was started with a .S command.
```

If the text shown above were stored in the file named 'rawtext', the command

```
nroff -mh rawtext
```

would produce the following output on your terminal:

Starting a Paragraph in MH

Some people use the .P macro command to start a paragraph because they prefer indented paragraphs. This paragraph was started with a .P command.

Other people use .S to start a paragraph because they abhor indentation. This paragraph was started with a .S command.

The nroff command given above uses the argument "-mh" to inform nroff that the file 'rawtext' contains text interspersed with some hypothetical macros.

Using a macro package with nroff/troff can involve a few surprises. Notice in the above example that the macro commands are honored only at the beginning of a line; commands that are embedded in midline are just copied to the output.

Another surprise in formatting text with nroff is that lines of the raw text that begin with blanks or tabs cause a break. A break is a discontinuity in the text filling process. As an example, the following few lines show some some raw text containing a line with leading white space:

```
.P
A line beginning with white space will cause a break.
A break is a discontinuity in the text filling
process.
    This line begins with white space.
```

If the raw text shown above is processed with nroff/troff using the hypothetical macros the following will be output:

A line beginning with white space will cause a break. A break is a discontinuity in the text filling process.
    This line begins with white space.

The third sentence in the example appears on its own line because the leading blanks in the raw text caused a break. Without the leading blanks in the raw text the third sentence would have been filled normally at the end of the second sentence. Breaks are caused automatically by many nroff/troff commands.

Besides the problem of lines that begin with white space, you should be wary of lines that naturally start with periods or single quotes. Both the period and the single quote are used to signal the start of nroff/troff commands, and a line that begins with either character must be a valid command.

Whenever you use a macro package you have to tell the text formatter what package you are using. The "-mNAME" option of nroff/troff informs the formatting program that it should include the macro package "NAME". The command

```
nroff -mm file1 file2 ...
```

will use the mm macros for the named files and the command

```
nroff -ms file1 file2 ...
```

will use the ms macros.

Since nroff usually writes its results on the standard output you can use output redirection to save the results in a file. The command

```
nroff -ms rawtext > results
```

will process 'rawtext' using the ms macros and put the formatted text in the file named 'results'. Note that troff does not normally write to the standard output.

Several options are available for nroff/troff. The "-s" option causes the program to stop after every page to allow you to change paper, the "-o" option allows you to control which pages are printed, and the "-n" option allows you to control the number assigned to the first page. As discussed above the "-m" option allows you to specify which macro package you are using.

The nroff program allows you to specify the terminal type using the "-T" option. If you don't use the "-T" option, then the terminal type is derived from the shell variable $TERM.

Nroff and troff are painfully slow programs. At some installations they are disabled during business hours to keep text processing fanatics from overloading the system. Text processing in general works best if you keep your text files reasonably small. Files over 10 pages are hard to edit and they take a long time to format. It is easy to work with small files at the beginning of a project and then combine them toward the end. A large project such as a book might involve hundreds of files if you keep them small. Consider the make program (see Chapter 12) for managing groups of files and use well chosen names.

11.3 Tbl — Format Tables

One of the most difficult things to process using a conventional (non-UNIX System) word processor is tabular data. Tables of data are hard for many reasons. The width of the columns is hard to judge. Getting column items to align or center is often hard, and when you get near the end of the table you almost always discover something back toward the beginning of the table that has to be adjusted. Drawing a box around the table or underlining certain items or rows or separating the columns with lines is nearly impossible with most systems. Cutting and pasting using real scissors and glue is the usual answer.

Of course the answer in the UNIX System is not a pair of scissors. The program tbl is a companion program to nroff/troff. Tbl is a program that creates a nroff/troff script for producing a table. If you create documents containing tabular data, then you should learn to use the tbl program.

The difference between a nroff/troff script generation program (tbl) and a macro package (ms, mm) is important. A script generation program is a UNIX System command. Tbl input files contain tabular data embedded within normal nroff/troff text. Tbl converts the tabular data into nroff/troff commands so that the output text contains only nroff/troff text. To convert the tabular data into a nroff/troff script the size and types of the items in the table must be analyzed. This sort of analysis is beyond the power of a macro package. A macro package is much simpler conceptually because each macro expands consistently into a known sequence of native nroff/troff commands.

Tbl is constructed so that tabular data and normal text data may be inter-mixed in one file. The start of tabular data is indicated by the command ".TS" and the conclusion of the table is indicated by the command ".TE". The tbl commands and the tabular data are located within the confines of the ".TS" and ".TE" commands.

The tbl program converts the tabular information that appears between the table start and the table end commands and converts it into a gruesomely unreadable sequence of nroff/troff commands. The contents of the file outside of the table start, table end commands is not effected by tbl. Once the file is pro-cessed by tbl it still must be processed by nroff/troff. A typical invocation of tbl in conjunction with nroff is

```
tbl reportdata | nroff -ms > prettyreport
```

in which the 'reportdata' file is first processed by tbl and then piped to nroff for further processing using the ms macros before being output to the file 'pret-tyreport'.

Table processing is performed outside of the nroff/troff context because a specialized application such as table processing does not belong in a general purpose text formatting program. Nroff/troff doesn't have to know about tables and tbl doesn't have to know about formatting. The ease with which tbl can be used with nroff is testimony to the UNIX System philosophy of letting programs work together to solve difficult problems.

11.4 Eqn – Format Equations

Another difficult job for most text processors is entering mathematical equa-tions. Mathematics is difficult because of the special symbols and because mathematics presents a two-dimensional problem as opposed to the one-dimensional problem of standard text processing. Because nroff is tied to stan-dard printers, producing equations using nroff is awkward. However, troff does have the capability to produce camera-ready copy of mathematical equations.

Eqn is a nroff/troff script generator. Eqn takes an equation specification placed between the commands ".EQ" and ".EN" and generates the appropriate nroff/troff script. An equation is specified in eqn by writing the equation almost mnemonically. The fraction one half is generated by writing the eqn command line

```
1 over 2
```

To make eqn approachable by people who don't know mathematics (e.g., typ-ists) eqn is devoid of mathematical knowledge. Users of eqn must paint a pic-ture of the equation in words in order to instruct eqn to produce a script which nroff/troff can interpret to produce the equation.

A typical invocation of eqn is

```
eqn eq.doc | troff
```

If nroff is being used you might use

```
neqn eq.doc  |  nroff
```

Note that eqn is used with troff and neqn is used with nroff.
    Eqn and tbl can be used together by increasing the length of the pipeline:

```
tbl  sigplan.ent  |  neqn  |  nroff
```

Tbl should come before eqn in order to minimize the data that is passed through the pipelines.

PART

2

ADVANCED
UNIX SYSTEM TOPICS

CHAPTER

12

Make and the
Source Code Control System

Coordination is a major problem in large programming projects. When several (or dozens or hundreds of) programmers work together communication among the programmers consumes significant amounts of time and effort. Decreased efficiency in large programming projects has become an accepted fact in the software industry. However, the most costly result of poor coordination among programmers is a poor product. Some of the most entrenched bugs in large programming projects are related to very subtle failures in coordination between the teams of programmers.

The UNIX System is not an error-free software system, but it is an inspiring example of extremely reliable programming. Part of the reliability of the UNIX System is due to its very modular design. Most UNIX System utilities are small and simple and much easier to maintain than the large and involved utilities that are common in other systems. Another lesson that can be learned from the UNIX System is that reliable software is easier to develop using an operating system with very powerful tools. Many of the programs in the UNIX System's software tool kit are standard utilities for manipulating text files because text files are the original form of all software. Other programs in the UNIX System tool kit are for analyzing the binary files that are produced by the compilers (see Chapter 16). However, the UNIX System's most original software tools are for formalizing much of the knowledge about a software system — knowledge that is usually locked in the subconscious of the major software developers. These tools are the subject of this chapter.

The first section of this chapter explains some of the problems that are common to large programming projects; the last two sections concentrate on the UNIX System utility program Make and the series of utility programs that comprise the Source Code Control System.

12.1 Large Programs

Some programming languages allow a program to be divided into separate units (loosely referred to here as modules) that are worked on separately. Most programming languages are very good at precisely defining and maintaining the integrity of the individual modules; the problem lies in the relationship of one module to another. Separate modules usually are entwined by a network of interdependencies and a change in one module can render another module obsolete.

Several types of problems can occur when program modules are placed in separate files. Consider a very low level module which returns mutually agreed upon values to some higher level module. In a large programming project the two modules would probably be in separate files so that they could be compiled separately. If the low level module is changed so that it returns a different set of values, then naturally the higher level module must also be changed.

One technique for coordinating various modules is to put definitions needed by several modules into a common file called an include file. In the case mentioned above the include file would define the values that the low level module passed to the high level module. Since all of the modules reference the same include file you might think that both modules would automatically be synchronized.

Although include files solve many of the major problems of program modularization, they occasionally lead to an even more subtle problem — timing. Once you have a common include file and separate program modules you run the risk of changing something in an include file without recompiling all of the affected program modules. If a program module includes a certain file, then we say that the program's object file depends both on that include file and on the program source file. If either the include file or the program source has been modified since the object was created, then the object file is out of date.

In a large programming project the order and extent of compilation depends on the internal references of the modules. Very modern languages (e.g., MODULA) are designed so that large groups of files are automatically coordinated based on the internal references of the modules. The UNIX System program Make can be used to enforce relationships between modules when languages other than MODULA are used. Make accepts a specification which defines the relationships between modules and defines the actions that must be performed to update modules. Based on the specification and the modification times of the relevant files, Make will automatically maintain the modules.

Programs usually go through a shakedown phase where most of the errors are caught and fixed. The errors that remain after the initial shakedown are usually entrenched and much more costly to remove than errors that are caught early. After a certain point in the life of a major piece of software fixing errors becomes very difficult because each fix is likely to cause several unexpected problems.

In the early stages of a software project errors can be fixed with little regard for the integrity of the whole because the whole is not yet sound. However, in a mature product each change must be considered extremely carefully because the product as a whole is (we hope) basically sound. The Source Code Control System (SCCS) is a series of UNIX System programs that make it easier to maintain and document a program as it evolves throughout its lifetime.

Another problem in large programming projects is the need for different versions of a program. Naturally SCCS is useful for maintaining different versions of a program.

Make and SCCS are the UNIX System's two most powerful tools for maintaining large software projects. They are important tools both for programs built to run under the UNIX System and for programs developed for use on other systems.

12.2 Make

Make is a program that accepts a specification of the interdependencies of the various modules of a program. Information about the relationships of one module to another allows Make to infer what compiled modules are out of date based on the modification dates of the files. The specification contains commands that are executed when a certain module is found to be out of date. The commands usually perform some action to update the module.

As a very simple case consider a main program module stored in a file called 'network.c' which uses a few subroutines whose source code is contained in the file 'subrs.c'. Let's assume that both 'network.c' and 'subrs.c' include a file of common definitions called 'netdefs.h'. These relationships are shown graphically in Figure 12.1. (Include files are discussed in Section 15.7.)

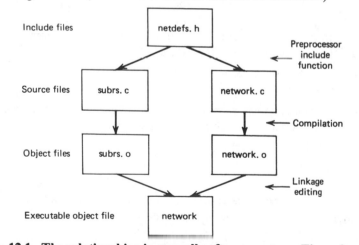

Figure 12.1. The relationships in a small software system. The software for the network program is contained in six key files: 'netdefs.h', which contains common definitions for the software system, 'subrs.c' and 'network.c', which contain C source code, 'subrs.o' and 'network.o', which contain the object code compiled from the source code, and 'network', which contains the executable program.

The specification of dependencies for Make is placed into a file called a Makefile. In a Makefile a dependency is specified by placing dependent modules to the left of a colon and the independent modules to the right of a colon. Let's try to determine the dependency for the 'subrs.c' module.

Since the 'subrs.c' module contains a compiler directive which includes the 'netdefs.h' file, the actual text that will be compiled is the text from 'netdefs.h' and from 'subrs.c'. Since 'subrs.c' isn't a complete program we can't perform a complete compilation, instead we perform a partial compilation. The result of the partial compilation will be placed in a file called 'subrs.o'. The ".o" suffix indicates that the file 'subrs.o' is an object file. (An object file is the result of a compilation. See Chapter 16.)

Since 'subrs.o' is created by compiling the text in 'subrs.c' including 'netdefs.h' we say that 'subrs.o' depends on those two files. This can be expressed in a Makefile as

```
subrs.o : subrs.c netdefs.h
```

In addition to the dependency specification in a Makefile you need to insert the UNIX System commands that will update an outdated module. The UNIX System command (or commands) is placed indented on the line following a dependency specification. Thus the entire specification for the dependencies and the script for recreation of the object module 'subrs.o' is

```
subrs.o : subrs.c netdefs.h
        cc -c subrs.c
```

The "-c" option to the C compiler directs the compiler to perform a partial compilation of the file 'subrs.c' and to place the object code in the file 'subrs.o'. (A complete compilation is not possible because the file 'subrs.o' doesn't contain a complete program: it merely contains support subroutines.) Similarly, the specification for the 'network.o' object module is

```
network.o : network.c netdefs.h
        cc -c network.c
```

The program 'network' depends on the two object modules 'network.o' and 'subrs.o' and it can be created as specified in this Makefile entry:

```
network : network.o subrs.o
        cc -o network network.o subrs.o
```

The "-o" option to the C compiler instructs the compiler to put the executable output in the file 'network' rather than into the default file 'a.out'. All of this taken together leads to the following Makefile for maintaining the 'network' program:

```
network : network.o subrs.o
        cc -o network network.o subrs.o
network.o : network.c netdefs.h
        cc -c network.c
subrs.o : subrs.c netdefs.h
        cc -c subrs.c
```

This file is used by the Make program to create a table of dependencies and a similar table of remedies for rebuilding obsolete files. We can use this Makefile to recompile the appropriate modules every time we change (using the text editor) a source or include module. For the following example, we assume that the Makefile specification given above is stored in a file named 'Makefile'. (The name 'Makefile' is one of the default file names that the Make program uses for Makefiles.) Let's first change some definition in the 'netdefs.h' include file and then enter the command

    make network

The goal of the Make command given above is to see whether the file 'network' is out of date and, if it is, to create a new version. The Make command first opens the file named 'Makefile' and creates a table of dependencies; from the table of dependencies Make figures out which items in the table are out of date (Figure 12.2). Remember a file is out of date if it depends on something modified more recently than itself. Since everything in our example depends on the include file 'netdefs.h' all of the following files would be out of date: subrs.o, network.o, and network.

Next Make would execute the following commands in order to recreate the outdated files:

    cc -c subrs.c
    cc -c network.c
    cc -o network network.o subrs.o

The final product is the new version of 'network'.

Changing a single module provides a better example of the usefulness of Make. Let's suppose that the source code in the file 'subrs.c' is changed (Figure 12.3). Now the command

    make network

would lead Make to discover that two files are out of date: subrs.o and network. Make would execute the UNIX System commands

    cc -c subrs.c
    cc -o network network.o subrs.o

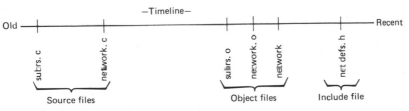

Figure 12.2. A timeline for the network software system. According to the make specification in the text, this timeline indicates that the three object files ('subrs.o', 'network.o', and 'network') are obsolete because they are older than the include file, 'netdefs.h'.

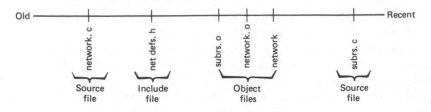

Figure 12.3. Another timeline for the network software system. In this example, only two of the object files are obsolete: 'subrs.o' is obsolete because it is older than 'subrs.c' and 'network' is obsolete because it depends on the obsolete file 'subrs.o'. Notice that 'network.o' is not obsolete.

in order to create a new 'network' program. Notice that Make performs the minimum amount of recompilation in order to produce an up to date version of 'network'.

In this simple system consisting of two source code files and one include file, using Make doesn't lead to much of an advantage. However, maintenance of a system consisting of dozens of source code files and a rambling hierarchy of include files is much easier using Make.

You might have noticed that the Makefile specification given above is rather verbose. Since the object file 'subrs.o' usually depends on a source file named 'subrs.c' Make contains internal rules to create 'subrs.o' from 'subrs.c'. For example, Make knows that the file 'subrs.o' is created by compiling the file 'subrs.c' using the "-c" compiler option. The Makefile given above could be rewritten to take advantage of Make's internal rules as follows:

```
network : network.o subrs.o
        cc -o network network.o subrs.o
subrs.o network.o : netdefs.h
```

Make has a system of named variables that are very similar to the named variables that are available in the UNIX System shell. If you include the line

```
CSOURCE = network.c subrs.c
```

in a Makefile, then subsequently you can use the word $(CSOURCE) to refer to all of the source files. As an example, consider the following Makefile dependency and command line:

```
listing : $(CSOURCE)
        pr $(CSOURCE) | lpr
```

Using this feature the UNIX System command

```
make listing
```

will produce a printed listing of all of the source code files on the lineprinter. In all of the examples of Make given previously the UNIX System command was executed only if certain items were out of date. In this example the UNIX Sys-

tem command will always be executed because there is no file called 'listing', so
it is presumed to be out of date and the command is executed.

As a similar feature consider the following excerpt from a Makefile:

```
network.lint  :  $(CSOURCE)
          lint $(CSOURCE) > network.lint
```

The command

```
make  network.lint
```

will process the C source programs using lint and place the output in the file
'network.lint'. Although a wide variety of tasks related to programming can be
performed with the assistance of Make, the most important use of Make is documentation of the interdependencies of a complicated source code system.

12.3 Source Code Control System

SCCS is used to control and document text files by creating something analogous to an audit trail. The premise of SCCS is that most program source code
files evolve and change over long periods of time as program bugs are fixed and
enhancements are added. SCCS is in part a system to document these changes,
in part a system for controlling who has the ability to make changes, and in part
a system for recovering old versions of a file. The SCCS system can be used on
any type of text file. However, since SCCS usually is used with program source
files most of the comments that follow will assume that the SCCS text is actually
a program.

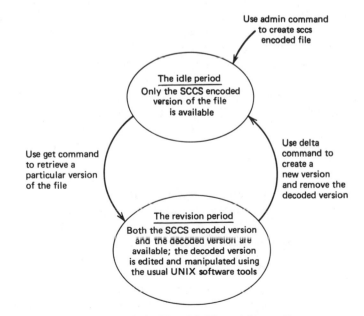

Figure 12.4. The SCCS revision cycle.

SCCS works by keeping an encoded version of a text file in a special SCCS format file. The encoded format contains enough information to recreate old versions and to keep track of who is working on (or allowed to work on) specific revisions of the file. All SCCS format files are named using the prefix "s.". Thus the SCCS file 's.network.c' is the encoded version of 'network.c'.

Let's generally describe the revision cycle using SCCS before we show some specific examples of using the SCCS programs. The complete cycle for a mature software product usually consists of a long idle period between revisions followed by a revision of the software.

During the idle period between revisions only the SCCS format version of a file exists. When a revision becomes necessary the get command is used to retrieve a version of a file from an encoded SCCS format file. The actual revisions are made to the retrieved version of the file. If the file is a program source file, then the programmer will probably go through a series of changes, compilations, and tests to verify the changes made to the file.

During the course of a revision, the SCCS format encoded file and the recovered file both exist. When the revisions are complete the new information contained in the recovered file is added into the SCCS format encoded file using the delta command. A natural consequence of updating the SCCS format encoded file using the delta command is the removal of the unencoded file. Leaving the open format version lying around between revisions is dangerous because changes might be made to it in the false belief that the master copy was being updated. Therefore, only the SCCS format version of a file is available during the idle period.

It is best to apply the SCCS system at a mature point in the life cycle of a software project. If the SCCS system is imposed too early, many of the early versions of the software will involve repair of obvious flaws and inclusion of obviously necessary features. If, however, the SCCS system is applied too late in the lifetime of a software system, then much of the necessary information will be missing.

The SCCS system can be initiated for a software system using the admin command. Besides the ability to create an SCCS format file, the admin command is able to control parameters of existing SCCS files. The command

    admin -n s.SCCSsample

will create 's.SCCSexample' and install standard parameters in the file. Other than the SCCS system information, the file is empty and it is catalogued using the version number 1.1. (A variation on this command can create a file which is not created empty.) Before we can put some text in this empty file we have to retrieve the file using the command

    get -e s.SCCSsample

The flag "-e" indicates that we should retrieve a file suitable for editing. The get command prints the version (1.1) of the retrieved file and the number of lines (0) in the retrieved file. All of this work has merely started the SCCS record keep-

get   Retrieve a version of an encoded file.
admin   Perform administrative functions on encoded files.
delta   Place a new version into an encoded file.
prs   Print an encoded file.

Figure 12.5. The programs in the SCCS system.

ing system and fetched a blank file. We can use the standard UNIX System text
editor to add text to the file.

```
ed SCCSsample
a
Doctor Foster went to Gloucester
In a shower of rain;
He stepped in a puddle,
Right up to his middle,
And never went there again.
.
wq
```

Now, assuming the revisions are complete we can save the new version of the
file using the command

```
delta s.SCCSsample
```

The changes will be saved under the version number 1.2 since the delta command automatically increments the version number. The delta program will
display the prompt "comments?" on the terminal and then read a comment line
from the terminal to add to the file. The comments are used to specify the reason for the revision. In this example let's suppose that the comment "Placed
rhyme in file" is entered. The delta program will remove the file 'SCCSsample'
once its contents are safely added to the file 's.SCCSsample'. Delta prints out a
statistical summary of the changes and an error message that we can ignore concerning id keywords.

Now let's try retrieving version 1.2 of 's.SCCSsample' and then add some text
in order to create version 1.3. The command

```
get -e s.SCCSsample
```

will retrieve the latest version and the editor can be used to modify the file.

```
ed SCCSsample
$a
   - Book of Nursery and Mother Goose Rhymes
by Marguerite deAngeli, Doubleday, 1953.
.
wq
```

will add two lines to the retrieved file. We can use the command

```
delta s.SCCSsample
```

to save the new version (1.3). Finally, let's suppose we enter the comment "Added the citation" when the delta command requests a "comment?".

Figure 12.6 shows the contents of the file 's.SCCSsample' after the preceding operations have been performed. Figure 12.6 is included here to give you an intuitive feel for the inner workings of the SCCS system; there is no reason for you to understand all of the lines. As you can see from Figure 12.6 the power of the SCCS system comes at some expense in storage use. Our seven-line text file contains 30 lines when stored in the SCCS encoded format.

```
<^a>h32774
<^a>s 00002/00000/00005
<^a>d D 1.3 82/04/17 11:57:30 kgc 3 2
<^a>c Added the citation
<^a>e
<^a>s 00005/00000/00000
<^a>d D 1.2 82/04/17 11:56:05 kgc 2 1
<^a>c Placed rhyme in file
<^a>e
<^a>s 00000/00000/00000
<^a>d D 1.1 82/04/17 11:47:26 kgc 1 0
<^a>e
<^a>u
<^a>U
<^a>t
<^a>T
<^a>l 2
Doctor Foster went to Gloucester
In a shower of rain;
He stepped in a puddle,
Right up to his middle,
And never went there again.
<^a>l 3
   - Book of Nursery and Mother Goose Rhymes
by Marguerite deAngeli, Doubleday, 1953.
<^a>E 3
<^a>E 2
<^a>l 1
<^a>E 1
```

Figure 12.6 The file 's.SCCSsample'. The contents of the file 's.SCCSsample' following the operations mentioned in the text provide a clue to the inner workings of the SCCS system. All of the lines except the seven that are the actual contents of the file start with the control-A nonprinting character, which has been shown in this figure with the notation "<^a>".

Any of the three versions of 's.SCCSsample' can be retrieved using the get command. Enter the command

```
get -s -p -r1.2 s.SCCSsample
```

to have version 1.2 of the file displayed on your terminal. The "-s" flag suppresses the normal output of statistics, the "-p" flag indicates output to the terminal, and the "-r1.2" indicates that we want to see version 1.2 of the file 's.SCCSsample'. The latest version can be displayed on the terminal by entering the command

```
get -s -p s.SCCSsample
```

Although only a few of the features of SCCS have been shown in this example, the use of SCCS in controlling source code throughout the mature lifetime of a software product should be apparent.

CHAPTER

13

The Shell
Programming Language

The shell is probably the most important UNIX System utility program; unfortunately, it is also one of the most poorly understood and one of the most poorly documented utilities. The UNIX System shell is both an interactive command interpreter and a command level programming language interpreter. This is one of the most powerful features of the UNIX System.

Some computer systems have simple and effective interactive command interpreters, but they lack the ability to program sophisticated command sequences. Other computers have elaborate command level programming languages but no provisions for simply running a program. The UNIX System combines both abilities in the shell.

We have already discussed the shell (Chapter 4) and you should have already used the shell interactively. Most interactive users exercise only a few of the shell's capabilities. Typical interactive use of the shell involves entering simple commands ("ls"), using the shell's filename generation facilities ("ls *.doc"), specifying I/O redirection ("ls > myfile"), and specifying pipelines ("ls | wc -l"). These techniques are powerful and extremely useful but they are only a small part of the shell's capabilities.

There is a very important difference between controlling a task interactively and creating a program to perform a task automatically. When you control a task interactively you can use your intellect to react to the situation as it develops. Programs have no intellect. Their reactions must be determined in advance and coded into the program. Anyone who has written a large program knows that anticipating all of the possible circumstances is very difficult.

Let's use an example to clarify the difference between interactive and automatic procedures. Suppose you want to examine a file on your terminal and you recall that the name of the file is 'groc.lst' or perhaps 'grocery.l' or something similar to that and you remember it is in your 'data.lsts' directory or

150

perhaps in your current directory or maybe in your 'groc.proj' directory. Interactively it is easy to browse through the directories and locate the file and then use the cat program to display the file on your terminal. Writing a program to find and display the 'gro...' file is very difficult. What is a sufficient criterion for locating the file? What should the program do if zero (or several) candidates are located? A program to locate and print 'gro...' would have to include answers to these and other questions.

The interactive procedure is a simple sequence of commands whereas a program to produce the same effect is a complicated logical structure. Experience shows that sophisticated control structures for repeating sequences of instructions and for testing certain conditions makes it easier to write good programs. The UNIX System shell contains these control structures. Experience has also shown that it is very useful to have items (called variables) whose value can change during the course of a program. The UNIX System shell contains variables.

One of the major differences between Version 6 of the UNIX System and Version 7 is the shell. The Version 6 shell is a good interactive command interpreter, but it is a weak programming language. The Version 7 shell combines all of the Version 6 interactive features with a powerful programming language. The features discussed here are from the Version 7 shell, which is commonly called the Bourne Shell after its creator, S. R. Bourne.

The first five sections of this chapter are useful for most UNIX System users. You should read the remainder of the chapter if you intend to write shell programs or if you really want to know more about the shell. Read Chapter 14 if you want to see some examples of shell programs. Most UNIX System users don't write complicated shell programs and most users don't need to understand the shell at the level that is presented in this chapter.

13.1 Executing a Shell Program

Any command or sequence of UNIX System commands stored in a file is called a shell program or a command file. Usually the term command file is used when the file contains a simple sequence of commands and the term shell program identifies a file containing a more complicated arrangement of commands (often using the shell's conditional commands and other advanced features). There are three ways to get the shell to execute a command file. The first method is very simple. Since the shell normally reads commands interactively you can use input redirection to get the shell to read commands from a file.

```
sh  <  lsdir
```

Here the shell is reading commands from the file 'lsdir'. (The function of the shell commands stored in 'lsdir' is unimportant in this example.) Any program that is normally controlled from the standard input can instead be controlled from a file by using input redirection.

Because the shell often reads commands from disk files (rather than interactively) a special capability is built into the shell. If the shell is invoked with the name of a file as an argument, then the shell will read commands from that file.

    sh lsdir

Many commands are built so that you can specify a file name as a command line argument or use input redirection. However, not all commands allow both forms of expression. The advantage of specifying a file as a command name argument is that you can pass arguments to the command. The command

    sh lsdir /bin /etc

will cause the shell to execute the commands in the file 'lsdir'. The 'lsdir' shell program can access the "/bin" and the "/etc" arguments. As you will see later, arguments to shell programs can be very useful.

    The third method is even more refined. The UNIX System text editor usually creates files with the execution privileges turned off because most text files contain letters and documents. Whenever the shell encounters a text file that has the execution privileges turned on the shell assumes that it contains a shell program. You can turn the execution privileges of the file 'lsdir' on by using the change mode command.

    chmod a+x lsdir

(See Section 9.3.) Once the execution privileges are turned on you can execute the commands in a file by simply typing the name of the file.

    lsdir

The shell will balk if you try to execute a file that doesn't have the privileges turned on.

    One advantage of this third method is that you can execute a shell program by merely entering its name as a command. You don't have to treat shell programs differently from any other programs. Another advantage is that the shell will search for executable commands in all of the usual directories (often '/bin', '/usr/bin', etc), but when you enter a command (e.g., "sh lsdir" or "sh < lsdir") the command file must reside in the current directory (or be specified using a path name). You can pass arguments to shell programs the same way that you pass arguments to ordinary programs.

    lsdir /usr/lib /usr/man/doc

Shell programs that are going to be used frequently should be made executable so that users can execute them easily.

13.2 Shell Variables

A programming language uses variables to store values. The name "variable" suggests that the stored values can change during the course of execution. The UNIX System shell variables can store strings of text. A variable can be set by entering an assignment command.

    ux = u.UNIX

The assignment command listed above assigns the value "u.UNIX" to the shell variable named "ux". The name of a shell variable must start with a letter and it may contain letters, digits, and underscores. Since "ux" is a variable its value can be changed by using another assignment statement.

    ux = UNIX

If you want to assign a value to a variable that contains internal spaces or tabs or newlines then you need to quote the value.

    hero = "John Paul Jones"

The readonly command allows you to mark a variable so that its value cannot be changed. The readonly command is used to mark variables.

    readonly ux

Now that the variable "ux" is readonly the command

    ux = uu.UNIX

will produce the error message "ux: is read only." Use readonly wisely as it is permanent during the life of the shell. If you want a list of the current readonly variables, enter the command

    readonly

The variables that you create are local to the current shell unless you mark them for export. Variables marked for export will be made available to any commands that the shell creates. The command

    export ux

will mark the variable "ux" for export. The export mark sticks until the shell terminates. You can get a list of the current exportable variables by entering the command

    export

When you assign a value or a mode to a variable you use the name of the variable. However, when you use the value stored in a variable you have to place a currency symbol before the name of the shell. The currency symbol informs the shell that the following name refers to a variable, not a file or literal. The echo command can be used to display the values of certain variables. The command

    echo $ux

will echo the word "UNIX" since the value of the variable $ux is "UNIX". A variable that has not been explicitly set contains the null string. Therefore the command

    echo $abc

will echo nothing.

You should use curly braces to surround the name of a variable when the name is immediately followed by characters that are not part of the name. The command

    echo ${ux}tm

will echo the word "UNIXtm". Another way to separate variable names from surrounding characters is by using double quotes. The command

    echo "$ux"tm

will also echo the word "UNIXtm". See Section 13.5 for an explanation of quoting to understand why this works.

Five shell variables are automatically set by the shell:

1. The variable $? contains the value returned by the last executed command.

2. The variable $$ contains the process number of the shell.

3. The variable $! contains the process number of the last background process that the shell invoked.

4. The variable $# contains the number of arguments (positional parameters) to the shell. (See Section 13.10.)

5. The variable $- contains the flags that were passed to the shell when it was invoked or flags that were set using the set command.

These automatic variables can be used the same way as user created variables. The command

    echo $$

will print the process id number of the shell. The pid number can be verified using the ps command.

13.3 Using Shell Variables Interactively

Besides their obvious value in shell programs, shell variables can be very useful interactively. Suppose that there is a certain directory (we'll use '/usr/td/c/mon/src/doc') containing some files that you are using, but for some good reason you decide to remain in your current directory and reference the files in '/usr/td/c/mon/src/doc' using absolute pathnames. It is clumsy to enter commands that reference the '/usr/td/c/mon/src/doc' directory because they are so hard to type. You can simplify matters by storing the directory name in a variable and typing the variable name instead of the full directory name.

    docdir = /usr/td/c/mon/src/doc

You can verify that you typed the directory name correctly by entering the command

    echo $docdir

You can get a list of the files in the directory by using the command

    ls $docdir

You can type a particular file (we'll type 'sema.txt') in the directory by using the command

    cat $docdir/sema.txt

You can even use command name generation as in the following command which produces a long format listing of all of the files whose name ends in ".txt".

    ls -l $docdir/*.txt

If you had to run a program called 'mkdoc' that resided in the $docdir directory you could create a new variable to store the absolute pathname of 'mkdoc'. You could either enter the command

    mkdoc = /usr/td/c/mon/src/doc/mkdoc

to create the "mkdoc" variable or you could use the slightly shorter command

    mkdoc = $docdir/mkdoc

Now the command

    $mkdoc $docdir/sema.txt

will run the '/usr/td/c/mon/src/doc/mkdoc' program with the argument" /usr/td/c/mon/src/doc/sema.txt". Variables can occasionally simplify common interactive tasks.

13.4 The Search String

When you enter a command, the first thing that the shell does is search for the program. But where does it look? Many UNIX System installations contain thousands of directories and it would be too time consuming to look everywhere. To focus the search the UNIX System shell maintains a search string. The search string is a list of directories where the shell looks for your commands.

Most search strings include the current directory, the '/bin' directory, and the '/usr/bin' directory. In the UNIX System it is customary to store most of the frequently used commands in '/bin' and the '/usr/bin'. The search string can be modified so that additional directories are searched whenever you enter a command. If the command is not found in any of the directories in the search string, then the shell prints a message complaining that the program was not located.

You can display the current search string by entering the command

    echo $PATH

The response might be

    :/bin:/usr/bin

This search string specifies searches of the current directory, then the '/bin'

directory, and finally the '/usr/bin' directory. The directories in the search
string are separated by colons. Any null directories (two colons in a row or a
leading colon) in the search string are taken to mean the current directory. The
search string that specifies searches through '/bin' and then '/usr/bin' is

   /bin:/usr/bin

If you wanted to look in '/bin' first, and then in the current directory, and then
finally in '/usr/bin', the search string would be

   /bin::/usr/bin

Since the search string is just a shell variable you can set it interactively. The
command

   PATH = :/bin:/usr/bin:/usa/kc/bin

would create a search string containing all of the usual directories plus the directory '/usa/kc/bin'.

   If your login directory contains a file called '.profile', then the shell commands in that directory will be executed when you log in. The commands in
'.profile' are usually used to adjust the terminal handler to your terminal, initialize environmental variables such as $PATH, and execute any commands that
you want executed. If you want a unique search string, you should place the
appropriate command in '.profile'.

   It is important to search as few places as possible and to search them in the
optimal order. People with very large search strings often have much poorer
system response because the shell is busy searching dozens of directories each
time a command in entered. In a related matter it is important to keep the sizes
of directories manageable. It takes much less time to search a directory containing just a few files than a swollen directory that contains hundreds of files. The
time that the shell spends searching for commands is significant, and careful
control of your search string and directory sizes can minimize that time.

   Search strings are very important when a group of people all need access to a
body of programs. For example, if a group of people all use a set of teletext programs, then all of the teletext programs should be put in a directory (perhaps
'/usr/teletext/bin'). Everyone who uses the programs should modify their
search string to include the teletext directory. If instead the teletext programs
were placed in '/bin' or '/usr/bin', then every user on the system would constantly be penalized because it would take longer to search through the standard
directories, hence it would take longer to execute each command. This is an
example of users' ability to control their environment to create a more productive atmosphere.

13.5 Quoting

Unfortunately, most of the special characters used by the shell are also used by
other programs. There just aren't enough characters and symbols to go around.
When you enter commands interactively or when you place commands in a file

and execute the file the shell is the first program to acquire the information. If the information contains any of the shell's special characters, then you can expect the shell to alter the information unless it is quoted.

When you enter a command involving pipes

```
ls | wc -l
```

the vertical bar indicates a pipe operation and the shell spawns two processes, ls and wc with the standard output of ls connected to the standard input of wc. When you enter a command involving logical comparisons between two shell variables, as in

```
expr $var1 \| $var2
```

the vertical bar is a mathematical symbol, not a pipe fitting. When the vertical bar is used as a math symbol we have to be very careful to quote it so that its meaning as a pipe fitting is removed. In the example given immediately above the vertical bar is quoted by the backslash character.

There are three methods of quoting in the UNIX System shell:

1. The backslash (\ ) quotes the character that immediately follows.

2. Characters enclosed by single quote marks (') are quoted. No interpretations occur.

3. Characters enclosed by double quote marks (") are quoted except for backslash, accent grave, double quote, and currency symbol. Command and parameter substitution occur within double quotes.

When a single character has to be quoted it is usually easiest to use a backslash as in the example above. When a group of characters must be quoted and you don't want any interpretations to occur, then it is easiest to use the single quotes, the strongest form of quoting in the UNIX System shell. The double quote marks are a weaker form of quoting. Command and parameter substitution occur within double quote marks, therefore the characters that control command and parameter substitution (`, $) need to be quoted if you want to suppress these substitutions. Backslash and of course the double quote are also special within double quotes.

If you enter the command

```
echo '$HOME'
```

or the similar command

```
echo \$HOME
```

the word "$HOME" will be printed, but if you enter the command

```
echo "$HOME"
```

the name of your home directory will be printed. (See next section.)

Quoting is also used to make a single word out of a sequence of characters that contains blanks. If you enter the command

```
macedonian = Alexander the Great
```

then $macedonian will be assigned the value "Alexander" and then the shell will report an error in locating the program called "the". Instead you could enter the command

    macedonian = 'Alexander the Great'

or you could enter the command

    macedonian = "Alexander the Great"

or you could enter the command

    macedonian = Alexander \ the \ Great

All three versions assign the value "Alexander the Great" to the shell variable $macedonian.

13.6 The Set Command

The set command is used to print a list of the variables that have been created. The command

    set

produced the following output on my system:

    HOME = /usa/kc
    PATH = :/usa/kc/bin:/bin:/usr/bin
    IFS =

    PS1 = $
    PS2 = >
    TERM = vt100

All of these variables are created during the login process and they are an important part of your UNIX System environment. Some systems contain additional variables to support local features. (Note: the automatic variables $$, $?, $!, $#, and $- are not listed by the set command.) Let's discuss each variable individually:

1. The "HOME" variable contains the name of your home directory.

2. The "PATH" variable contains the search string that the shell uses when it searches for your commands. The search string is discussed in Section 13.4.

3. The "IFS" variable contains the internal field separators, usually space, tab, and newline. The internal field separators separate the words of commands.

4. "PS1" and "PS2" are the primary prompt strings used by the shell. "PS1" is the normal prompt used by the shell and "PS2" is used for additional input to complete obviously incomplete commands.

5. The "TERM" variable contains the brand name of your terminal. Some commands need to know what type of terminal you are using in order to produce correct output.

When an interactive shell first starts executing it reads and executes the commands in the file '.profile' in the user's home directory. Typically the commands in '.profile' adjust the system's treatment of your terminal using the stty command and adjust some of these variables to suit your preferences. For example, if the '.profile' file contains the assignment

```
PS1 = "Yes boss ->"
```

then the system will address you with the "Yes boss ->" prompt rather than the standard prompt. Of course you can also reassign PS1 (or any of the parameters) interactively.

The set command can also be used to control several internal modes of the shell. For example, the command

```
set -v
```

will cause the shell to turn verbose mode on. All shell input lines will be printed as they are read. Verbose mode can be turned off by the command

```
set +v
```

Most of the flag arguments that can be controlled using the set command can also be supplied as command line arguments when you are invoking the shell to execute a series of commands in a file. The command

```
sh -v lsdir
```

will invoke a shell to execute the commands in the file 'lsdir' using the verbose mode. The effect is the same as if the command "set -v" were the first command in 'lsdir'. See the UNIX System manual for a complete list of the shell options that can be controlled using the set command or command line arguments.

13.7 Simple Conditionals

The ability to make a decision is the hallmark of intelligence. Decisions imply a choice among options; a selection of one path in preference to others. When a decision is made in a program one sequence of commands is executed and the other possible sequences are ignored. The structures that enact decisions in a programming language are called conditionals.

The primitives of a system are the operations that are built into the system. In computer programming languages such as BASIC and FORTRAN the primitives are machine operations on binary quantities. The control flow in a BASIC or FORTRAN program is based on the results of the primitive operations. The primitives of the shell command programming language are the UNIX System utility programs. Therefore, in the shell command programming language the control flow is based on the success or failure of the executing programs.

When a UNIX System program executes successfully it returns a zero exit status. By convention, if an executing program encounters serious problems, it returns a nonzero exit status. If I enter the command line

```
cd  /usa/kc
```

on my system I will make my home directory the current directory, and the exit status of cd will be zero. However, if you enter the same command on your system, the shell will probably print "/usa/kc: bad directory" (because there is no '/usa/kc' directory on your system) and the exit status of cd will be one. The exit status of a pipeline is the exit status of the last command in the pipeline. The exit status returned by a command (or pipeline) can be used to control the flow of execution in a shell program.

Most systems contain the special programs true and false. The only function of the program true is to return a true (zero) exit status. Similarly, the only function of the false program is to return a false (zero) exit status.

The Bourne shell has several conditional operators. The simplest conditional is the double ampersand ("&&") operator. When two commands are separated by a double ampersand the second command will execute only if the first command returns a zero exit status. The command

```
test -d  /usa/kc && echo success!
```

will type out the message "success!" if the file '/usa/kc' is a directory. The test program is used to test various conditions. The "-d" flag argument specifies that test should determine whether the following argument is a directory. A variety of other conditions can be tested; see the description of the test command in the UNIX System manual.

The opposite of the double ampersand is the double bar operator (" | |"). When two commands are separated by the double bar operator the second command will only execute if the first command returns a nonzero exit status. The command

```
test -d  /usa/kc | |  echo failure!
```

will type out the message "failure!" if the file does not exist or if the file exists but is not a directory.

13.8 Simple Commands, Pipelines, Lists

We have already defined a simple command to be a command and its arguments. There are two other fundamental units in the UNIX System shell: pipelines and lists. You need to understand pipelines and lists because they are used in shell control structures.

A pipeline is a simple command or group of simple commands connected by pipe fittings (the vertical bar or caret). Each of the following lines is a pipeline:

```
ls  -l  /bin  /usr/bin
who  |  wc  -l
a^b^c^d
ps
```

In the UNIX System a list is a sequence of pipelines; therefore, the four pipelines just mentioned form one list. In the list shown above the list elements (the pipelines) are on separate lines. (In UNIX System jargon, we say that the pipelines are separated by the newline character.) The following list is equivalent to the first:

```
ls -l /bin /usr/bin ; who^wc -l;a|b|c|d ; ps
```

In this list the elements are separated by semicolons. The following characters can be used to separate the elements of a list:

1. ; or the newline character to indicate sequential execution.

2. && to indicate conditional (true) execution of the following pipeline.

3. | | to indicate conditional (false) execution of the following pipeline.

4. & to indicate background (asynchronous) execution of the preceding pipeline.

The list is a basic structure in the UNIX System. A list can be as simple as a single command or as complicated as you choose to make it. The value returned by a list is the exit status of the last pipeline in the list. It is important to understand the differences between a command, a pipeline, and a list:

1. A simple command executes one program.

2. A pipeline is a sequence of simple commands joined by pipe fittings. The simplest pipeline is a simple command.

3. A list is a sequence of pipelines. The simplest list is a single pipeline (which may be a simple command).

13.9 The If Conditional

The double ampersand conditional and the double bar conditional are useful for creating very simple conditional structures. However, the shell has many much more sophisticated conditionals. One of the most important shell features is the Bourne shell if conditional, which is a greatly improved version of the Version 6 if conditional. The syntax of the if conditional is:

```
if  if-list
    then  then-list
elif  elif-list
    then  then-list
else  else-list
fi
```

The words "if", "then", "elif", "else", and "fi" are keywords. Keywords are words that the shell (or any programming language) uses to indicate built-in structures such as the if conditional statement. The words "if-list", "then-list", "elif-list", and "else-list" denote lists of the UNIX System commands. The "elif .. then .." part is optional, the "else" part is optional, and there can be as many "elif .. then .." parts as necessary. Therefore the simplest if conditional is

```
if  if-list
    then  then-list
fi
```

The UNIX System shell's if conditional behaves similarly to the if statement in many programming languages. Let's use a simple example to show how the if statement works. Imagine there are four programs named winter, spring, summer, and fall which return a true exit status during their season and false otherwise. Also imagine a set of programs which print the chores that should be performed during each season. Our shell program to print chore reminders is

```
if  winter
    then
        snowremoval
        weatherstrip
elif  spring
    then
        startgarden
        mowlawn
elif  summer
    then
        tendgarden
        painthouse
        mowlawn
        waterlawn
elif  fall
    then
        harvest
        mowlawn
else
        echo  Something  is  wrong.
        echo  Check  the  4  season  programs.
fi
```

During the spring season the spring command will be true and the startgarden command and the mowlawn programs will be executed. During the fall season the fall command will return a true status and the harvest command and the mowlawn command will be executed. If none of the season programs exit with a true status, then the else part of the conditional will be executed causing an error message to be printed.

Now let's show a more realistic example. Suppose some continuously running program writes a diagnostic to an errorfile each time it encounters errors during an operation. Another program runs once each hour to log the errors. If the errorfile exists, then this second program should copy the errorfile to a line-printer at headquarters; if the errorfile doesn't exist (because no errors occurred), then the second program should send an "all is well" message. The following shell command file would perform this simple task:

```
date > /dev/lp-to-hdq
if test -r errfile
    then
        cat errorfile > /dev/lp-to-hdq
        rm errorfile
else
        echo "No errors this hour" > /dev/lp-to-hdq
fi
```

Notice that date, cat, and echo redirect their standard output to the line-printer-to-headquarters device. You might think that the errorfile should be copied or moved to the special lineprinter interface file. However, copy (cp) and move (mv) are disk operations that move (or copy) an ordinary file from one place on the disk to another. Instead of relocating a file you want to redirect the output so that the executing program writes data to the special file. When a program writes data to a special file the operating system actually delivers the data to the I/O device, a printer in this case.

13.10 Shell Program Arguments

We have already seen the importance of writing programs that perform general functions. Most programs that perform general functions can be directed to perform more specific functions by supplying them with command line arguments. For example, the command

```
ls
```

will output a list of the files in the current directory. If you want a more specific list, such as a list of all of the files in the '/bin' directory, you have to enter a more specific command. The command

```
ls /bin
```

will output a list of all of the files in the '/bin' directory. The argument "/bin" is used by the ls program to direct its attention to the '/bin' directory.

In shell programs the command line arguments are made available in a series of numbered variables. $1 is the variable that contains the first command line argument, $2 contains the second argument, etc. The numbered variables are often called positional parameters because $1 refers to the argument in the first position, etc. The special variable name $0 always refers to the zeroeth argument, which is the name of the executing shell program. An additional feature is the special name $#, which refers to the number of arguments to the command (see Section 13.2.)

Consider a few simple examples of the use of positional parameters. Suppose you need a program that acquires four arguments and then echoes those arguments in the reverse order. If the program (we'll call it 'rev-4') were invoked as

```
rev-4  20  30  40  50
```

it would respond "50 40 30 20". Our program will check the number of arguments and print an error message if there are too few or too many. If the number of arguments is OK, then the arguments will be printed in the reverse order.

```
if test $# = 4
      then echo $4 $3 $2 $1
else echo $0 usage: arg1 arg2 arg3 arg4
fi
```

In this simple shell program we use the test command to see if the automatic variable $# indicates that the program was executed with four arguments and we use the positional parameters $1, $2, $3, and $4 to represent the actual arguments. As a convenience some versions of the UNIX System allow any expression enclosed in square brackets to be evaluated by the test command. On these systems the line containing the if condition in the example immediately above could have been written equivalently as "if [$# = 4]". The square brackets are often used to make things more readable but the test program is actually performing the operations in either case. (Note that the UNIX System expr command can also be used to perform arithmetic comparisons.)

The for conditional (see Section 13.16) provides a more flexible method for working with the positional parameters.

13.11 The While and Until Conditional Loops

The while and until conditionals allow you to repeat a group of commands. Let's first examine the while conditional. Its syntax is:

```
while  while-list
   do  do-list
done
```

The keywords here are "while", "do", and "done". First the while-list is executed. If the while-list returns a true exit status, then the do-list is executed and then the operation restarts from the beginning. If the while-list returns a false exit status, then the conditional is complete.

Suppose that you must write a shell program that waits for a certain file to be removed. (Some other program is responsible for removing the file.) The while command can wait for a condition to become true. Since we want other UNIX System users to get some processing time, we should delay a few seconds between tests rather than test continuously. The following shell program waits for a file named 'lockfile' to vanish:

```
while test -r lockfile
  do sleep 5
done
```

This program tests to see if the file named 'lockfile' is readable. If it is, then the command "sleep 5" suspends execution for five seconds. When 'lockfile' is removed the test fails and the command completes.

Notice that the foregoing shell program separates the command lists by placing them on separate lines. We could also enter the program on a single line and use semicolons to separate the lists.

```
while test -r lockfile ; do sleep 5 ; done
```

The until conditional is a variant of the while structure. Whereas the while structure repeats while the while-list returns a true value, the until structure repeats while the until-list returns a false value. The syntax of the until structure is:

```
until until-list
  do do-list
done
```

The only new keyword is "until".

Suppose you have to write a shell program that waits until a certain file is created. One method would be to use the while structure and negate the test:

```
while test ! -r proceedfile ; do sleep 1 ; done
```

The exclamation point argument to the test program negates the readability test so that test returns a true indication if the file is not readable. Another method uses the until structure:

```
until test -r proceedfile ; do sleep 1 ; done
```

Using this method the loop will continue until the test command returns a true value (until the file 'proceedfile' i screated).

13.12 Structured Commands

Conditional structures such as while and until are executed by the shell almost as if they are a single command. The entire structure is scanned by the shell before any part of it is executed. Try entering the following line interactively on your system:

```
until test -r stopfile ; do
```

The command is obviously incomplete so the shell prompts you for further input (usually with a ">"). Complete the command by typing

```
echo Hello ; sleep 2 ; done &
```

The final ampersand indicates that the entire until command should run in the background. The command will type "Hello" every two seconds until your create the stopfile. Since your command is running in the background the shell should be ready to accept another command. When you tire of seeing the greeting on your terminal, type the following command to create a file called 'stopfile':

> stopfile

Since it might take you longer than two seconds to enter the command you will probably be interrupted in midstroke by a greeting or two. Just remember that the system is keeping track of the characters that you are typing even while it (the system) is periodically typing the "Hello" greeting. As soon as you successfully create the stopfile the background greeting process will terminate. (You should remove 'stopfile' so that your directory doesn't become cluttered.)

All Bourne shell conditionals are structured commands. In a structure all of the alternative processing paths are part of the structure; control flow is local to the structure. The opposite of a structure is the goto construct. In a goto statement the alternative processing paths are not part of the statement; control flows to a nonlocal statement.

Modern programming languages favor control structures over the goto construct. Goto's are out of favor because their nonlocal control transfers lead to incomprehensible programs. The Bourne shell doesn't include the goto statement because it would violate the convention of processing one command (or structured command) at a time.

13.13 Command Substitution

The shell allows you to take the standard output of a command and use it within a shell procedure. When a command is surrounded by accents grave (`) that command is executed by the shell and the resulting text is substituted in place of the command. For example, you could deposit the current date and time into a variable called now by executing the following command:

now = `date`

It might help to think of this process in two stages. In the first stage the date program is executed and the resulting text is substituted. Conceptually this leaves us with the shell command "now= '09:30 Jan 1, 1980 '". This command is executed causing the text to be stored in the variable $now. The command

echo $now

will print the date that is stored in the shell variable $now.

Command substitution is often used to provide arithmetic with shell variables. The expr command can perform arithmetic operations on its arguments. If you enter the command

expr 5 + 13

then "18" will be printed on your terminal. Many of the operators that you use in expressions (parentheses, asterisks, ampersands, etc.) are special characters to the shell and you have to be very careful to escape them (see Section 13.5). If a shell variable is assigned a numeric value as in

```
count = 10
```

then the value can be increased by one by using command substitution:

```
count = `expr $count + 1`
```

The expr command will receive the arguments "10", "+" and "1". The result is "11", which is stored in the shell variable $count.

Now that we can do arithmetic on variables we can rewrite the reverse arguments program (mentioned in Section 13.10) to reverse any number of arguments.

```
count = $#
cmd = echo
while test $count -gt 0
    do
        cmd = "$cmd  \$$count"
        count = `expr $count - 1`
    done
eval $cmd
```

This program is a bit difficult because it uses many of the facilities of the shell. The program consists of a while conditional loop that executes once for each argument, starting at the final argument and sequencing down to the first argument. The argument being processed is indicated by the variable $count; its initial value is the number of the last argument and then its value is decreased by one each time through the loop.

Each trip through the loop adds some text to the variable $cmd. Initially the variable $cmd contains the text "echo". If the program were invoked with four arguments, after the first trip through the loop the variable $cmd would contain "echo $4", after the second trip the variable would contain "echo $4 $3", and so on. The loop terminates when the variable $count is decremented to zero.

The word "\$$count" in the first statement of the do-list deserves some attention. The goal is to create a text string consisting of a currency symbol followed by the current value of the $count variable. Since the currency symbol is a special symbol to the shell it has to be escaped with a backslash. This explains the first backslash and the first currency symbol. The second currency symbol is just the start of the reference to the variable $count.

The hardest part of the program is the line beginning with the word eval. Eval is a special command that provides an extra layer of substitutions on its arguments and then executes the arguments. At the completion of the loop the shell variable $cmd contains an echo command to output the reversed list of arguments. For the four-argument case the shell variable $cmd would contain "echo $4 $3 $2 $1". The eval causes the echo command to be reevaluated and executed, resulting in the output of the arguments in reverse order.

If the program is stored in a file called 'revargs' and 'revargs' is made executable using the chmod command, then the command

```
revargs n o t
```

will output "t o n". Revargs is not very good for palindromes but there are situations where the order of arguments has to be adjusted.

13.14 Shell Substitutions

Thus far we have discussed all of the substitutions that the shell performs. Let's summarize all of the substitutions in the order in which they occur. The order becomes very important in situations where one word undergoes several substitutions.

1. Command substitution. All of the commands that are surrounded by accents grave are executed and the resulting text is substituted in place of the command, as discussed in Section 13.13.

2. Parameter (or variable) substitution. All of the words in the program that begin with a "$" are replaced, as discussed in Section 13.2.

3. Blank interpretation. The results of the preceding substitutions are scanned for field separators. The usual field separators are blanks, tabs, and newlines. Any word that contains a field separator is divided into multiple words. Field separators in quoted words are ignored, and null words (except for explicitly quoted null words) are discarded.

4. File name generation. The shell examines each word for the metacharacters "*", "?", and "[". If any of the words contain these metacharacters, that word is replaced by an alphabetically sorted list of file names that match the pattern or by the original word if there are no matches. File name generation is discussed in Section 4.8.

A great deal of the power of the shell lies in its ability to perform text substitutions. However, the technique is confusing for people who are used to programming languages such as FORTRAN and BASIC, which are oriented toward numbers. The substitutions that occur in the shell are more similar to the general text handling capabilities that are built into programming languages such as LISP and SNOBOL.

13.15 Here Documents

A here document is used to temporarily redirect the standard input within a shell program. The notation for a here document resembles standard input redirection.

```
cmd args  <<symbol
( the here document )
symbol
```

The start of the here document is indicated by the "<<" notation. The following symbol is remembered and is used to indicate the end of the here document. The here document can be as many lines as necessary. A line consisting of the symbol indicates the end of the here document. The shell makes the here document available to the command as the standard input.

Consider the problem of handling errors in a large shell program that runs during the wee hours of the morning. You could have the shell program write an error message to a file and give someone the responsibility of looking at the file every day. A better method would be to send mail to the responsible person so that the notification is automatic.

If the following command were included in the error handling section of the shell program, then the named person ("opsmanager" in this case) would get mail describing the problem:

```
mail opsmanager <<!
************* PROBLEMS AGAIN *****************
The midnight error has struck again! The
tdata file was missing - all processing
stopped.
!
```

An alternative solution would be to put the message in a separate file and then use ordinary input redirection. The here document enables you to keep everything in one file.

13.16 The For Structure

The UNIX System shell contains a for structure, which allows a group of commands to be executed once for each word in a list of words. The general form of the for structure is

```
for name in word1 word2 ...
    do do-list
    done
```

The do-list will be executed once for each word in the list of words (word1, word2, etc.). The current word in the list will be assigned to the shell variable $name. The keywords are "for", "in", and the familiar "do" and "done".

The following example shows a silly use of the for structure.

```
for fruit in apples pears oranges mangos
    do
        echo $fruit are fruits
    done
```

If you execute this program it will print "apples are fruits" followed by "pears are fruits", and so on. This form of the for structure often is used to perform some function for each file in a group of files or for each directory in a group of directories.

The for structure can also be used without the keyword "in" followed by the list of words.

```
for  name
    do  do-list
    done
```

In this form the do-list is executed once for each positional parameter (argument) of the shell. This is the simplest method for sequencing through the arguments to a shell program.

We can use the second form of the for structure to rewrite the reverse argument's shell program.

```
list = ""
for  arg
    do
        list = "$arg  $list"
    done
echo  $list
```

In this argument reverse shell program the for structure sequences through the arguments to the shell, placing each argument in front of the previous arguments stored in the variable $list. The reversed list is printed at the conclusion of the program.

13.17 The Case Structure

The shell's case structure is a fancy multiway branch based upon pattern matching. The general form of the case structure is

```
case  word  in
    pattern1)  pat1-list  ;;
    pattern2)  pat2-list  ;;
    ...
esac
```

The word is compared with all of the patterns. The first match causes the corresponding pattern-list to be executed, and execution of the structure is complete. The patterns can be composed of the usual shell metacharacters: "*" to match any sequence of characters, "?" to match any single character, and square brackets to delimit a class of characters. Several distinct patterns can be included in one pattern-list by using the vertical bar to indicate alternation. The usual meaning of the vertical bar (pipe connection) is suppressed during a case statement.

The following shell program attempts to determine the breed of an animal.

```
for breed
do
   case $breed in
      arabian|palomino|clydesdale)echo $breed is a horse ;;
      jersey|guernsey|holstein) echo $breed is a cow ;;
      husky|shepherd|setter|labrador) echo $breed is a dog ;;
      siamese|persian|angora) echo $breed is a cat ;;
      *) echo $breed is not in our catalog ;;
   esac
done
```

Notice that the final pattern is "*", which will match everything. Only one of the pattern-lists can be executed on one pass through the case structure. If this program is stored in an executable file named 'breeds', then the command

```
breeds husky holstein terrier
```

will produce the messages "husky is a dog", "holstein is a cow", and "terrier is not in our catalog". The case structure is often used in conjunction with the for structure.

13.18 Break and Continue

The shell's break and continue statements are used to alter the action of for loops, while loops, and until loops. The break statement causes the shell to break out of the enclosing loop while the continue statement causes the shell to branch to the beginning of the enclosing loop and start another iteration.

As a first example let's rewrite one of the argument reverse shell programs. You might recall that the original version used a while loop.

```
count = $ #
cmd = echo
while test $count -gt 0
   do
      cmd = "$cmd  \$$count"
      count = `expr $count - 1`
   done
eval $cmd
```

The program could be written equivalently using a break statement.

```
count = $ #
cmd = echo
while  true
    do
        cmd = "$cmd  \$$count"
        count = `expr $count - 1`
        if test $count -eq 0
            then break
        fi
    done
eval $cmd
```

In this program a break statement offers little advantage because there is only one loop exit criterion and only one exit point. The break is the only clean solution when a loop has several exit points or when the exit criterion is quite involved.

We could also rewrite this problem using a continue statement.

```
count = $ #
cmd = echo
while  true
    do
        cmd = "$cmd  \$$count"
        count = `expr $count - 1`
        if test $count -gt 0
            then continue
        fi
        eval $cmd
        exit
    done
```

The last two statements of the loop ("eval $cmd" and "exit") are executed only once, at the conclusion of the processing. They are skipped on all of the initial passes through the loop. The exit statement terminates processing in a shell program; it is usually made to be ineffective when entered interactively.

CHAPTER

14

A Few Shell Programs

One of the most interesting features of the UNIX System is the shell. The shell is a powerful interactive command interpreter entwined within a sophisticated high level programming language. The primitive operations in the shell programming language are the UNIX System commands. Hence the entire power of the UNIX Operating System can be used in a shell program.

Programmers usually are trained to work with conventional programming languages. However, shell programming requires a different sort of thinking. Because the shell is so important to the UNIX System we next consider a few examples of shell programs. All of these examples are designed to work on Version 7 of the UNIX System and they use the Version 7 shell features.

Simple shell programs can be written by nonprogrammers, but sophisticated shell programming — in fact all programming — is still a job for experts. The first section of this chapter explains some of the issues that you should consider when you are considering the shell language for a given application. Simple shell programs are commonly used UNIX System commands conveniently stored in a file. One example is shown in Section 14.2. Other shell programs are conceptually simple but involve many commands. A good example is the accounting problem which is developed in Section 14.3. Finally, in Sections 14.4 and 14.5 we see examples of shell programs that use some of the shell's programming language features.

14.1 When Do You Use the Shell Programming Language?

There are no firm rules for deciding when to use the shell programming language to write a program. When program execution speed is important more efficient languages should be used because there is a large execution speed penalty for using the very high level features of the shell. However, execution speed is not the only criterion for deciding the programming language to use for a given problem.

The shell programming language should be used when the problem solution involves many of the operations that are standard UNIX System commands. There are UNIX System commands to search through files, to sort files, to transform files, create files, move files, and so on. If the problem can be expressed in terms of the basic operations that are already built into the UNIX System, then a strong case can be made to use the shell programming language.

Once you become fluent in shell programming you begin to view problems in terms of the potential for shell language solutions. Many problems that don't appear at first to be amenable to shell language solutions actually can be performed elegantly by shell programs.

Another way to evaluate the suitability of the shell programming language is to examine the basic data that are involved in the problem. If the basic data are either lines of text or files, then the shell may represent a good solution. If the basic data are numbers or characters, then the shell is probably not a good solution.

The final criterion that we mention in relation to using a shell program is program development cost. It costs a lot of money to develop a program in a compiled language such as C or FORTRAN. Interactive languages make it easier to test and experiment, so for programs that are going to be used only once or twice it may be much cheaper to put up with the slow execution speed of shell programs in order to take advantage of the easy development of shell programs.

14.2 How Many Users?

When a UNIX System becomes slow and unresponsive either the system is about to fail or there are too many people competing for the computer's limited resources. The easiest way to roughly determine the load on the system is to see how many people are using the system. If you execute the command

    who

then a list of the users will be printed. To determine how many users are on the system we want to use the wc program to count the lines in the output of the who command. The command

    who | wc -l

will print a count of the number of users. The "-l" option to wc specifies that wc should count only lines; normally wc counts lines, words, and characters. If you want to be fancier, you can use the command

    echo `who | wc -l` users on the system

to produce the same count followed by the message "users on the system". If the command is placed in the file 'nusers' and 'nusers' is made executable, then the command

    nusers

will produce the message "20 users on the system" when there are twenty logged on users.

How would you solve this problem using the C language? A C solution to this problem would be difficult because you would have to be able to decipher the contents of the file '/etc/utmp' (the file where logins are recorded) in order to find out how many people are using the system. Since the who command already knows how to examine '/etc/utmp' this is an example of a problem that is solved easily using existing UNIX System tools but is fairly hard to solve using C.

14.3 Updating an Accounting File

The accounting information in my department is stored in a large file. At the end of each fiscal year many accounts are marked obsolete and their records must be removed from the file so that the file remains small enough to be manageable. However, even with the yearly culling of the obsolete account information the file remains very large, containing approximately 30,000 lines of text.

One approach to the problem is to do the removal by hand using the UNIX System text editor since the file is an ordinary text file. The secretary responsible for the update estimated that it would take at least a week to perform the update using the editor. The records for each account are grouped together so it is fairly easy to use the standard editor to update the file. However, updating a 30,000-line file in a week implies an update rate of about 1000 records an hour, or 20 records a minute. The possiblities for error are large when you are deciding to delete or retain records 20 times each minute. Moreover, 30 hours of time on our local UNIX System represents a sizable cost, as does a week of secretarial time.

Another approach is to write a special program to do the update. Since the program will be run only once a year efficiency is not a major consideration. The shell seems to be a natural solution because the items of interest are lines of text. Another reason to use the shell is that it is important to minimize program development time. Obviously there is no saving if it takes a week to write the program.

The first step in solving this type of problem is determining a specific criterion for deciding which records are to be removed and which should remain. It would not be enough for the secretary to tell you to remove all of the old records; instead you need a very specific criterion. In our case the secretary prepared a list of all of the accounts that were to be brought forward into the new accounts file for the new year.

For each account number in the list prepared by the secretary we want to find and extract all records from the account file and put the records in a current accounts file. One easy way to do this is to execute one extraction command for each account number in the secretary's list. Therefore, we want to transform the list of account numbers to be brought forward into a list of extraction commands. The UNIX System command grep will be used to do the extraction. Once we have this list of commands we will execute it to actually perform the

extraction. The final step is to clean up any miscellaneous files that we have
created and check the results.

Before we perform the operation let's look at the two files that we have been
given as input. The list of current account numbers ('currents') is just a list of
numbers:

```
48150
48677
56789
56790
```

Only a few entries are shown. The account file ('acctfile') contains the following
information:

jmx	48150	mathiasson	gt	0	general maintenance
jmg	48150	mathiasson	gt	0	electrometer
tmg	48150	mathiasson	gt	0	general maint
jmm	48309	pickett	gt	1000	y-axis amp
jmm	48309	pickett	gt	0	y-axis amp repair

Of course only 5 of the 30,000 lines are shown here.

We can extract the records for account number 48150 by using the command

```
grep 48150 acctfile
```

If the string "48150" occurs in some field other than the account number field,
we will get extraneous output. Thus this is not an absolutely safe method — it
would be inappropriate for some applications. However, for the application at
hand this is an adequate solution provided that someone who is familiar with
the accounts examines them carefully.

The grep command normally places its output on the standard output, so we
will have to redirect the output to a file. Since grep includes a lot of regular
expression matching that we don't need for this job, we should use the similar
program fgrep, which runs faster. See the UNIX System manual for a description of grep and fgrep.

Taking all of this into consideration leads to this command to extract the
records for account number 48150 from from the old accounting file and add
them to the end of the new accounting file:

```
fgrep 48150 acctfile >> nuacctfile
```

(Remember that the ">" notation for output redirection overwrites the target
file whereas the notation ">>" specifies that the output should be appended to
the end of the target file.)

We have a file of account numbers as shown above and we want to transform
it into a file of extraction commands:

```
fgrep 48150 acctfile >> nuacctfile
fgrep 48677 acctfile >> nuacctfile
fgrep 56789 acctfile >> nuacctfile
fgrep 56790 acctfile >> nuacctfile
```

The easiest method probably is to use the UNIX System text editor, and if I were going to perform the job only once I would use that technique. However, if you are going to perform the extraction many times, then you should use the UNIX System stream editor. The stream editor reads an input file and applies transformations to the file line by line. The stream editor is very similar to the standard UNIX System editor so it is relatively easy to use if you are familiar with the standard editor. See the description of the UNIX System stream editor (sed) in the manual.

The editing script for the stream editor can be supplied in an auxiliary file or on the command line. For our very simple transformation we will supply the editing script on the command line. The editing script accepted by the stream editor is very similar to the editing commands accepted by the standard UNIX System text editor. However, since the special characters for controlling the editor and the special characters for the shell overlap we will have to quote the characters in the script so that they are passed to sed rather than acted on by the shell.

If we were using the UNIX System text editor, we could use the editor substitute command

```
s/.*/fgrep & acctfile >> nuacctfile/
```

to change a line consisting of an account number (e.g., "48150") into a line containing the shell command "fgrep 48150 acctfile >> nuacctfile". The same syntax applies to the stream editor. The only difference is that the substitute command has to be quoted. The flag "-e" to sed indicates that the next argument is the editing script. Hence the command to transform the list of account numbers in the file 'currents' into a list of shell commands is

```
sed -e "s/.*/fgrep & acctfile >> nuacctfile/" currents
```

The complicated thing between the quotes is the editor substitute command. The only problem with this command is that the output appears on the terminal. We can save the output in a file by using the following command:

```
sed -e "s/.*/fgrep & acctfile >> nuacctfile/" \
    currents > shellcmds
```

(We use a backslash at the end of the first line in order to continue the command onto the second line.) If you execute this stream editor command, you will find that the file 'shellcmds' has the following contents:

```
fgrep 48150 acctfile >> nuacctfile
fgrep 48677 acctfile >> nuacctfile
fgrep 56789 acctfile >> nuacctfile
fgrep 56790 acctfile >> nuacctfile
```

Of course the actual script is much longer but I don't want to bother you with endless columns of commands. Each command in the file 'shellcmds' is a command that will extract all of the records for one particular account and add them to the end of 'nuacctfile'. Since the file 'shellcmds' is quite long it should probably be run at night or on the weekend. When I ran it one weekend it took about one hour of CPU time.

The conclusion is that it was cost effective and easy to write a shell program that saved about one week of secretarial labor. Notice that none of the advanced features of the shell were needed. The only UNIX System feature that we used that is not available on almost all operating systems is I/O redirection. In this example, the UNIX System shell made it easy to provide a solution, but the same result could have been accomplished on most operating systems.

14.4 Listing Subdirectories

The UNIX Operating System contains the ls command to list all of the files in a directory, but it lacks the built-in capability to list all of the directory files in a directory. Whenever you are poking around in an unfamiliar part of the file system you are likely to want to know the names of the subdirectories of the current directory.

Section 8.8 explained that the command

```
ls -l /   |  grep  '^d'
```

will list all of the directory files in the root directory, because in a long format listing, all the lines for directories start with the character "d". We can extend this simple command line so that we can list the subdirectories of any directory, not just the root directory, by using shell program arguments. We want to use a positional parameter in place of the name of the root directory to make this a more general solution:

```
ls -l $1  |  grep  '^d'
```

If this command is placed in the file 'lsdir' and 'lsdir' is made executable, then the command

```
lsdir  /bin
```

will produce a long format list of the subdirectories of the '/bin' directory.

If no arguments are supplied, then the positional parameter $1 will be unset and the ls program won't receive any directory names as arguments so the files in the current directory will be listed. This is very nice behavior. The command

```
lsdir
```

will list the subdirectories of the current directory just as the command

```
ls
```

will list the files in the current directory.

Obviously the lsdir command expects just one argument. If you enter the command

```
lsdir  /etc  /lib
```

only the subdirectories of '/etc' will be listed. We can fix this deficiency by using a for loop:

```
for i
    do
    ls -l $i | grep '^d'
    done
```

If this improved version is placed in the file 'lsdir', then the command

```
lsdir /etc /lib
```

will list the subdirectories of both '/etc' and '/lib'.

What happens with this improved version of lsdir when no arguments are supplied? With no arguments the for loop will never execute and no output will be generated. In order to correct this deficiency we need to put a test at the beginning of the file 'lsdir' to make sure that there is at least one argument:

```
if test $# = 0
    then lsdir .
else
    for i
        do
        ls -l $i | grep '^d'
        done
fi
```

This last version of lsdir checks to make sure that there is at least one argument. If there is at least one argument, then the for loop is executed but if there are no arguments, then the command "lsdir ." is executed to list the subdirectories of the current directory. Notice that lsdir is calling itself, a technique known as recursion. Shell programs are allowed to execute other shell programs (nesting) or to execute themselves recursively.

What other techniques could be used to perform this same function? The UNIX System program named test can be used to test files to see if they are directories. The command

```
for i in /etc/*
    do
    if test -d $i
        then echo $i
    fi
    done
```

will test all of the files in the '/etc' directory to see if they are directories and the names of all of the files that pass the test will be printed using the echo com-

mand. Using this alternative technique for identifying directories we can
rewrite the last version of lsdir:

```
if test $#  =  0
    then lsdir .
else
      for i
        do
        for j in $i/*
            do
            if test -d $j
               then echo $j
            fi
            done
        done
 fi
```

Can you think of any alternative methods for generating a list of the subdirectories of a given directory? Are these methods more or less efficient than the
method we have shown? Which of the two approaches that we have shown is
more efficient, and which approach is more general and flexible? How hard
would it be to write a C program to list subdirectories?

14.5 Listing Files in the Current Subtree

Everyone who uses the UNIX System occasionally misplaces a file. Perhaps
you can't remember the exact name of the file, or you put it in some unknown
directory. In any case the file is missing and you want to find it. Perhaps the
easiest way to find a file is just to list all of the files in the current file system subtree. (The current subtree consists of the current directory and all of its subdirectories, their sub-subdirectories, etc.) Very often you will know that the file
is in a certain part of the file system but you won't know exactly where. (Typically the file is in some unknown subdirectory of your home directory.)

The find command is used to find files. You can use arguments to find files
with certain names, or to find files that have been modified more recently than a
certain date, or to find files with certain privileges, and so on. If you don't use
any of the special options, then find will find all of the files in the subtree.

The simplest form of the find command is

```
find . -print
```

This will print all of the files in the current subtree. The dot indicates that the
search should start in the current directory (remember that dot is always the
name of the current directory) and the option "-print" indicates that the file
names should be printed. (See your UNIX System manual for a complete
explanation of the find command and all of its options.) You could memorize
the syntax for the find command or you could put the command in a shell command file that we will call 'lstree'. Whenever you want a list of all of the files in

the current subtree you can enter the command

    lstree

instead of the command

    find . -print

Many shell programs are this simple; they are just a useful but complicated command placed in a file.

A variant on this problem is the problem of listing all of the directories in the current subtree. As a first solution let's use the find command. The find command contains a test for directories. The command

    find . -type d -print

will find and print all of the directories in the current subtree. The argument "-type" indicates that we are trying to find certain types of file—directories in this case as indicated by the "d" argument. We could place this command in a file and enter the name of the file whenever we want a list of the directories in the current subtree.

Let's show another way to solve this problem. We can use the shell's for loop to perform tests on each file in a directory. The command

```
for i in *
do
      if test -d $i
         then echo $i
      fi
done
```

will test all of the files in the current directory and print the names of all of the files that prove to be directories. In order to list all of the directories in the current subtree we need to use recursion. Recursion is a technique where a routine calls itself. We can modify the command listed above so that it descends into each directory and then calls itself to list the directories in that directory, and descend still further, and so on. We will put the following commands in the file 'lstree1':

```
if test $# = 0
      then dirname = .
else  dirname = $1
fi
for i in *
do
      if test -d $i
         then echo $dirname/$i
                 (cd $i ; lstree1 $dirname/$i)
      fi
done
```

The argument to 'lstree1' is used to keep track of the pathname leading to the directory being examined. When 'lstree1' is invoked without arguments, then the variable $dirname acquires the value ".", otherwise $dirname acquires the value of the first argument to 'lstree1'. The interesting line in this program is "(cd $1 ; lstree1 $dirname/$i)". When you surround a list of shell commands in parentheses the commands are executed in a subshell. We want the cd command and the lstree command executed in a subshell because it would bk disastrous to perform a cd in the midst of a for loop. When the subshell completes the cd command and the lstree1 command it exits and control returns to the original shell in the original directory.

Let's look at yet another method. Instead of a for loop to generate a list of all of the files in the current directory we can use the ls command in combination with the read command. This time we will store the program in the 'lstree2' file.

```
if test  $#  =  0
     then  dirname = .
else  dirname = $1
fi
ls  | (
     while  read  i
     do
     if  test  -d  $i
        then  echo  $dirname/$i
              (cd  $i  ;  lstree2  $dirname/$i)
     fi
     done )
```

This program is similar to the previous except that the for loop is replaced with the ls command. In this version we generate a list of the files in the current directory using the ls command. The list is piped to the list of commands enclosed in parentheses. The read command reads lines from the pipe and places them in the variable $i. The end of the program is the same as 'lstree1'.

It is left to the reader to evaluate these three approaches.

CHAPTER

15

C and the UNIX System

The C programming language and the UNIX Operating System are very closely associated. Over 90 percent of the UNIX System kernel and the great majority of the UNIX System utility programs are written in C. C is a middle level programming language. It is much easier to use and much more productive than assembly language yet it lacks many of the expensive facilities of very high level languages (e.g., PL/1).

C was developed by Dennis M. Ritchie in the early 1970s for work on the early versions of the UNIX System. C evolved directly from B, a language designed by Ken Thompson. The major difference between B and C is that objects in B are limited to native machine words whereas C contains several basic types of object: characters (or bytes); short, long, and native integers; and floating point numbers. The typing in C allows it to adjust to a variety of machines. For example, on the PDP-11 the short and native integers are 16 bits and the long integer is 32 bits, whereas on the Interdata 8/32 the short integer is 16 bits and the native and long integers are 32 bits.

Ken Thompson's B evolved from BCPL, a systems programming language designed by Martin Richards. BCPL introduced many of the features for which C is famous, including the marriage of pointers and arrays and the terse style of expression. The evolution of BCPL into B into C has transformed a systems programming language into a general purpose language. C occasionally is called a systems programming language because it has been used very successfully for systems programming, but in fact C is an extremely general purpose language.

C is general purpose in part because it lacks many of the features that direct a language to a specific application. C lacks a built-in I/O subsystem, it lacks built-in operations on higher level objects such as records and arrays, and it lacks dynamic facilities for storage management. When these facilities are needed they are provided as external subroutines.

In a simple single-user computer system the application programs are either allowed or encouraged to access many computer resources directly. This is not possible in a multiuser computer system such as the UNIX System. In the UNIX System the kernel is responsible for supervising all transfers between programs and I/O devices and files. System calls are the mechanism that programs use in order to access the services of the operating system. The UNIX System contains system calls to perform I/O, to work with certain status elements that the system maintains, and to create new processes.

This chapter discusses the interface between the C programming language and the UNIX Operating System in a general manner that will be interesting to nonprogrammers who are curious about how programs interface with the system; it also provides a general introduction for programmers who want to become familiar with the UNIX System. The first section discusses subroutines and the next few sections discuss some of the more interesting system calls. The final sections discuss the C compiler and a program called lint, which can be used to perform tests on a C program.

The result of a compilation of a C source program is an object file. An object file contains machine instructions that correspond to the original C source program as well as various other information that makes it possible to combine object files from several compilations in order to produce a file containing a complete program image which can be executed. The following chapter discusses object files, separate compilation, and several of the UNIX System's utilities for manipulating object files.

All of the details for using system calls are provided in Section 2 of the UNIX System manual and the details for using the standard subroutines are provided in Section 3 of the manual. This chapter is not an introduction to programming in C and very little knowledge of C is required to read this chapter.

15.1 Standard Subroutines

Many features are omitted from the C programming language that are built into other languages. For example, C does not contain any built-in capacity for manipulating character strings. Instead common string functions are provided in the standard subroutine library. Many people who are used to higher level programming languages (PL/1 or PASCAL) are surprised that you have to call subroutine in C in order to compare two character strings. In PASCAL you would use the statement

```
IF  Str1  =  'Hello'  THEN  ....
```

to compare the variable "Str1" with the constant string "Hello". The equivalent in C is

```
if  (strcmp(Str1,"Hello"))  ....
```

The standard subroutine "strcmp" is used to compare two character strings.

The standard subroutines are used to provide string manipulation functions, common arithmetic functions, a variety of conversions from one representation of numbers to another, and a few common algorithms such as the quick sort. The object versions of the subroutines are stored in the standard subroutine library 'libc.a' in the '/lib' directory. '/lib/libc.a' is usually searched by the C compiler so that programmers need not make special arrangements to use the standard subroutines.

One of the most interesting C subroutines is printf. Printf is used to produce formatted output. You can output a message in a program by using the subroutine call

```
printf("The world is not safe for democracy. \ n");
```

The argument to printf in this case is a constant string. (The " \n" at the end of the string is C shorthand for a newline character.) Printf usually is used to output the value of variables. The first argument to printf is a format string and the following arguments (if there are any) are objects to be output. Normal characters in the format string are just copied to the output while the conversion specifiers in the format string cause one of the following arguments to be converted to a printable form and then output. The conversion specifiers consist of a percent symbol followed by one or more characters which detail the conversion. Using printf is much easier than describing it so we will show some examples. If x, y and z are integers, then their values can be printed in decimal format by using

```
printf("Values of x, y, and z: %d %d %d \ n",x,y,z);
```

The "%d" conversion specifier indicates decimal output conversion of an integer. If "Strptr" is a pointer to a character string, then the following will print the address of the string (in the octal radix) followed by the contents of the string:

```
printf("%o %s",Strptr,Strptr);
```

"Strptr" appears twice as an argument because it is needed twice, once for the "%o" octal conversion and once for the "%s" string conversion. Printf can be used to output long numbers, floating point numbers, and characters. On many UNIX Systems there are versions of the printf subroutine that will output to a file or to a character string.

When a programmer includes a standard subroutine in a program the actual computer instructions for executing the subroutine are stored in the executable program module. Thus the size of the executable program depends somewhat on how many subroutines are included in the program. Some of the subroutines are notoriously large and consume a lot of space. However, since the subroutines are contained in the body of the executable program there is very little time wasted in calling a standard subroutine.

15.2 Input/Output System Calls

Device independence is one of the most important ideas in the UNIX System. It means that a program can access a disk file as easily as a terminal or a paper tape punch or a printer. Disk file and special I/O devices are accessed using one set of system calls. I/O devices, like ordinary disk files, have names. For example, the name '/dev/pt' refers to a paper tape device and the name '/dev/lp' refers to a printer.

Even the exceptions to the idea of device independence are handled in a very straightforward manner. Obviously you cannot randomly access a sequential device such as a terminal, so any attempts to do so will lead to an error. But an error is the correct response in contrast to many systems that do horrible things when a program attempts to manipulate an I/O device in an unexpected way.

From the point of view of a program performing I/O, all I/O requests are handled synchronously. A program requesting input is suspended from the point of making the request until the input has been completed. Writing operations are more complicated. When a program wants to transfer a few characters to a terminal the program will be suspended from the time of making the request until the time that the characters are accepted by the system and started on their journey. However, synchrony as practiced in the UNIX System doesn't mean that the characters will have arrived at their destination by the time the program resumes execution; it just means that the characters have been swallowed by the UNIX System and are at least about to start the journey. What synchrony does mean is that I/O requests almost certainly take a while, and large requests take longer than small requests.

Each I/O connection that is available to a program is identified by a number known as a file descriptor. Most UNIX Systems allow each program to have between 10 and 20 files open simultaneously. Remember that in the UNIX System a file can be either a disk file or a terminal or some other I/O device or even a connection to another program.

One of the unusual and often baffling features of the UNIX System is the fact that child programs inherit the open files of their parents. Most of the programs running on a typical UNIX System are started by the shell. By convention, three files are opened automatically by the shell for the use of child programs. Since the shell is the parent of all of the commands that you execute interactively the standard connections established by the shell are very important in the UNIX System.

The first connection that is available is identified by file descriptor zero and it is usually called the standard input. The standard input usually is connected to your terminal's keyboard, although it can just as easily be connected to a disk file or a paper tape reader. The standard input is the usual source of interactive input to a program.

The second connection that is automatically opened by the shell is identified by file descriptor one and it is usually called the standard output. The standard output usually is connected to your terminal's display, although it can also be redirected to any writeable file. The standard output generally is used by programs for their main text output. For example, the ls command writes its list of files on the standard output.

The third connection, identified by file descriptor two, is called the standard error output. It usually is connected to your terminal and it is the channel that receives most error messages. It is sometimes used so that error messages are directed to a terminal when the main output of a program is directed elsewhere, and it is sometimes used so that error messages are collected in a disk file when programs are run from long shell command files.

If no alternative arrangements are made, then all three standard channels are connected to your terminal's special file. If the shell command line contains a ">", then the standard output is redirected to some other file; if the command line contains a "<", then the standard input is redirected from some other file. The standard error connection can be redirected by using the "2>" notation in a shell command line.

The three standard connections can be used or ignored by an individual program. They are merely a convenience that allows the powerful redirection facilities of the UNIX System. A program can write output to your terminal without regard to I/O redirection by opening the file associated with the terminal ('/dev/tty') and performing I/O.

The system calls for performing I/O include

open   establish a connection with a file that already exists

creat   create a file and then establish a connection with that file

pipe   create a connection that can be used in a pipeline between two processes

dup   create another connection to a file that has at least one existing connection

fcntl   perform several control operations on files

read   read data from a file

write   write data into a file

close   sever a connection with a file

A file descriptor is returned when a program executes an open, create, pipe, or dup system call and by some operations involving the fcntl system call. The returned file descriptor then can be used to perform input and/or output operations on the file using read and write. The read and write system calls simply transfer data between data regions in the process and the file. The UNIX System also includes routines for performing higher level input and output (printf and scanf) and for performing locally buffered input and output (putchar and getchar). Any files that remain open when a program terminates are automatically closed.

Pipes are established between processes by using the pipe system call in conjunction with system calls for creating processes. This very interesting feature of the UNIX System is discussed below in Section 15.4.

15.3 Status System Calls

Most operating systems have a host of items that must be controlled and moni-
tored in order to fine tune the performance of the system. Some examples are
the priorities of executing programs, the privileges of programs, the protection
attributes of files, the environment in which a program executes, and the mounting and unmounting of file systems (data sets).

In many operating systems status items are controllable only from the system
console via a hardcoded command interpretor. Since the UNIX System does
not come with a hardcoded command interpretor the only way to control and
monitor these items is by using an ordinary program. Any executing program
can request, for example, that its execution priority be increased or decreased.
Any program can decrease its execution priority, but only programs run by the
superuser can actually increase their priority. In the UNIX System any program
can request control of system status functions, but only certain program requests
are allowed by the kernel.

Controlling the access modes of a file is another example. In the UNIX System a program can execute the chmod system call in order to control the modes
(read, write, and execute for owner, group, and other; see Chapter 6) of a file.
The following short C program will use the chmod system call to make the file
named 'nopeeking' inaccessible (no privileges to anyone) until some future
change in modes:

```
# define  NOACCESS  0
main()
{
chmod("nopeeking",NOACCESS);
}
```

The program will change the modes only when run by the owner of the file
'nopeeking' or by the superuser.

The system calls that control or monitor certain status items include

time	read the date
stime	set the date
getpid	determine the process identification number
getuid	get the user identification number
getgid	get the group identification number
chown	change the ownership of a file
chmod	change the mode of a file
chdir	change the current working directory
link	create a link to a file
unlink	remove a link to a file
mount	mount a file system

umount   unmount a file system

nice   change priority of a process

stat   get file status

Several other status related system calls exist on various versions of the UNIX System.

15.4 Process Control System Calls

One of the strengths of the UNIX System is its set of system calls for creating and coordinating processes. All of these systems calls (except exit) would be superfluous in a system that allowed only one process at a time. The system calls for controlling processes are basic but effective. They include

fork   duplicate a process

exec   change the identity of a process

exit   terminate a process

kill   send a signal to a process

signal   specify an action that should be performed when a signal is received

wait   wait for the termination of a child process

In many systems it is possible to chain programs together so that one program follows another. The equivalent operation in the UNIX System is called an exec and several versions of the exec system call are available for replacing the current process with a new process. The created process is called the successor and the process that called exec is known as the predecessor.

The UNIX System would be a very weak system if exec were the only system call for creating a process. The exec system call doesn't increase the number of processes but merely changes the form of a process. To increase the number of processes in the UNIX System you must use the fork system call. The fork system call creates a new process that is an exact copy of the calling process (except for a few parameters concerning the identity of the process such as the process identification number). The created process is called the child and the process that called fork is called the parent. The parent process is not destroyed by the fork system call. Following the fork both processes compete for system resources (e.g., execution time).

Probably the most common use of fork is to create a child process that immediately executes the exec system call. The effect of a fork followed in the child by an exec is for the parent process to create a child process with a new identity. This is much more interesting than just creating a duplicate.

Often a child process is created to accomplish some specific task and the parent wants to wait for the task to be completed before continuing. One obvious example is the shell which uses the fork-exec pair to execute almost all of the commands that you enter. (A few commands are handled specially by the

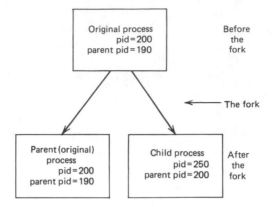

Figure 15.1. The fork system call. The fork system call is used to duplicate a process. After the fork the two processes are identical except for a few key parameters which describe the process. ("pid" is the process identification number.)

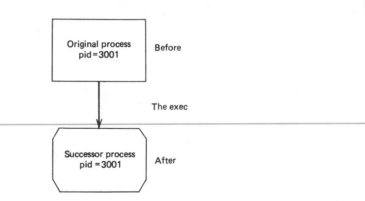

Figure 15.2. The exec system call. The exec system call is used to change the identity of a process.

shell.) Unless you use the ampersand character to specify background execution, the shell (parent) executes the wait system call to wait for the completion (death) of the child process. (Similarly, when you use the ampersand to force background execution the shell doesn't wait for the child process to complete.)

The kill system call is used to send signals from one process to another. (The name "kill" is poorly chosen.) A signal is a mutually agreed upon value that communicates some piece of information from one process to another. One of the common uses of the kill system call is to send the SIGKILL signal to a process. A process that receives SIGKILL terminates itself. About a dozen other standard signals are used in the UNIX System.

Since only one process is actually running at a given instant in time, it is a sure bet that the target process of the kill system call is suspended (or occasion-

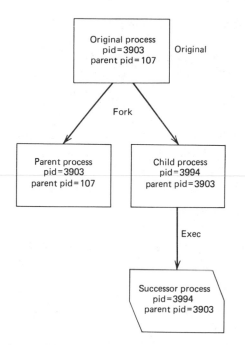

Figure 15.3. Creating a child process with a different identity. In the UNIX System a fork often is followed by an exec in order to create a new process with a different identity. This technique is used by the shell to execute your commands.

ally nonexistent). The signal sent by the kill system call doesn't take effect until the target process is activated. Whenever a process starts executing after a suspension the system automatically checks a list of signals to see if any signals have arrived. If there have been arrivals, then appropriate action is taken. For example, the appropriate action to take following the arrival of the SIGKILL signal is to execute the exit system call. The system call named signal is used to specify the action that should be taken if a given signal arrives. Taken together the kill-signal pair of system calls allows a simple yet powerful interprocess communication system.

One insidious consequence of the fact that processes respond to signals only when they awake is that processes that are endlessly waiting for something can never die. Such processes are common in the UNIX System systems with buggy device drivers. Although they cause no harm individually, a large accumulation of endlessly waiting processes usually spells doom for the system because the kernel's process table eventually fills up.

The UNIX System also includes the exit system call which causes the demise of the calling process. Exit is called automatically in response to a variety of signals and at the end of the main module in a C program. The exit call can be used explicitly anywhere in a program and it automatically closes all of the process's open files.

Let's conclude our discussion of the process control system calls with a discussion of pipes. Pipes are connections between related processes. The first stage in creating a pipe is for a process to execute the pipe system call. Two file descriptors are returned, one for reading and one for writing. Next the process forks in order to create two processes and usually the child process execs to change its identity. Throughout forks and execs the open files established by the pipe system call remain open. After the forking and execing, one of the processes uses the read descriptor and the other process uses the write descriptor. When the shell establishes a pipe connection between two processes the shell arranges for the pipe descriptors to have the values zero and one, usually associated with the standard input and the standard output.

15.5 Passing Arguments to Programs

An argument is information that you specify on a command line in order to control the operation of a command. For example, when you enter the command

    cc myprog.c

the word "myprog.c" is an argument that directs the C compiler to compile the code contained in the file 'myprog.c'. This section discusses the mechanism that is used in the UNIX System to pass command line arguments to programs.

One of the most valuable features of the UNIX System is that arguments for a program can be placed right on the command line. Passing arguments to programs on a command line is not unique to the UNIX System. However, the UNIX System is unique in the amount of processing done by the shell in order to generate the arguments, and the arguments are especially easy to use in the UNIX System. The next few paragraphs discuss how the arguments are actually passed and then the last few paragraphs in this section present an example of a C program accessing command line arguments.

In the discussion here we ignore all of the work done by the shell or some other program to generate a list of arguments to be passed to a command. In Section 13.14 we discussed file name generation, parameter substitution, and command substitution. The net effect of all of these chores is the generation of a list of arguments to be passed to a command.

Let's start this discussion at the point where some program (typically the shell) has an array of character strings (the arguments) and the name of a program to be executed using the exec system call. As usual in these matters the program forks once in order to create a new process and then the child process prepares to perform the exec.

Several versions of the exec system call allow an array of character strings to be passed to a program. When the exec system call containing the array of arguments is executed the kernel of the operating system acquires the array of arguments from the calling program. Then the successor program is loaded into memory (remember that the calling program is overlaid in a successful exec) and the array of arguments is placed in the memory space of the successor program.

Two parameters are made available to the program, a count of the arguments and a pointer to an array of pointers to the arguments. The two parameters, like all parameters for C routines, are on the stack and the actual arguments are in high memory. Be careful not to confuse parameters which are values that are available for routines with arguments which are character strings that are passed to a program.

Once all of this is complete the program starts to run. It might seem strange to use just two parameters to access virtually any number of arguments. The advantage of using two parameters is uniformity; the program doesn't have to know in advance how many arguments it may receive. The main routine of a program has to declare the two parameters. The first argument is an integer and the second argument is a pointer to an array of character strings. Here is a short program which prints out its arguments one on a line:

```
main(argc,argv)          /* echo arguments one per line */
int argc;
char *argv[];
{
int i;
for(i = 0;i<argc;i+ +)
        printf("%s \ n",argv[i]);
}
```

C language programmers will recognize this as a program which prints an array of character strings. If you don't know C, then don't worry about the exact syntax of the program. This program is stored in the file 'showargs.c'. The command

```
cc -o showargs showargs.c
```

will compile 'showargs.c' and place the executable output in the file 'showargs'. If you run showargs you will discover that the name of the program is always printed before the "true" arguments. This is because the name of a program is considered to be argument number zero. Notice therefore that argc is always at least one. If you wanted to print only the arguments other than the name of the program, you would have to change the for loop to start at one instead of zero.

The two parameters are often named argc (argument count) and argv (argument vector), although these names are strictly optional. The "argc" parameter is often declared equivalently

```
char **argv;
```

(C fanatics can probably explain why this is equivalent.) The order of the declarations is important; the argument count must be first.

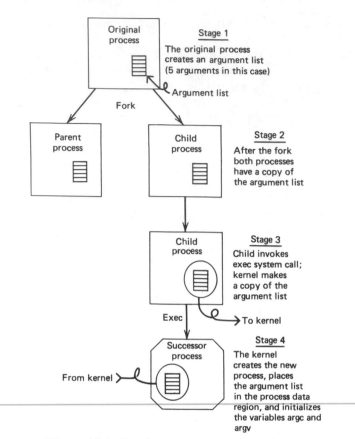

Figure 15.4. Passing arguments to a program.

15.6 The Implementation of System Calls

The system call interface has been designed to appear the same as the subroutine interface. Parameters may be passed to a system call and a value can be returned. The basic difference is that the code that is executed during a subroutine is linked into the executable program module, whereas the bulk of the code that is executed during a system call resides in the kernel address space (rather than in the program's address space). Therefore, adding a new system call to a program will have little effect on the size of the program while adding a new subroutine to a program may increase the size of the program by thousands of bytes.

There is very little time wasted in calling a subroutine. However, executing a system call is a time consuming process. System calls on the PDP11 version of the UNIX System work by means of a trap instruction. A trap is an instruction whose effect is somewhat similar to that of a hardware interrupt. The trap leads to a large change in context which is time consuming and often causes the calling process to be suspended or even swapped out.

The bottom line is that system calls are time consuming and they should be used sparingly. Probably the biggest waste of time occurs when large numbers of bytes are read or written using single byte transfers. For example, the following simple program counts the number of blanks in a file using single character read operations:

```
/* count blanks in a file reading char by char */
main(argc,argv)
int argc; char *argv[];
{
int fd;
int count = 0;
char c;
fd = open(argv[1],0);
if (fd < 0)
        { printf("Cannot open %s. \ n",argv[1]); exit(1); }
while(read(fd,&c,1) = = 1)
        if (c = = ' ')
                count + +;
printf("There are %d blanks in %s. \ n",count,argv[1]);
}
```

Written this way the program executes the read system call to read each character. When I ran the program to count the number of blanks in a file containing about 20,000 characters it took an average of 33 seconds to run on a lightly loaded PDP11/70. About 95 percent of the time was spent executing the 20,000 system calls. If this program were needed only once, then it might be considered acceptable. However, the UNIX System includes buffered I/O which works perfectly for this application. Using the standard buffered I/O routine getchar in place of read results in the following program:

```
#include <stdio.h>
main(argc,argv) /* count blanks using buffered I/O */
int argc; char *argv[];
{
FILE *fd;
int count = 0;
char c;
fd = fopen(argv[1],"r");
if (fd = = NULL)
        { printf("Cannot open %s. \ n",argv[1]); exit(1); }
while((c = getc(fd)) != EOF)
        if (c = = ' ')
                count + +;
printf("There are %d blanks in %s. \ n",count,argv[1]);
}
```

This version is more complicated because it uses the standard buffered input package. (See the descriptions of fopen and getc in Section 3 of the UNIX System manual.) However, the slight increase in coding is more than offset by the enormous increase in speed. When this version was run it required about 1 second and it spent only one third of its time executing system calls. The difference is that this second version executed only about 40 system calls to scan the 20,000 character file.

The UNIX System does buffer files at the system level so that there is no unreasonable penalty for reading files conveniently, but there is no excuse for reading large quantities of input a byte at a time using a system call such as read rather than a buffered input routine such as getc.

15.7 Separate Compilation

The C language is designed so that the source code for an entire program can be dispersed into a number of files. Placing the source code in separate files is intended to encourage modular design, development, and debugging. Small programs (up to a few hundred lines of code) such as the the echo program or the blank count program shown earlier in this chapter can be stored easily in a single file. Larger programs (several hundred lines and up) are usually stored in several files.

A file containing just a few subroutines (typically a few hundred lines of code) is much easier to understand and work on than a massive file containing thousands of lines of code. A program contained in a single file can be partitioned into several files by collecting groups of subroutines or data structures and placing the groups into the separate files. A logical entity such as a subroutine or a data declaration cannot be split into two files.

Separating a program into several files introduces several new problems. One problem is the need for the subroutines in one file to know about the subroutines and data declarations in the other files. The C language contains a special type of declaration called an external definition. The purpose of an external definition is to reference and describe items that may not be defined in the local file. If the number of references to items in other files is small, then a few external definitions can be placed in the file. However, if the number of references to items in other files is large, it might be best to create a file that contains external definitions for everything in the program and use the include feature of the C compiler to include the file. Files are included by using the include directive. In a C language program the line

```
# include  "defs.h"
```

will include the contents of the file 'defs.h' in a program.

Another problem is the need for certain constants and tokens to be known throughout the program. For example, in a program that manipulates lists of items the maximum number of items in the list is a key constant that needs to be known by all of the subroutines. In C the define directive can be used to create a named constant. The line

define LISTLEN 20

in a C program will define a constant called "LISTLEN". Wherever the name "LISTLEN" is encountered in a program the text string constant "20" will be substituted. An include file usually contains all of the definitions that are used throughout a large file. The define directive is actually a macro replacement facility. It can have parameters and can be used to generate complicated sequences of C code.

All of the lines in a C program that begin with a sharp are assumed to be directives such as include or define. All of these directives are processed by a part of the C compiler known as the C preprocessor. The C preprocessor also performs other chores such as removing the comments from a program. Occasionally you want to see the output of the C preprocessor in order to see if it is doing what you want it to do. You can also use this technique to check for a comment which has unwittingly extended past its intended limit. The shell command

cc -P myprog.c

will run the preprocessor on the file 'myprog.c' and leave the output in the file 'myprog.i'.

The normal goal of the C compiler is to compile an entire program in order to produce an executable module. If you have partitioned a large program into several files, you can perform a complete compilation by mentioning all of the files in the command line

cc fileA.c fileB.c fileC.c

If everything works well and no errors are detected, then four files will be produced: a file named 'a.out' which contains the executable program and the files 'fileA.o', 'fileB.o', and 'fileC.o' which contain the object code for the individual source files.

The object codes for the individual source files are retained in order to reduce the amount of work in subsequent compilations. If 'fileA.c' is updated but 'fileB.c' and 'fileC.c' are unchanged, then the only object file that is out of date is 'fileA.o'. The object modules 'fileB.o' and 'fileC.o' can be used as is because the source code that they depend on has not been changed. The entire system can be recompiled by performing a partial compilation on 'fileA.c' and then relinking the three object files to produce a new 'a.out' executable file. This will be accomplished by entering the command

cc fileA.c fileB.o fileC.o

One very useful feature of the C compiler is that it knows what types of suffix are used on what types of file. Based on the suffix ".c" the C compiler knows that 'fileA.c' is a source program that must be compiled, and based on the ".o" suffix the C compiler knows that 'fileB.o' and 'fileC.o' are object files that only need to be linked (with 'fileA.o') to produce an executable 'a.out' file.

Remembering which files are obsolete and which are not obsolete can be very difficult. One solution is to always keep the object files up to date. Whenever a source file is changed the corresponding object file is immediately recreated. The term partial compilation is used to describe a compilation where the goal is to compile just one module, not a complete software system. The "-c" option of the C compiler is used to perform partial compilations. The command

```
cc -c fileA.c
```

will produce an up to date 'fileA.o'. If the "-c" option were not used, the C compiler would issue an error message when it realized that the source code in 'fileA.c' did not contain a complete program.

The 'a.out' can be produced from a set of up to date object files by entering the command

```
cc fileA.o fileB.o fileC.o
```

Another way to keep track of which object files are obsolete is to use the UNIX System program make, which looks at the dates of all of the files in a software system in order to determine what needs to be recompiled. See Chapter 12 for more information on the make program.

15.8 Lint – Check C Programs

The C programming language is very lax about checking for certain errors in programs. Many of these problems arise from the fact that when a program is divided into separate modules the compiler relies on the external definitions for determining the types of object in other modules. If the external definitions are inaccurate, then suspicious code is generated. Problems also arise from the use of pointers, a technique that tends to obscure the basic type of an object.

In short the C compiler assumes that the code you have written embodies the operations you want to perform, and if an operation is logically possible then in most cases the C compiler attempts to produce the corresponding machine instructions. The attitude of the C compiler is that you are smarter than the compiler and whatever you dictate should be attempted.

Fortunately the UNIX System also contains a much more suspicious program. The UNIX System program lint is used to check C programs for many types of error including objects whose types are defined differently in different files, objects or values that are never used, variables that are apparently used before their value is established, and other dubious practices. Lint does not produce object files – it merely produces warnings and comments on your coding practices. Occasionally the warnings produced by lint do not indicate trouble, but in general the warnings mean that something is wrong or nonportable. Many companies are requiring that all software written for them be able to survive analysis by lint with no complaints.

One problem with using one program to compile a program and one program to perform checks on a program is the possibility that the two programs will get out of synchronization. Features in the C language that are recognized and working in one of the programs may be absent or not working in the other.

There are several advantages to performing these checks in a separate program rather than in the compiler. One advantage is that exhaustive analaysis can be performed in a separate program — analysis that would be too time consuming in a compiler. Another advantage is the fact that lint can analyze a software system as a whole, a very desirable feature for a language that encourages separate compilation.

CHAPTER

16

Programmers' Utilities

The UNIX System has several utility programs for manipulating the binary files that are produced by the UNIX System compilers. These utilities are used primarily by programmers. The UNIX System's language compilers (C, FORTRAN, PASCAL, etc.) translate a text file containing a program source into an object file which contains binary information. Since object files contain binary information, not text information, they cannot be manipulated using the standard UNIX System utilities for text files. Instead certain standard transformations are performed on object files using the utilities described in this chapter.

Some UNIX Systems contain programming systems that allow a programmer to compile programs on a UNIX System for execution on some other system. Such programming systems are called cross-systems and there is no standard for the format of the files that are produced. The manipulation of executable files produced by cross-compilation systems is not discussed in this chapter and the utilities discussed here cannot be assumed to work on such files.

The first section of this chapter discusses the production of object files using the C compiler. Producing object files using FORTRAN or PASCAL (or other compiled languages) is essentially similar. The final sections describe various utilities for working with object files.

16.1 Compilation

An object file is the result of a compilation of a high level language program or it is the result of an assembly of an assembly language program. All of the object files produced by the standard UNIX System compiled languages can have four sections: the header, the program (instructions and data), the relocation information, and the symbol table (Figure 15.1). The header and the program are always present. The header specifies the sizes of the various sections and it indicates whether the relocation information and the symbol table are present. The relocation information and the symbol table are useful for com-

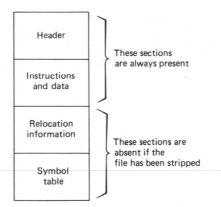

Figure 16.1. The structure of an object file.

bining object files to form executable programs and for debugging executable programs.

The program source code for very short programs often is contained in a single file. It is possible to compile such a program to immediately produce an executable object file. The default executable file name in the UNIX System is 'a.out'. The command

    cc myprog.c

will compile the C language program 'myprog.c' using cc (the C compiler) and place the output in the file 'a.out'. If 'myprog.c' contains unresolved references to other program modules or if it contains source code errors, then 'a.out' will not be made executable. When no errors are detected and there are no unresolved references then 'a.out' is made executable. You can have the executable output placed in the file of your choice if you use the "-o filename" option.

    cc -o myprog myprog.c

In this case the output is placed in 'myprog' rather than in 'a.out'.

The program source code for large, complicated programs usually is stored in several files in order to simplify program development and maintenance. A compilation of just one (of several) source code files is called a partial compilation. The object file resulting from a partial compilation is named 'file.o' if the source file is named 'file.c'. (Object files are often called ".o" (dot oh) files.)

The C compiler option "-c" instructs the compiler to perform a partial compilation. The major difference between a partial compilation and a complete compilation is that unresolved external references are not considered an error during a partial compilation. The command

    cc -c fileA.c

will produce the object file 'fileA.o'. The result of a partial compilation is never made executable.

A complete compilation of a program stored in several source code files can be performed using any mix of object and source files so long as each separate program module is represented. Thus a program stored in the source files 'fileA.c', 'fileB.c', and 'fileC.c' could be completely compiled from the C language source files by using the command

```
cc fileA.c fileB.c fileC.c
```

If all of the source code files have been compiled separately to produce object files, then a complete compilation can also be performed using the command

```
cc fileA.o fileB.o fileC.o
```

This command will execute much faster than the previous one because there is much less to do; the major work is combining the object files to produce an executable file. It is also possible to mix object files and source files in a single complete compilation:

```
cc fileA.c fileB.o fileC.c
```

In this command we assume that 'fileB.c' has already been compiled to produce 'fileB.o'.

16.2 Size – Print Object File Characteristics

The size program prints the size of the program section of an object file. The program section consists of three parts, the instructions (often called text although there is no relation to text files), the initialized data, and the uninitialized data. The size program prints in decimal the sizes of these three parts followed by the sum of these sizes printed in both octal and decimal.

The size printed by the size program reflects just the size of the program section of an object file, not the size of the entire object file. The "ls -l" command will reveal the entire size of an object file.

The command

```
size file?.o
```

will print the sizes of all of the object files in the previous example.

16.3 Strip – Remove Symbol Table from Object File

The strip command is used to remove the relocation information and the symbol table from an object file. This results in a significant reduction in size of the file. The command

```
strip myprog
```

will remove the relocation information and the symbol table from 'myprog'. The same effect could be achieved during compilation by using the "-s" option of the C compiler:

```
cc -s -o myprog myprog.c
```

Stripped files are harder to debug. There is no point in stripping the result of a partial compilation because a stripped file cannot be combined with other files to form an executable program.

16.4 Nm - Print Object File Symbol Table

The nm (list symbol table names) program examines the symbol table in the named object files. The object files examined by nm must not have been stripped using the strip command. Without any options the nm program prints a list of everything in the symbol table:

```
nm  myprog
```

This form of nm has little use unless you pipe the output to grep to select certain items or unless you examine very small object files. Most programs contain many more symbols than you would expect.

Nm prints the symbols one per line. The first field on the line contains the value of the symbol (if it is defined), the second field is a letter that indicates the type of the symbol, and the final field is the name of symbol. In C, and in most other high level languages, from the compiler's point of view the "value" of a symbol is its address, therefore the "value" printed by the nm program is the symbol's address. The type letter is in lower case for local symbols and in upper case for external symbols.

The most important type letters are D and B for initialized and uninitialized data, T for text, A for absolute, and U for undefined. A complete list of the type letters can be found in the UNIX System manual.

One of the most useful options for nm is "-u", which causes nm to print a list of the undefined symbols:

```
nm  -u  fileA.o
```

Undefined symbols are those symbols that were used but never declared in a program. The program source files are usually a better source of information, but when things become unexplainable you can try examining the symbols in the object files.

The "-g" option causes nm to print a list of the externals in the symbol table:

```
nm  -g  fileA.o
```

The list of externals tells you what items are defined in the file.

16.5 Ar – Archive Files

The UNIX System librarian program is called ar (archive). A library (alternatively called an archive) is a file that contains a set of files. Although the UNIX System libraries can contain any type of file, most libraries contain object files. Individual files are not modified when they are added to a library.

Object files frequently are combined into libraries to make them easier to reference. For instance, all of the object files for the standard C subroutines and system calls are contained in a single library, '/lib/libc.a'. Other libraries contain subroutines for graphics, mathematical functions, and so on. If a program requires several of the graphics subroutines, it is much easier to mention the graphics library than to mention each graphics subroutine by name.

The ar program can be used to print a table of the files in the archive, to add files to the archive, and to extract copies of files in the archive. Let's first create an archive to contain the object files 'fileA.o', 'fileB.o', 'fileC.o'.

```
ar rv libfile.a file?.o
```

The options for the ar program ("r" and "v" in this case) are not preceded by a hyphen as in most other UNIX System programs because ar always requires at least one option. The "r" option indicates that the specified files should be added to the library 'libfile.a'. The file 'libfile.a' will be created if necessary. Usually the "r" option is used to add files to an existing library, but it can also be used to create libraries. The "v" option specifies the verbose mode; a message is printed for each operation performed by ar. It is a good idea to use the verbose oqtion when you are using ar interactively.

Following the execution of the command listed above the library 'libfile.a' will contain 'fileA.o', 'fileB.o', and 'fileC.o'. The command

```
ar t libfile.a
```

will print a table of the contents of the archive. The three files should be listed.

The order of files in an archive is often important. The command

```
ar mva fileA.o libfile.a fileC.o
```

will move (the "m" option) 'fileC.o' after (the "a" option) the 'fileA.o' in the library 'libfile.a'. (As usual the "v" option specifies verbose mode.) The command

```
ar t libfile.a
```

will reveal the new order: 'fileA.o', 'fileC.o', 'fileB.o'. Alternatively, 'fileB.o' could be moved to the beginning of the archive by using the command

```
ar mvb fileA.o libfile.a fileB.o
```

This command moves (the "m" option) 'fileB.o' before (the "b" option) 'fileA.o' in the library 'libfile.a'. The command

```
ar t libfile.a
```

will reveal the new order: 'fileB.o', 'fileA.o', 'fileC.o'.

Probably the most common ar option is "r", replace. If 'fileB.c' were changed and recompiled, the copy of 'fileB.o' outside of 'libfile.a' would be more recent than 'fileB.o' in the library. The command

```
ar rv libfile.a fileB.o
```

would replace the outdated version inside the library with the new version. The after and before ("a" and "b") options can be used during a replace to change the ordering; without these options the ordering is not changed during a replace operation.

Sometimes you want to acquire a copy of a file from an archive. Copying out of an archive is more common with archives containing source code or text than with archives containing object files. The command

    ar xv libfile.a fileB.o

will extract (the "x" option) a copy of 'fileB.o' from the library. The archive is not changed by an extraction; the only change occurs outside of the archive in your current directory where the copy of the archive member is created.

16.6 Ld – Combine Object Files

Ld is the UNIX System's linkage editor program. It is not an editor for text files; it is an editor for object files. Ld combines object files, usually in order to produce an executable output file. Occasionally ld combines files so that they can be used in further linkage editing sessions.

Object files are linked by combining all of the program sections to form one big program section. Then the information in the symbol tables and relocation sections is used to adjust all of the cross references. When object files are combined in a library the individual files are not changed; when object files are combined using ld the individual sections of the object files are merged into one larger object file with the same four sections (header, program, relocation, symbols).

Most UNIX System users do not use the ld program directly. Instead they use one of the compilers (cc, f77, pc), and the compiler automatically calls the ld program. Compilers generally consist of several passes. The last phase in a full compilation is linkage editing. Linkage editing is not performed during partial compilations.

You can control the operation of the ld program by supplying the ld program options to your compiler. The compiler will pass them along to ld. For example, the "-s" option for ld causes ld to strip the relocation information and the symbol table from the output file. The command

    cc -s myprog.c

will pass the "-s" option on to the ld program. Ld will strip the output.

Some programs are regularly executed simultaneously by several users. Typical examples are the shell and the editor. When one program is being executed simultaneously as several different processes it is not necessary to keep several copies of the program's instructions. However, it is necessary to keep one copy of the program's data for each executing process.

A program where the instructions (text) can be shared between several processes is called pure executable. The linkage editor will create a pure executable program if the option "-n" is present. The disadvantage of pure programs is memory utilization — they require a little more memory than impure programs. If only one copy of a pure program is executing, somewhat more memory is used, but when several copies are running there is a net savings because there is only one copy of the text. The command

```
cc -n -o nprocs nprocs.c
```

will produce a pure executable program 'nprocs'. The file command can be used to discover which programs are pure executable. (The information is in the header of the object file.) The command

```
file nprocs
```

will print the message "pure executable" instead of the message "executable", which is printed for impure programs. From the program user's point of view there is no difference between a pure program and an impure program. They execute the same and it is impossible to discover that other people are sharing the program's text. On systems without memory protection and memory mapping this feature is likely to be absent.

    Another frequently useful option is "-i", which arranges for the program text and the program data to reside in separate address spaces. On computers that support separate instruction and data address spaces the "-i" option allows for larger programs.

CHAPTER

17

Yacc and Lex

This chapter discusses two of the UNIX System's most intriguing facilities, yacc (Yet Another Compiler Compiler) and lex. Yacc and lex are widely referenced in the UNIX System literature and they are very important in the creation and maintenance of some of the key UNIX System utilities. Unfortunately relatively few UNIX System users understand what they do. This chapter describes yacc and lex at the "What is this stuff good for?" level. If you want to use yacc or lex, then you need to dive into the reference manuals and papers that describe the details.

Recognizing command languages is one of the most common problems in computer programming. Many computer applications involve a language that is used to control some process. Examples of command languages that are used in the UNIX System include the shell programming language, the C programming language, and the dependency specification used by the make program.

Some command languages are very easy to recognize but others require significant programming effort. Although it certainly is possible to write a C (or FORTRAN or PASCAL) program to recognize a complicated command language, much better techniques have been developed. This chapter introduces some of these techniques.

17.1 Lexical Analysis and Parsing

Recognition of a complicated command language usually is divided into two phases: lexical analysis and parsing. Low level objects such as numbers and operators and special words are recognized during the lexical analysis phase, whereas higher level objects such as statements in a programming language are recognized during the parsing phase. There is some leeway in deciding just which objects will be recognized during lexical analysis and which will be recognized during parsing. Experience is often the best guide.

We use the term lexical analyzer to describe a program which performs lexical analysis and we use the term parser to describe a program which performs parsing. Lexical analysis and parsing are explained in more detail in the remainder of this section. Lex and yacc, the UNIX System's utility programs for producing lexical analyzers and parsers, are discussed in the last two sections of this chapter.

The input to the lexical analysis phase is a stream of characters. These characters might come from a terminal where someone is interactively entering commands to control some process or they might come from a file or they might even come from the output of another program. In any case the lexical analysis program scans the input according to a set of rules. When the lexical program recognizes an object it outputs an indication of the type of object that it has just encountered. The indication is usually called a token. Given the input

        25   * (16/2   )   +   15

a lexical analyzer might output something analogous to

    NOLNONRON

Here the token "N" stands for a number, "O" stands for an operator, "L" stands for a left parenthesis, and "R" stands for a right parenthesis. The sequence "NOLNONRON" doesn't mean much to you or me — we prefer the original form — but it is just perfect for a parser that is attempting to deduce the form of an arithmetic expression.

The purpose of the lexical analysis phase is to smooth out many of the irregularities of the input, such as the spacing and the length of items, in order to produce an output which codes the sequence of items that have been encountered. Another input which would produce the "NOLNONRON" lexical sequence is

    0x19*(0x10/0x2) + 0xF

In this expression the numbers are in the hexadecimal radix instead of the decimal radix shown above and the spacing of elements is different. Yet the basic expression is the same so the lexical output is the same.

The parser phase of analysis is responsible for understanding the higher level properties of the input. If the sequence shown above (NOLNONRON) is encountered during the course of an analysis, then the parser is responsible for verifying that the sequence represents a valid expression and for producing an appropriate sequence of actions.

The goal in specifying a parser is to list a set of rules that a command language must follow. If a command conforms to the rules, then some appropriate action is taken; if the command doesn't fit the rules, then it is in error. For example, if we were working with an arithmetic command language, we would want our rules to allow commands such as "7", "1 + 1", "5/8", and "6*7*14" and to exclude blunders such as "6 7", "5 + *8", and "7k4".

Assuming that a good definition of number is already available, we might define an arithmetic expression as follows:

expression:
        number
        |
        expression "+" expression
        |
        expression "-" expression
        |
        expression "*" expression
        |
        expression "/" expression
        ;

In the list above the vertical bar indicates an alternative rule and number stands for any number. A colon is used to start the list of alternatives and the semicolon ends the list. The standard arithmetic operators for addition, subtraction, multiplication, and division are shown in quotes because they must appear literally in an expression. The definition shown above states that an expression is either a number or it is two expressions being added, subtracted, multiplied, or divided.

By defining an expression in terms of itself we have created a definition that works for any size expression. Computer scientists have developed techniques for writing parsers that follow this type of rule. (In a more useful example precedence rules would have to be added to our definition in order to resolve the ambiguity of an expression such as "5*8 + 1".)

The basic difference between a lexical analyzer and a parser is that a lexical analyzer follows rules to recognize certain sequences or groups of characters whereas a parser follows rules that may be self-referential to recognize more complicated constructs.

17.2 Lex

The lex program is used to generate a lexical analysis routine. Lex reads as input a specification of the lexical analyzer and it produces either a C or a RATFOR subroutine as its output. The output must be compiled and combined with other programs in order to use the lexical analyzer. As described in the previous section the lexical analyzer takes a stream of characters as input and produces a stream of tokens as output. These three transformations are shown in Figure 17.1.

One of the important things to understand about both lex and yacc is that they produce subroutines, not full programs. The advantage of producing a subroutine is that it is possible to add application specific code before, during, and after the lexical analysis or parsing. Programs similar to lex and yacc which produce full programs tend to be hard to adapt to a wide variety of uses.

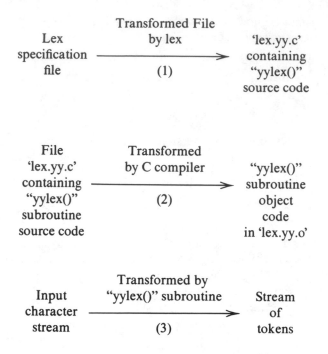

Figure 17.1. The elements of the lex system using C as the generated language.

The lexical rules that lex transforms into a program resemble the rules for forming regular expressions using the UNIX System text editor. The rule

[0-9]

is a single character regular expression that matches one digit. The rule

[0-9] +

matches a sequence of digits. The rules that are used in lex are a more powerful superset of the rules used in the editor for specifying text pattern matches. For every rule in a lex specification it is possible to code an action in the target language. The action code will be performed every time the rule leads to a pattern match. For example, the following line from a lex specification would generate code that would print the message "found a number!" every time a number is encountered in the input:

[0-9] +   { printf("found a number! \ n"); }

This type of code is interesting but of limited practical value. A more general approach when lex is being used as part of a language translator is to return a value each time an item is recognized. The value is called a token (as discussed above) and some routine is responsible for repeatedly calling the lex generated subroutine "yylex" to acquire each token.

If the name "NUMBER" were defined appropriately, then the following line from a lex specification would generate code that would indicate that a number had been encountered in the input stream.

```
[0-9]+           { return(NUMBER); }
```

But what number? Obviously the code also has to indicate what number has been encountered. The usual method (variations are possible) is to put the value in an integer variable. In our case we will call this variable "yylval". In order to understand the following you should know that Lex makes the matched text (the digits in this case) available in a character string called "yytext" and that the standard C subroutine "atoi" converts a character string of digits into an integer value.

```
[0-9]+ {
         yylval = atoi(yytext);
         return(NUMBER);
      }
```

This code is quite representative of the contents of many lex specification files. Notice that both the value and the type of the object are made available in this specification.

A more complete example should make these ideas clearer. The example will be a lexical analyzer that can recognize the following items:

1. Numbers (digit strings).

2. The words "set", "bit", "on", and "off".

3. Either a newline or a semicolon.

The analyzer will ignore spaces and tabs.

The first thing that we need to do is to define the tokens that the analyzer will return. We will use the token names "SET", "BIT", "ONCMD", "OFFCMD", and "NUMBER" to represent these items. The token name "ENDCMD" will be returned whenever a newline or a semicolon is recognized and the token "UNKNOWN" will be returned whenever something not identified by the rules is encountered. The following list of tokens is placed in the file "y.tab.h" so that it is available to both the analyzer subroutine and the program that calls the analyzer subroutine:

```
#  define  SET  257
#  define  BIT  258
#  define  ONCMD  259
#  define  OFFCMD  260
#  define  NUMBER  261
#  define  ENDCMD  262
#  define  UNKNOWN  263
```

The particular values for these tokens are chosen so that they do not interfere with values assigned to the ASCII character set.

A lexical specification consists of at least two sections: the declaration section and the rules section. The two sections are separated by a pair of percent symbols. C language declarations in the declaration part of the lex specification must be enclosed by "%{" and "%}" delimiters. The following is the lex specification to recognize the items listed above:

```
%{
/*
 * a lex specification to recognize
 * numbers, 4 words, and delimiters
 */
#include "y.tab.h"
extern int yylval;
%}
%%
[0-9]+      {                             /* rule 1 */
            yylval = atoi(yytext);
            return(NUMBER);
            }
;           return(ENDCMD);               /* rule 2 */
\n          return(ENDCMD);               /* rule 3 */
set         return(SET);                  /* rule 4 */
bit         return(BIT);                  /* rule 5 */
on          return(ONCMD);                /* rule 6 */
off         return(OFFCMD);               /* rule 7 */
[ \t]+      ;                             /* rule 8 */
.           return(UNKNOWN);              /* rule 9 */
```

A few of the rules are worth discussing individually. Rule 8 causes spaces and tabs to be ignored. The notation "[\t]+" indicates a sequence of spaces and tabs and since the action part is null any such sequence will be ignored. Rule 9 uses the metacharacter "." to match anything that has not already been matched. Lex works through the rules from the top down so Rule 9 will apply only when all of the other rules fail.

Lex is quite happy to receive an ambiguous specification. When there are several rules that all seem to apply, the rule that specifies the longest match is applied unless several rules specify a match of the same length in which case the topmost rule is applied. Rule 9, which specifies a one character match, is the last rule in the specification and thus clearly has the lowest priority.

It would be fairly easy to write a C language subroutine to recognize the items shown above. However, even for a very simple set of items the lex specification is shorter (and easier to change) than the equivalent C program. For someone who knows lex this specification is easier to write than the C version. This specification only hints at the power of lex and for many applications the equivalent C program would be quite difficult. More demanding applications provide even more incentive to use lex rather than a customized C program.

If this lex specification is placed in the file 'lexdemo.l', then the following shell command will produce the file 'lex.yy.c', which contains a C subroutine "yylex()":

```
lex lexdemo.l
```

The name 'lex.yy.c' is the standard name of the lex output file, somewhat as 'a.out' is the standard name of the executable output of the C compiler. The file 'lex.yy.c' can be compiled to produce an object file using the command

```
cc -c lex.yy.c
```

Now that we have a lex subroutine we need a method for testing it. In the next section of this chapter you will see how this lexical analysis subroutine can combine with a parser created using yacc. However, for now we just want to see how it responds to various inputs. The following C language program was written to test the "yylex()" subroutine. The program repeatedly calls "yylex()" and then prints a message that depends on the returned token.

```c
#include "y.tab.h"

int yylval;
extern char yytext[];

/*
 *              DEMONSTRATION
 * call yylex() to acquire tokens
 */
main()
{
int token;
while(token = yylex())
        switch(token)
        {
        case NUMBER:    printf("Number: %d \ n",yylval); break;
        case SET:       printf("Set \ n"); break;
        case BIT:       printf("Bit \ n"); break;
        case ONCMD:     printf("On \ n"); break;
        case OFFCMD:    printf("Off \ n"); break;
        case UNKNOWN:   printf("Unknown: %s \ n",yytext);
                        break;
        case ENDCMD:    printf("End marker \ n"); break;
        default:        printf("Unknown token: %d \ n",token);
                        break;
        }
}
```

This main subroutine is just a multiway branch that prints a message based on the value of the token. If the C main routine (in the file 'lextst.c') and the "yylex()" subroutine are compiled,

```
cc  lextst.c  lex.yy.o
```

then the resulting executable program will accept the input

```
set  bit  5          on;set20
```

to produce the output

```
Set
Bit
Number: 5
On
End  marker
Set
Number: 20
End  marker
```

As another example the input

```
set  bit  3  On
```

will produce the output

```
Set
Bit
Number:  3
Unknown:  O
Unknown:  n
End  marker
```

17.3 Yacc

The UNIX System utility program yacc is used to create a parser subroutine. Yacc accepts a syntax specification and then produces either a C or a RATFOR source code for the parser subroutine. The parser subroutine must be compiled and then combined with a program which calls it to parse an input. The parser subroutine calls a subroutine named "yylex()" to acquire tokens. Notice that this works smoothly with lex since lex produces a subroutine named "yylex()". However, any subroutine named "yylex()" can be used, not just one produced by lex. The three transformations involved in using yacc are summarized in Figure 17.2.

The major difference between a lex specification and a yacc specification is the format for the rules. In the lex specification the rules are regular expressions similar to those used in many text editors. The rules in a yacc specification consist of chains of definitions that often are self-referential.

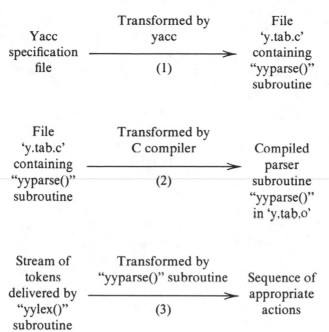

Figure 17.2. The various elements in the yacc system using C as the generated language.

For example, a command might be defined as

cmd: SET BIT numb ONCMD ENDCMD
          |
          SET BIT numb OFFCMD ENDCMD
          ;

Definitions in yacc are introduced by a colon. The vertical bar separates alternatives in the definition and the semicolon indicates the end of a definition. Tokens (returned by "yylex()") are usually capitalized and names that are defined within the yacc specification are usually lower case.

Since the two alternative definitions of cmd are almost identical, it would be wise to consolidate them as follows:

cmd: SET BIT numb onoff ENDCMD
          ;

Now of course we must supply a definition for onoff that shows that onoff stands either for the token ONCMD or for the token OFFCMD and we need a definition for numb.

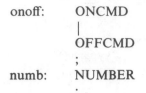

```
onoff:     ONCMD
           |
           OFFCMD
           ;
numb:      NUMBER
           ;
```

Yacc specifications are the embodiment of top-down design. At the top of the specification is the most general definition, and subsequent definitions in the file expand and elaborate on the established definitions. Definitions that relate directly to the tokens returned by "yylex()" usually are found near the end of the file.

For each rule in a yacc specification there may be an associated action. Like actions in lex, the yacc actions are executed whenever input corresponding to the given rule is encountered. Since rules in yacc may be written in terms of other rules there is a mechanism in yacc for returning values from one rule to another. You can see why returning values from one rule to another is necessary by examining the definitions for cmd and onoff. Obviously the action for cmd needs to know whether onoff stands for the ONCMD token or the OFFCMD token and it needs to know the value of numb.

A low level rule (e.g., numb) can return a value to a high level rule (e.g., cmd) by assigning a value to the pseudo variable $$.

```
numb:      NUMBER
           { $$ = yylval; }
           ;
```

A high level rule can pick up a value by examining the pseudo variable $1 for the first member of the definition, $2 for the second, and so on.

```
cmd:       SET BIT numb onoff ENDCMD
           {
           printf("Val %d returned by numb rule. \ n",$3);
           }
           ;
```

Now that the basic elements of a yacc specification have been discussed it is time to give an example. In many areas of programming it is necessary to interactively assign values to elements of complicated data structures. For example, a program that controls a physiological stimulator may contain a data structure that controls the timing and amplitude of the stimulus. To use the program the data structure must be loaded with the appropriate values. The process might be controlled interactively through a command language

set trial 3 amplitude 10;set bit 5 on trial 3 csr

The yacc specification that follows is the skeleton for this type of application. Instead of controlling an entire abstract data structure, what follows can set bits on or off in an integer variable or assign values to the variable. Each time a command is successfully recognized the value of the variable is printed. The commands that are recognized by the following yacc specification include

```
set  bit  3  on
set  10
set  bit  4  off  ;  set  bit  0  on
```

Just as in a lex specification, the first part of a yacc specification contains declarations and the second part contains rules. The sections are separated by the "%%" delimiter. The third part of this yacc specification consists of a very simple main subroutine in C which calls the generated "yyparse()" subroutine to actually perform the parsing.

The declaration part consists of C language definitions enclosed in "%{" and "%}" delimiters and token declarations. In order for yacc and lex to agree on token definitions, yacc can output a file of defined values for declared tokens. In our case this is the file 'y.tab.h', which was included into the lex specification. Lex and yacc work easily together.

The following yacc specification is longer and more difficult than most examples in this book. However, if you understand the ideas presented here and you are familiar with C, then you should not find it too complicated to understand.

```
%{
/*
 *  Yacc  Specification  File
 *    - The  First  Part -
 *         Declarations
 */
int  testvar  =  0;
int  yylval;
# define  Off  0
# define  On  1
%}
%TOKEN  SET,BIT,ONCMD,OFFCMD
%TOKEN  NUMBER,ENDCMD,UNKNOWN
%%
/*
 *  - The  Second  Part -
 *              Rules
 */
session:    /*  Rule  1  */
            |
            cmds
            ;
```

```
    cmds:   cmd                          /* Rule 2 */
            |
            cmds cmd
            ;
    cmd:    ENDCMD    /* Rule 3 - Alternative 1 */
                      { /* the null cmd */ }
            |
            error          ENDCMD   /*   Rule 3 - Alternative 2 */
            |
            SET BIT numb onoff ENDCMD /* Alternative 3 */
                      {
                      if (($3 <= 15) && ($3 >= 0))
                          {
                          if ($4 == Off)
                               testvar = testvar & ~(1 << $3);
                          else
                               testvar = testvar | (1 << $3);
                          }
                      else printf("Illegal bit number: %d \ n",$3);
                      printf("Testvar - %o \ n",testvar);
                      }
            |
            SET numb ENDCMD      /* Rule 3 - Alternative 4 */
                      {
                      testvar = $2;
                      printf("Testvar - %o \ n",testvar);
                      }
            ;
    numb:   NUMBER    /* Rule 4 */
                      { $$ = yylval; }
            ;
    onoff:  ONCMD     /* Rule 5 - Alternative 1 */
                      {$$ = On;}
            |
            OFFCMD    /* Rule 5 - Alternative 2 */
                      { $$ = Off; }
            ;
%%
/*
 *   - The Third Part -
 * Support Subroutines
 */
main()
{
yyparse();
}
```

If this specification is stored in the file 'yaccdemo.y', then the command

    yacc -d yaccdemo.y

will produce the C language source file 'y.tab.c' and the file of token definitions 'y.tab.h'. The command

    cc -o yaccdemo y.tab.c lex.yy.c

will produce the file 'yaccdemo', which can be executed in order to use the program.

Several of the rules are straightforward. Rules one and two simply explain that a session is either a null event or a sequence of commands, and a sequence of commands (cmds) is either a single command or several commands.

Most of the real work is in rule three. Alternatives three and four of rule three implement the two types of command, the bit setting commands and full assignment commands. Alternative one allows null commands. Null commands occur rather easily, as in

    set bit 3 on;

and they should not be illegal. (This input leads to a null command because the command "set bit 3 on" is terminated with a semicolon and then the newly initiated command is abruptly terminated with a newline.)

The second alternative of rule three illustrates a simple error recovery technique. The name "error" is built into yacc and anytime an input error is encountered it is as if the error token were recognized. Errors will occur in our simple language for inputs similar to

    bit set 3 on

because the key words are out of order. They also occur for inputs similar to

    please set bit 3 off

because the word "please" is not recognized. In all of these situations the effect of an error is to complete alternative two of rule three by waiting until an ENDCMD token (either a semicolon or a newline) is encountered. The effect is to throw away the tail of a mangled command, a simple but adequate option for our simple command language. More sophisticated error handling schemes can be implemented.

CHAPTER

18

The System Manager's Utilities

Managing a computer system involves more than just turning the power on before the users start logging in each morning. The system manager is responsible for maintaining the integrity of the system, installing new software, adapting software to local conditions, performing periodic backups of users' files, recovering lost data, and informing the users of new services and features. At some installations these responsibilities are widely distributed; at other installations there is a single person who accepts these responsibilities.

Many of the operations performed by the system manager should be inaccessible to ordinary users. In the UNIX System this is accomplished by providing a special privilege level called superuser. The UNIX System superuser is not restricted by the normal file access system and is allowed to perform all of the system maintenance functions. All of the programs discussed in this chapter should be owned by "root" and the programs that can alter the state of the system (volcopy, fsck, fsdb, etc.) should be executable only by the owner, that is, someone with the superuser privilege.

A person can acquire the superuser privilege by logging in using the name "root" or by executing the su command. In either case the user must enter the superuser password before the superuser privilege is granted. The superuser password should be known only by trusted and experienced UNIX System programmers.

Maintaining the integrity of the system is probably the most challenging activity for a system manager; performing periodic backups is probably the most bothersome. This chapter does not explain how to fix every conceivable file system problem, or how to set up a comprehensive backup policy. You must learn by a combination of trial and error and improvisation. If you have exemplary backups, then damage to the file system is not very important, and if you can patch even the most corrupt file system, then your need for comprehensive backups is diminished. The strongest defense against lost data is to keep good backups and to understand the procedure for repair of the file system because eventually every UNIX System installation has file system corruptions. It is well beyond the scope of this book to provide a complete guide to UNIX System management. The goal of this chapter is to provide an introduction to some of the procedures and utilities that are provided for the system manager.

18.1 Security

The security of a system is its reliability in the face of adversity. If a system unexpectedly crashes or loses files or allows unauthorized access to files, then it is insecure. A secure system works reliably and maintains and protects users' files. Security is a relative criterion; the world has yet to see the first completely secure computer system.

The reliability of the UNIX System (its crash resistance) is high. UNIX Systems generated from standard software modules often run for months without a crash. This record compares very favorably with the reliability of the computer hardware. UNIX Systems that are composed of standard software modules intertwined with locally modified software modules usually are less reliable.

The UNIX System is not a fault tolerant computer system. It imposes heavy demands on computer hardware and it is not forgiving (or informative) when hardware malfunctions. The later UNIX Systems include error logging and they tend to be better at spotting hardware malfunctions before they become serious.

There are three basic reasons computer systems lose files: the hardware malfunctions, the operating system software malfunctions, and the computer user malfunctions. Hardware malfunctions are inevitable, operating system malfunctions are likely, and computer user malfunctions are assured. The goal of computer manufacturers and operating system designers is to minimize the data loss caused by hardware and software; at the very least these losses should be small compared to accidental file erasures by users. One paradox of the UNIX System is that from a user's point of view all I/O transactions are synchronous, whereas from the system's point of view all I/O is buffered and asynchronous. The implication of the data buffering performed by the kernel is that data loss is likely whenever the computer stops unexpectedly. This type of loss is undesirable but unavoidable if one wants to maintain the efficiency of the system.

Another aspect of system security concerns the malicious or the mischievous user. Although beating the system is a natural human instinct, beating a multiuser computer system usually means interfering with other users and thus is strongly discouraged. Some simple precautions will prevent the great majority of problems.

In older UNIX Systems a user can usually cause a stoppage of service by gobbling up some resource (process table entries, file system storage space, etc.). It is always easy to examine the process table after the stoppage and discover the source of the problem so most of the difficulties here are caused by buggy programs. These techniques are less effective in Version 7 of the UNIX System because you need superuser privilege in order to gobble most resources.

There are several common sense policies for protecting the security of a system. Obviously you should limit the number of people who know and use the superuser password. You should also limit access to the system console, and you should not leave the system console (or any other terminal) unattended and logged in with superuser privilege. Whenever the computer is running it should be attended by someone who is trusted. For instance, someone using the computer alone at night can trivially break the security system by halting the computer and then rebooting the computer to single-user mode.

You should also prevent users from importing (by mounting tapes or disks) programs that run in privilege mode. One of the easiest ways to break the UNIX System's security is to import a privileged version of the su command (superuser; see below) that doesn't require a password. Programs owned by root that use the set user id mode (su, mail, etc.) are dangerous. These programs should have write privilege denied so that they cannot be altered by an ordinary user. The find program can be used to locate all of the programs in a system that use the set user id mode.

18.2 Su – Become Superuser

The UNIX System superuser is the most privileged user. The superuser is able to perform many operations that are denied to ordinary users. Most of the operations discussed in the remainder of this chapter must be invoked by the superuser. In addition, several of the commands mentioned in other parts of this book function differently when invoked by the superuser. For example, ordinary users can use the date command to display the date and time, but the superuser can also use the date command to set the date and time.

Ordinary users are constrained by the UNIX System's file access mode protection system. However, the superuser is not constrained by the protection system. The superuser can change the mode of any file or access any file in any way. Inadvertent superuser commands can do great damage because the normal constraints don't apply. The superuser privilege should be limited to a few careful and trusted individuals.

There are two ways to acquire the superuser privilege. One way is to log in using the special name "root". The other method is to log in using your normal login name and then execute the su (superuser) command. In either case the system will ask you to enter the super-user password. If you enter the correct password, the system will display a different prompt (usually a sharp) while you are operating with superuser privilege. At the conclusion of the operations requiring the superuser privilege you should strike Control-d. If you logged in as "root", then you will be logged off; if you used the su command, you will be returned to your normal identity.

18.3 Mount and Umount File Systems

The mount and umount (pronounced "you mount") commands are used to control the logical connection of the disk storage volumes to the file system. Before we can talk about these two commands we need to discuss a few terms. A file system is a collection of files and directories. Small disks (such as floppy disks) usually contain a single file system. Large disks usually are divided into several regions, each containing one file system. Large disks are subdivided into several file systems for convenience. Subdividing disks makes it easier to perform backups and to fix broken file systems. The UNIX System doesn't force you to subdivide large disks but most managers prefer subdivided disks.

The process of loading the UNIX System kernel into memory so that operations can start is called booting. The details of the booting procedure vary from one computer to another but in all systems the result is that the UNIX System kernel (usually stored in the file '/unix') is loaded into memory from the root file system. The root file system contains the most essential UNIX System utilities and files. At the end of the boot procedure only the files in the root file system are accessible.

The mount command is used to inform the UNIX System kernel of the existence of other file systems which should be incorporated into the accessible file system structure. A file system which exists but is not incorporated into the accessible file system structure is said to be unmounted. A file system which is incorporated into the accessible structure is said to be mounted.

Unmounted file systems are attached by logically connecting them to an accessible directory. Usually the directory is empty and specially provided for mounting the file system. For example, on a small system the root file system might be stored on the '/dev/rk0' device. It might contain the file 'unix' and the directories 'usr', 'etc', 'dev', and 'bin'. The 'dev' directory contains all of the special files for the special I/O device files, the 'bin' directory contains the most fre-

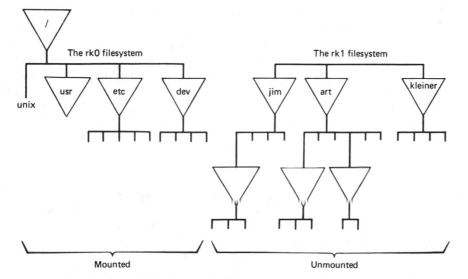

Figure 18.1. The rk0 and rk1 filesystems before rk1 is mounted.

quently used commands, the 'etc' directory contains files for system initialization and system management, and 'usr' is an empty directory. The files stored on the '/dev/rk1' device can be attached to the empty 'usr' directory using the command

```
/etc/mount  /dev/rk1  /usr
```

(Note that: the mount command is usually stored in the '/etc' directory. In some systems the search string for the superuser includes the '/etc' directory so you can use the name 'mount' instead of the name '/etc/mount'.) The first argument to the mount command (/dev/rk1) is the name of a special device containing a file system volume. The second argument (/usr) is the name of the directory where the file system will be connected. Immediately after booting the file systems appear as in Figure 18.1. Figure 18.2 shows the file system after it has been logically extended by mounting the '/dev/rk1' device on the '/usr' directory.

It is possible to mount a file system so that it can be read but not written. This capability is used frequently when you are recovering data from a backup and you want to be absolutely sure that the backup is not disturbed. When a file system is mounted read/write then the access dates of the files are modified whenever the files are accessed even if the files are not explicitly written. Mounting a file system read/only prevents this update, hence a file system should be mounted read/only when you don't want to disturb the access dates of the files. The command

```
/etc/mount  /dev/rk2  /mnt  -r
```

will mount the file system on the device '/dev/rk2' on the '/mnt' directory in read/only mode.

The UNIX System kernel usually is unaware of any write protect switches or mechanisms on the disk or tape drives. If you logically mount a file system as read/write and then use the switches on the disk drive to write protect the media, a flood of errors will occur each time a file is accessed because the write protect feature of the mechanism is preventing the operating system from updating the access dates of the files. If you use the write protect switches on a disk drive, you must also logically mount the file system read/only. The root file system can never be mounted read/only.

If the mount command is invoked without arguments

```
/etc/mount
```

then the names of all of the mounted file systems will be printed.

```
/dev/rk0 on / read/write on Thu Dec 3 19:08:21
/dev/rk1 on /usr read/write on Thu Dec 3 19:09:03
/dev/rk2 on /mnt read/only on Thu Dec 3 19:10:55
```

The root file system, '/dev/rk0' in this example, can never be unmounted. All other file systems can be unmounted, provided that nobody on the system is using them. The command

    /etc/umount /dev/rk1

attempts to unmount the '/dev/rk1' file system. If anyone has an open file on '/dev/rk1' or if anyone has a current directory on '/dev/rk1', then the umount command will complain that the '/dev/rk1' file system is busy. The only remedy is to find out who is accessing the file system (use the ps command) and then try again when the file system is idle. Occasionally a zombie process has an open file on a file system that you want to unmount. If you can't kill the process, you can't unmount the file system. The only remedy is to halt the system and then reboot.

Occasionally you need to access data on a disk that does not contain a valid UNIX file system. Disks or tapes without a file system can be accessed by using the special device file, but they cannot be mounted. Mounting is an operation that logically extends the file system, so it is limited to units actually containing a UNIX file system. Although tapes can contain file systems, usually they are treated as great big files without being mounted.

When you have mounted a file system you must be extremely careful not to remove the physical media (the disk) before performing the logical unmount operation. When a file system is mounted, certain vital information about the

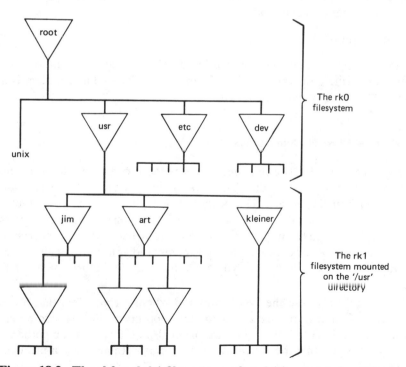

Figure 18.2. The rk0 and rk1 filesystems after rk1 is mounted on '/usr'.

locations of files on that file system is kept in memory with the kernel. Removing the physical media without performing the unmount may cause the memory resident information about the file system to be lost. One purpose of the unmount operation is to flush all of the memory resident information out to the physical media so that everything is consistent. Failure to logically unmount prior to physical removal is one of the major causes of corrupt (inconsistent) file systems in the UNIX System.

The root file system cannot be unmounted because it contains the programs and files that are necessary for system operation. Whenever you need to change the root volume you have to shut down the system, reload the root volume, and then reboot the system. It is therefore virtually impossible to run the UNIX System without two disks (or one disk and one tape).

When you perform a mount operation the information about the mount is recorded in two separate places. The UNIX System kernel contains a memory resident table of mounted file systems and the attachment is recorded in that table. Unfortunately the UNIX System contains no system calls that allow the contents of the internal mount table to be read by a user program, so it is impossible for a user program to really know what file systems are mounted. Thus whenever the mount command actually mounts a file system it places a record of the mount in an ordinary disk file (usually '/etc/mnttab') on the root file system. When this system works it works well, but anytime you have information stored in two separate places it is possible for the information to get out of sync. When you enter the command

```
/etc/mount
```

the information in the disk file is printed. Occasionally the internal system mount table (the gospel) contains different information. The problem is likely to persist until the system is rebooted.

18.4 Sync — Flush System Buffers

The sync command flushes the memory resident information about the file systems out to the physical media. You should always execute the sync command before you halt the system. UNIX System lore dictates that you should sync twice just to be sure. The completion of the sync command is not a guarantee that the information has in fact been written out to disk, although it certainly has been scheduled. After executing the sync command you should wait for the disk activity lights to cease (assuming you are at the console) before you actually halt the computer.

You should also use the sync command whenever you feel that a crash is inevitable. Perhaps you are about to run a program that uses some suspect feature of the UNIX System (beware of local modifications) or perhaps your intuition tells you that the system is about to crash. In any case a prudent sync never hurts.

There is one exception to the rule that you should run the sync command before you halt the computer. When you reconstruct the free list using the 'icheck' program or the 'fsck' program the information on the disk is more timely than the information in memory so you should not sync before you halt.

18.5 Mknod — Create Special Files

In the UNIX System special files are the link between the peripheral I/O devices and the operating system. There are two different interfaces to peripheral I/O devices: the block interface and the character interface. The block interface delivers data to a peripheral in blocks (512 byte chunks) and it is used primarily with disks and tapes. The character interface is primarily used to deliver data to peripherals one character at a time and it is used mainly with terminals, printers, paper tape readers, and other character-by-character devices. In addition to their block interface, disks and tapes usually have a character interface (also called the raw interface) that is used by many of the system maintenance programs.

Usually the special files are created when the system is generated or when the hardware configuration is changed. The special files usually are found in the '/dev' directory. If you enter the command

    ls -l /dev

you will get a long format list of all of the special files on your system. The mode field for all of the special files starts with either the "b" character to indicate a block special file or the "c" character to indicate a character special file. Here is a partial list of the special files on my system:

crw--w--w-	1	bin	sys	0,	0	Jan	8	09:13	console
crw-rw----	1	bin	sys	3,	1	Jan	2	12:01	kmem
c-w--w----	1	bin	sys	5,	0	Jan	7	23:15	lp
crw-rw----	1	bin	sys	3,	0	Dec	7	11:11	mem
brw-rw----	1	bin	sys	1,	0	Jan	8	09:13	mt0
crw-rw-rw-	1	bin	sys	3,	2	Jan	8	09:00	null
brw-rw----	1	bin	sys	2,	0	Jan	8	10:15	rk0
brw-rw----	1	bin	sys	2,	1	Jan	8	10:15	rk1
crw-rw----	1	bin	sys	4,	0	Jan	8	09:44	rmt0
crw-rw----	1	bin	sys	6,	0	Jan	8	10:15	rrk0
crw-rw----	1	bin	sys	6,	1	Jan	8	10:15	rrk1
crw--w--w-	1	bin	sys	1,	0	Jan	2	03:20	tty
crw--w--w-	1	bin	sys	0,	1	Jan	5	15:49	tty1
crw--w--w-	1	bin	sys	0,	2	Jan	8	10:17	tty2
crw--w--w-	1	bin	sys	0,	3	Jan	8	10:20	tty3

In a long format listing of an ordinary file the size of the file in bytes is printed after the owner and group information. A special file doesn't have a length because it is not a storage region but a link to an I/O device. Instead of the length the major and minor device numbers are printed.

The major device number indicates what type of hardware is associated with the file. The following table shows the major device numbers for the block and character special file listed above.

Major Device Number	Files
Character Special Devices	
0	console, tty1, tty2, tty3
1	tty
3	mem, kmem, null
4	rmt0
5	lp
6	rrk0, rrk1
Block Special Devices	
1	mt0
2	rk0, rk1

As you can see there are often several interfaces to one major device type. The four communication lines (console, tty1, tty2, and tty3) all have major device number 0. This means that there are four identical hardware devices in the computer to handle the four communication lines. To distinguish the four lines the four special files for the communication lines have the minor device numbers zero through three. The minor device number indicates which device when there are several identical devices.

What we have done in this section is look at the information in the '/dev' directory to deduce the major and minor device numbers used in this installation. To create the special files in the first place you must look in the system generation files (often in a file called 'conf.c'). Once you know the major and minor device number you can use the mknod command to create the special file. Let's suppose that you are creating the character special file for a paper tape device. Examining the system generation files reveals that the major device number is seven and the minor device number is zero (there is only one paper tape device). The command

```
/etc/mknod  /dev/pt  c  7  0
```

will create the character special file '/dev/pt' for the paper tape device.

On systems with named pipes (fifos) the mknod command is used to create the pipe. The command

```
/etc/mknod  /dev/fifo1  p
```

will create the '/dev/fifo1' fifo.

18.6 Df — Disk Free Space

The df (disk free) command prints a summary of the free space on the online file systems. The summary includes the number of free blocks and the number of free inodes. The command

    df /dev/rp3

will print the free space on '/dev/rp3'.

    /tmp on /dev/rp3 456 blocks 345 inodes

In this example we see that '/dev/rp3' is mounted on the '/tmp' directory and that there are 456 free blocks and 345 free inodes.

The same summary would be printed if you entered the command

    df /tmp

because df allows arguments to be file systems (such as /dev/rp3) or the name of a directory where a file system is mounted (such as '/tmp'). You cannot enter the name of just any directory; there must be a disk region mounted on that directory.

You can also use the df command without specifying a file system. In this case the free space on all of the mounted file systems will be summarized.

The system manager should run df periodically to monitor the free space on all of the file systems. Some systems need 20 or 30 percent free space, other systems only need 5 or 10 percent — experience is your best guide. Some systems impose limits on the disk space that is used by individuals. The du program can be used to check for compliance with these limits (see Section 7.16).

Individual users who are about to create very large files should use df in order to make sure that there is adequate room. You don't need superuser privilege to use df.

18.7 Volcopy, Labelit, Dump, Restor, Cpio — Backups

There are numerous approaches to the problem of performing periodic backups. The goal is to be able to recover lost data. Infrequent backups mean that the backup is usually old and out of date while frequent backups can be disruptive of normal system operations. Each system manager has to find the middle ground based on the frequency of data loss, the value of the data, and the amount of effort that can be expended in the backup process. Each manager also has to find a procedure that works with the available hardware. With a minimal set of disks then the normal users have to be off the system for the entire backup procedure. With more hardware the users have to be off the system for only part of the operation.

The UNIX System supports three major sets of backup utilities: the volcopy/labelit system, dump/restor system, and the cpio program. The volcopy program copies whole file systems from one place to another. Volcopy scrupulously checks the labels (installed using labelit) on the file systems to make sure that the correct volumes are mounted during the copy operation. The dump program performs an incremental file system save operation. Only the files that have been modified later than a certain date are saved. The restor program can examine the dumps created by the dump program to recover individual files or entire file systems. The cpio program creates a great big file which contains an image of an entire (or part of a) file system.

One advantage of the volcopy system is that the entire file system is saved every time a backup is performed. This redundancy makes for very secure backups. Another advantage of the volcopy system is that it can be used to make copies to either disks or tapes. A disk to disk backup operation, which is extremely fast, is preferred for the most frequent backups. The final advantage of volcopy is that it is extremely easy to recover lost data. Since an entire file system is saved, it is possible to mount the saved file system to recover a single file, or to copy the file system back from the backup medium, in order to recover an entire file system. Volcopy backups from disk to tape are good for long term archival storage of data, but they are inconvenient for day to day work because it is hard to remove a single file from a backup tape.

The advantage of the incremental dump system is that fewer data are transferred to the backup medium during each backup because only the recently modified files are saved. Thus the time spent performing backups is minimized. One disadvantage of the dump/restor system is that it performs dumps to tape only. Disk to disk backups must be performed using volcopy. Recovering individual files using restor is tricky since a missing file may be on any of several tapes depending on when the file was last modified. The restor program will browse through the assortment of dumped tapes and figure out which tape contains the missing file. Recovering file systems is also difficult because the backup is spread out over several tapes.

The cpio program is a very convenient way to save a file system on tape. Cpio can create a great big file which contains an image of an entire file system. Since tapes are usually manipulated as if they were a large file, the big file produced by cpio is ideal. Cpio also can be used to extract individual files from the archive, which makes it more convenient than volcopy operations to tape when single files need to be recovered. The find program has an option which automatically invokes cpio to perform a backup operation.

18.8 Dd – Convert Files

Data often are transferred between other computers and UNIX System computers using magnetic tapes. The main problem is converting between a foreign format and the UNIX System format. For example, punch card data often are transported from a mainframe system to a UNIX System. Punch card data transferred to tape usually are placed in blocks of 80 characters. To use such data in a UNIX System the coding has to be ASCII (most punch cards use EBCDIC) and the lines (card images) need a trailing newline character.

The dd program performs these conversions. In early versions of the UNIX System dd also is used for backups because it is a very efficient way to move data from one file system to another or from a file system to tape. In Version 7 of the UNIX System the programs volcopy and dump have superseded dd for backups, but dd is still used for conversions.

18.9 Fsck, Fsdb — Check File Systems

Sooner or later every file system becomes corrupt. The system manager is responsible for repairing corrupt file systems. There are lots of reasons for corrupt file systems including intermittent hardware failures, power line surges or other irregularities, problems with the disk media, and turning off the computer without executing the sync command. Corrupt file systems should be repaired immediately in order to limit the loss of data. Occasionally a file system is so corrupt that it must be discarded and recovered entirely from a backup, but usually only a file or two is lost and sometimes nothing is lost.

A file system is somewhat like a general ledger, and like a ledger, a file system should be consistent. In a corrupt file system something (perhaps a block of data) is not accounted for, or perhaps it is counted twice. Fixing a corrupt file system removes the inconsistencies. File systems should be checked every time a computer is booted and they should always be fixed as soon as a problem is noticed.

There have been several programs for repairing file systems. In Version 6 of the UNIX System the programs icheck, dcheck, check, ncheck and fcheck were used to check and repair file systems. These programs have been replaced in Version 7 of the UNIX System with the program fsck to check and repair file systems. In addition, Version 7 of the UNIX System contains the program fsdb to debug and perform subtle repairs on a file system. Fsdb can be used only by people who thoroughly understand the file system structure.

All file system checking and repairing should be done on unmounted (or quiescent) file systems. Fixing file systems using the predecessors of fsck is difficult because you need to use several programs and good judgment in order to repair a corrupt file system. Using fsck is much easier because fsck recommends solutions when it discovers problems with a file system. In most cases you should follow these recommendations unless you know enough about the file system to use fsdb.

Repairing the file system will make more sense if you understand the format of the UNIX file system. The philosophy of fsck is to prune the dead or dying files. Pruning is simple and effective but usually results in loss of data and occasionally results in more data loss than is strictly necessary. An adequate file backup system makes data loss less painful.

Occasionally files and their names become separated. This is possible in the UNIX System because the names of files are stored in directories while the rest of the information for files is stored in a structure called an inode. Files without names are called orphaned files and fsck will attempt to place them in a directory called 'lost+found'. You should create the 'lost+found' directory in the root of the file system before you use fsck and you should make sure that there are empty slots in the directory by copying some files into 'lost+found' and then removing the files. If the 'lost+found' directory is not present then orphaned files are discarded. In the 'lost+found' directory fsck will use a number as the name of the file. You should attempt to determine the real name of the file based on its contents and either restore the file to its rightful owner or remove it.

The command

    fsck

will check all of the file systems mentioned in the file '/etc/checklist'. Usually '/etc/checklist' contains a list of all of the active file systems. You can check an individual file system by using its name as an argument to fsck:

    fsck /dev/rk2

Every file system contains a list of free blocks. When a file is created the blocks of data in the file are gathered from the list of free blocks. Occasionally the list of free blocks is damaged; sometimes blocks that are free aren't in the list and occasionally blocks that used in an existing file are also mentioned in the free list. The "-s" option of fsck will rebuild the free list. The command

    fsck -s /dev/rk2

will rebuild the free list of /dev/rk2. (The "-s" option of fsck is the same as the "-s" option of the older icheck program.) When you rebuild the free list of a mounted file system (usually the root file system) you must halt the computer immediately after the rebuild and then boot the system from scratch. Halting the computer immediately (without the usual sync operation) prevents the UNIX System kernel from writing the old (bad) freelist out to disk. Usually when fsck discovers errors in the course of checking a file system it will ask for your permission to rebuild the free list.

18.10 Cron—Run Programs at Specified Times

The cron program is used to execute programs at specified times. The cron program usually is started shortly after the system is booted and there should only be one cron process running in a system. Cron reads commands from the file '/usr/lib/crontab' (the crontab). Each line in the crontab specifies a command and the time or times when it should be executed.

Cron periodically examines '/usr/lib/crontab' in order to keep up with new additions to the file. Thus the crontab file can be changed while cron is running.

Entries in the crontab file consist of five fields that specify the time that a command should be run followed by the command. In order, the five time fields represent minutes (0-59), hours (0-23), day of the month (1-31), month of the year (1-12), and day of the week (0-6 with Sunday as zero). The time fields are separated by spaces or tabs.

The following line in crontab causes the date to be printed on the console every 10 minutes.

    0,10,20,30,40,50 * * * * date > /dev/console

The numbers representing the time can either be a number in the range mentioned above, a list of numbers separated by commas (as in the example), or two numbers separated by a hyphen to indicate a range of times or an asterisk to indicate all legal values. The command to print the date on the console every hour weekday nights from six to 10 is

```
0  6-10 * * 1-5 date > /dev/console
```

The cron system is often used to run programs unattended during the wee hours, to perform periodic accounting operations, and so on. Some systems use cron to disable certain programs during the peak periods in order to improve system response.

18.11 Fifo Files

Fifo files are used to allow one program to transfer information to another program. Typically one program will write into a fifo and another program will read from the fifo. The fifo establishes a communication channel between the two programs. Information is stored in the fifo file only during the short period of time between one program's output to the fifo and the other program's input from the fifo. Fifos are available on few UNIX Systems.

Fifo files obviously are similar to UNIX System pipes. The advantage of using a fifo is that any two unrelated programs can use it to communicate. Pipes require the child programs at either end of the pipe to have the same parent. Usually this parent is the UNIX System shell. A fifo is used when it is not possible or convenient for the communicating processes to have the same parent.

Fifos can be created using the mknod (make node) command (discussed in Section 18.5). Fifos are owned by someone and access to them is governed by the usual three tiered protection system.

You have to create a fifo before you can use it. For instance, the following command reads data from the communication line '/dev/tty99' and then writes it out to a fifo file named 'fifo1.tel':

```
cat < /dev/tty99 > fifo1.tel
```

If the fifo file 'fifo1.tel' didn't exist when the command was entered, then the shell would have created an ordinary file named 'fifo1.tel' to receive the output of the cat command.

A command could pick up information from the fifo using input redirection:

```
sh < fifo1.tel
```

In these two examples we have used the shell's I/O redirection to access the fifo.

18.12 The Sticky Bit

Ordinary files are not stored contiguously on the disk. The information in a file is divided into blocks and the blocks are stored throughout the disk. If you are having a file typed on your terminal, the system's overhead in retrieving the file from the various places on the disk is very low because your requests to read the file are interleaved with other user I/O requests. However, if the system is loading the file for execution, the overhead of noncontiguous disk storage is high. The sticky mode helps to reduce this undesirable overhead for frequently executed programs.

When a program is temporarily suspended from execution the system may copy the program to temporary storage on disk. This process is called swapping. The temporary storage on disk is organized contiguously so that it can be accessed rapidly. In the UNIX System a special mode can be assigned to a file so that an executable image of the program is stored in the swap space when the program is not being executed. Since the program gets stuck in the swap space, the mode is called the sticky mode and the bit that controls the process is called the sticky bit.

Relatively few programs are assigned the sticky mode because swap space is a precious commodity which would be rapidly exhausted if all programs were assigned the sticky mode. Frequently used programs (e.g., the editor, ls, cat) are often assigned the sticky mode. On large systems where more swap space is available many programs are likely to have the sticky mode. On small systems where disk space is limited the sticky mode seldom is used.

The sticky mode can be assigned to a file only by the system manager. Users cannot assign the sticky mode to their own files. The sticky mode is indicated by the character "t" in the last position of the file type/mode field of the ls command's long format output.

18.13 Set User Id

Occasionally the sophisticated UNIX System access protection scheme gets in the way of valid access requirements. The classic example is the requirement posed by games programs. Many games programs want to keep an auxiliary file which contains some information that is private to the game. For example in an adventure program the list of messages in an auxiliary file should be hidden from inquisitive adventurers. The UNIX System mechanism to protect this sort of information is to make the auxiliary file owned by the creator of the game and restrict access to the file. However, when a person uses the game the information in the auxiliary file is needed.

The problem is simple; when you are not playing the game you should be prohibited from accessing the private game information. However, when you are playing the game you should, within the structure imposed by the game, be allowed access to the private information.

The set user id mode solves this problem. If a file has the set user id mode, you acquire all of the privileges of the file owner when you execute the program. The set user id mode is used for many games programs. When you are not playing the game you cannot access the protected game file, but when you are playing (executing) the game you have the access privileges of the game's creator. While you are playing the game, all of the access is structured by the rules of the game and the game program itself is responsible for preventing you from cheating.

The owner of a file can set the set user id mode for his own files. The set user id mode is indicated by the character "s" in place of the file owner's execution ("x") character in the type/mode field of the long listing.

The set group id mode for a file allows the person executing that file to acquire the same privileges as members of the owner's group. The set group id mode is essentially a fine tuning of the set user id system. The set group id mode is indicated by the character "s" in place of the file's group execution ("x") character in the type/mode field of the long listing. There is no set other id mode because it would accomplish nothing.

CHAPTER
19

The UNIX System Kernel

The UNIX System kernel is the master organizer of UNIX. The kernel schedules processes, allocates memory and disk storage, supervises the transmission of data between the main storage and the peripheral devices, and honors the processes' requests for service. This chapter examines the kernel in order to partially answer the question "How does the UNIX System really work?" Note that some of the more specific information presented in this chapter may not apply to all UNIX Systems.

Most of the information in this chapter has direct practical applications for the UNIX System managers and system programmers. The more theoretical aspects of the UNIX System, its avoidance of deadlock, its techniques for mutual exclusion, and so on, are discussed in the papers written by Ritchie and Thompson.

The kernel is the memory resident portion of the UNIX Operating System. Compared to other operating systems the UNIX System kernel provides a relatively small repertoire of services. The kernel never does anything directly for a user; all services are provided by utility programs which intercede between users and the kernel. This has worked out extremely well in the UNIX System. Utility programs are much easier to create, maintain, and customize than the UNIX System kernel and it is easy to add new utility programs years after the kernel has become relatively stable.

The UNIX System kernel contains about 10,000 lines of C code and about 1000 lines of assembly code. A program of this size can be understood and maintained by a single individual. Many UNIX Systems are distributed with the source code for the kernel and all of the utilities. This allows programmers to study and tinker with their own system. In contrast most other operating systems are too large to be understood or maintained by an individual and most other operating systems are distributed "as is" — tinkering is not allowed.

19.1 Overview

The UNIX System kernel consists of two major parts: the process management section and the device management section. The process management section allocates resources, schedules processes, and honors processes' requests for service; the device management section supervises the transmission of data between the main memory and the peripheral devices. One of the great triumphs of the UNIX System is the fact that widely different computers use almost identical process management sections.

The device management section for a given computer contains a module for every peripheral device that is attached to the computer. Every time a computer is attached to a new type of I/O peripheral a program module has to be added to the device management section. Whenever the UNIX System is moved to a different type of computer the device management section has to be largely rewritten because different computers usually have very different peripheral devices with different control principles.

The process of configuring the UNIX System for a particular set of peripheral devices and default options is called system generation. The major work of system generation is creating a list which describes the exact hardware environment and prescribes a certain set of options for the system.

Typical applications programs have a beginning, a middle, and an end, somewhat like a good novel. The UNIX System is more like a woven tapestry than a novel. The UNIX System does not have a single plot that runs from beginning to end; instead it has a number of interrelated threads that are woven in response to the needs of the moment. The fact that the kernel is not a simple sequential program makes it inherently more difficult to understand than most programs.

The UNIX System kernel maintains several important tables which coordinate the actions of the interrelated threads of execution. In fact the UNIX System is an excellent example of a program where the data structures the program. Understanding the UNIX System begins with an understanding of the tables of information that the kernel maintains. Surprisingly, most of the work of the kernel is routine table searching and table modification. The following sections of this chapter describe the major functions of the kernel and the relevant tables of information.

19.2 User Mode and Kernel Mode

At any given instant a computer is either executing a user program (a process) or executing system code. (I prefer to reserve the word process for entities that are in the kernel's process table.) We say that the computer is in user mode when it is executing instructions in a user process and it is in kernel mode when it is executing instructions in the kernel. Some computers have distinct hardware privileges for kernel mode (e.g., PDP-11). Other computers do not support two modes with hardware privileges (e.g., Z-80); the distinction is the source of the instructions, not the privilege level of the hardware.

Several mechanisms can prompt a switch from user mode to kernel mode. Perhaps the most important from the point of view of system integrity is the system clock. The system clock periodically interrupts (usually 60 times per second) whatever is going on. (An interrupt is a hardware signal that can divert the computer to a special software routine.) During the service routine for the system clock the process's priorities are reevaluated and a change of process is possible. In the absence of other interruptions, the system clock performs the basic time-slicing that enables a computer to be shared between many users.

Whenever a user program needs an operating system service it executes a system call. The implementation details of system calls vary from one computer architecture to another, but the immediate result is always a change from user mode to kernel mode. System calls that perform I/O operations often lead to a suspension of the calling process while the data are being transferred. A different user process will be performed in the interim if possible. Thus the natural I/O requirements of programs often drive the time-slicing mechanism.

The service requirements of the I/O peripherals is the third mechanism that causes a switch from user mode to kernel mode. I/O peripherals typically have a response time that is much longer than the normal instruction execution time of a computer. The details vary greatly from one computer architecture to another, but on most UNIX Systems there is an interruption each time a transfer is complete. (At various times a transfer is either 512 bytes, a single byte, or a variable-length string of bytes.) The transfer completion interrupt typically updates various status elements in certain tables and then possibly initiates another transfer.

19.3 Scheduling and Swapping

In a time-sharing computer system processes compete for execution time slices. Scheduling is the series of actions that decides which of the competing user processes to execute. Obviously scheduling is one of the key elements of a time-sharing system. The fundamental act of time-sharing is suspending a process and then restarting it at some later time. In most time-sharing systems (e.g., the UNIX System) the suspension/resumption activity occurs many times each second so that it appears externally that the computer is performing several functions simultaneously.

At most one user process is active at any given time. All of the other user processes are suspended. We can divide the set of suspended processes into two groups, those that are ready to run and those that are blocked. A blocked process is said to be sleeping until an event occurs. Usually the event is the completion of an I/O request, although process can also wait for (1) their children to die or (2) specified intervals of time or (3) signals from other processes. When the event occurs the sleeping process is awakened. Awakening a process marks it as ready to run; it doesn't mean that a process will immediately start to execute.

Ideally all of the user processes reside in memory and the role of the scheduler is to select the active process from the group of memory resident processes. Unfortunately, the memory on modern computers is not large enough to simultaneously store the typical number of processes that are active in a UNIX System. The solution is to store some of the suspended processes on disk, a procedure known as swapping. A process stored on disk must be reloaded into memory before it can execute. The scheduling system is responsible for two actions, scheduling the processes for execution and scheduling the processes for swapping.

The very simple explanation for a time-sharing system is that time is divided into a number of slices and the slices are parceled out to the processes. The UNIX System also takes into account the fact that processes waiting for I/O may not be able to take advantage of their given slice. To avoid discrimination against processes that perform I/O the UNIX System dynamically calculates process priorities in order to determine which inactive but ready process will execute when the currently active process is suspended.

Part of the priority calculation involves accumulated execution time starting when the process was last swapped in to memory. Processes that have accumulated a lot of execution time have less priority than processes that have been starved for execution time. Notice that processes that have just been swapped in and processes that have been waiting for I/O have not been executing so that they will have a relatively high priority. It is also possible for a user process to execute a system call which induces a bias in the calculation; ordinary user processes can only decrease their priority, but processes run by the superuser can increase or decrease their priority.

The net effect of this procedure is that I/O-intensive processes tend to execute until they can proceed no further. Computation-intensive processes tend to fill the gaps while the I/O processes are waiting for their I/O to complete. When everything is working the system tends to balance itself in order to keep the processor busy and give all of the processes some execution time.

In the UNIX System there is extremely little overhead for a suspended process. This crucial fact has had a profound impact on the nature of the UNIX System programming. In the UNIX System programs are written to do one thing well and large, complicated operations often are composed of several small programs working together. The low overhead of suspended processes has enabled many "operating system" functions to be exported from the UNIX System kernel and placed in ordinary programs. Consider the getty program. The getty program prints a login message on a communication line and then waits for a user to start logging in. There is a (usually suspended) getty process for every communication line in a UNIX System that is not being used by a logged in user. Many systems have 50 to 100 such getty processes. The UNIX System would be profoundly different if suspended processes required significant overhead.

19.4 Processes

The UNIX System supports two powerful illusions: that the file system has "places" and that processes have "life." The strong visceral connection of directories with "places" makes it possible for people to master the file system. Similarly, the illusion that processes have "life" and thus can perform useful work makes it easy to think about and control processes. We say that the shell runs programs, that the editor creates text files, that the ls program lists the contents of directories. All of these processes are described as if they were active, vital organisms. The gift of life that we bestow on processes is a convenient illusion. A computer scientist might describe a process as an execution of an abstract data structure. The energy in a computer is in the hardware, but the intelligence is in the programs so it is reasonable to transfer the life force to the software.

The idea of a process is the fundamental organizing concept in the UNIX System. Even though the instructions are executed by the CPU and stored in memory, even though the disks and tapes are spinning furiously, we say that the process is executing and we ignore the obvious — the computer is actually doing the work.

The UNIX System kernel exists to support the needs of processes. From a process's point of view the kernel's operations are a sort of overhead that must be endured; the view from within the kernel is that processes are just cataloged data structures that are manipulated according to a set of rules. The description of processes that follows might seem dull because the view from within is that processes are just data, more like an accountant's worksheet than a vital force.

A process is a program in a state of execution. For a given program there may be zero, one, or several active processes at a particular time. In this work we will confine the term process to entities that are cataloged in the UNIX System kernel's process table. Hence the activity of the UNIX System kernel is generally excluded as a process.

The vital information for processes is stored in two places: the process table and the user table (also called the per process data segment). The process table is always in memory. It contains one entry for each process; each entry details the state of a process. The state information includes the location of the process (memory address or swapped address), the size of the process, the identification number of the process, and the identification of the user running the process. Each UNIX System is generated with a certain number of entries in the process table — each process consumes one entry in the table and it is impossible to have more processes than there are entries in the process table.

Less timely information about each process is stored in the user table. One user table is allocated for each active process and only the user table of the active process is directly accessible to the kernel routines. See Figures 19.1a and 19.1b.

The process table is referenced during all of the life crises of processes. Creating a process involves initializing an entry in the process table, initializing a user table, and creating the actual text and data for the process. When a process changes its state (running, waiting, swapped out, swapped in, etc.) or receives a signal the interaction focuses on the process table. When a process dies its entry in the process table is freed so that it can be used by future processes.

The process table must always be in memory so that the kernel can manage the life crises of a process even while the process is swapped out. Many of the

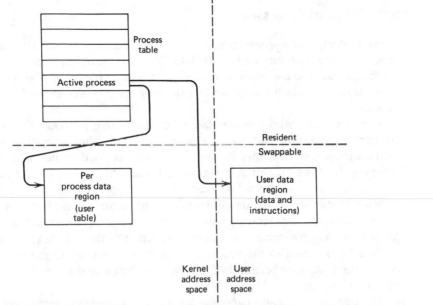

Figure 19.1A. The data structures for managing ordinary processes.

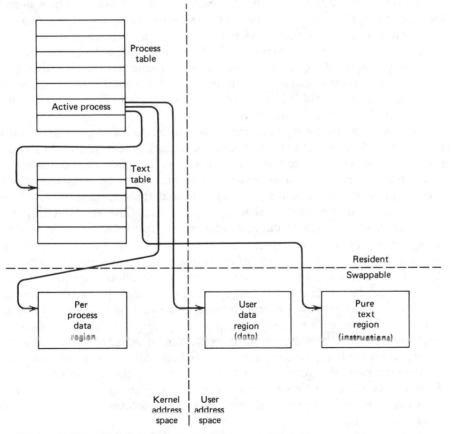

Figure 19.1B. The data structures for managing processes with pure text.

events in the life of a process occur while the process is inactive. For instance, a process is sleeping while waiting for I/O. The I/O completion causes the process to be awakened and marked as ready to resume execution. The information necessary to manage the wake-up of a sleeping process is contained in the process table.

The kernel allocates one user table for each active process. The user table contains information that must be accessible while the process is executing. While a process is suspended its user table is not accessed or modified. The user table is part of the process data region and when the process is swapped out to disk the user table is swapped with the rest of the process image.

Most of the user structure contains current information about the process. For example, the user table contains the user and group identification numbers for determining file access privileges, pointers into the system's file table (see Section 19.6) for all of the process's open files, a pointer to the inode of the current directory (see Section 19.6) in the inode table, and a list of responses for the various signals.

The current information about a process is manipulated very simply. If the process executes the chdir system call, then the value of the pointer to the current directory inode is changed. If a process elects to ignore a certain signal, then the appropriate entry in the table of signal responses is set to zero. Most of the manipulations of information in the user table are so simple that you might expect the program to perform the manipulation rather than the kernel. In part these simple manipulations are performed by the kernel for the sake of uniformity but the important reason is system integrity. On a computer with memory protection the user table is inaccessible to a process (except via system calls) even though it is part of the process image.

Some of the more common programs, such as the shell and getty, are usually being executed by several users simultaneously. Each process must have its own copy of the variable part of the process image but the fixed part, the program text, can be shared. In order to be shared a program must be compiled using a special option that arranges the process image so that the variable part and the text part are cleanly separated. Sharing program text allows the UNIX System to use the main memory of the computer more effectively. In order to keep track of the program text segments the UNIX System maintains a text table. When a program uses shared text the process table entry contains a pointer into the text table and the text table actually points to the location of the process text.

Let's conclude our discussion of processes by examining the two fundamental system calls which processes execute in order to create new processes. The fork system call is used by a process to create a copy of itself. The fork is the only mechanism in the UNIX System for increasing the number of processes. After the fork there are two processes, the parent and the child. The major difference between the two subsequent processes is the fact that the two processes have different process id numbers and different parent process id numbers. The two processes share open files and each process is able to determine whether it is the parent or the child.

The second major system call for creating processes is exec. The exec system call is used to transform the calling process into a new process. The total number of processes in the system isn't changed, only the character of the calling process is. After an exec system call the process id number is unchanged and open files remain open. The exec system call is similar to the chaining feature in other operating systems which allows a process to choose its successor.

A fork followed by an exec is commonly used by a parent process to create a child process with a new identity. This sequence is used by the shell each time the shell runs a program for you. The wait system call is commonly used in conjunction with fork and exec. The wait system call allows a parent process to wait for the demise of a child process. This is used by the shell when you execute a program in the foreground. The shell forks, the child process execs the required process, and the parent process waits for the demise of the child. When the child dies the parent prompts you to enter another command. The shell runs processes in the background simply by omitting the wait for the demise for the child process.

19.5 Booting, Process 0, Process 1

Now that some of the basic ideas of the UNIX System kernel have been introduced we can turn our attention to what happens when the kernel is first started. Several unique actions must be performed early in the course of execution in order to progress to the steady state condition discussed above. By the time process 1 is initialized and started the system is running normally and working according to the laws established by system calls.

The act of loading the kernel system image into memory and starting its execution is booting. Booting occurs whenever the system is started for the first time following the initial power up of the computer hardware and booting is also performed following crashes and intentional stoppages of the UNIX System.

Booting occurs in several phases. In the first phase the computer hardware arranges to have the first block of the disk in the bootstrap disk drive loaded into memory and executed. As you will discover in the next section, the first block of every file system is reserved for special purposes, usually a short bootstrap loader program. Thus in order to boot you must have a bootable disk (i.e., one with a valid loader program in the first block) installed in the bootstrap disk drive.

The purpose of the short loader program is to find and load the file named 'unix' in the root directory ('/unix'). The file '/unix' contains the machine instructions for the operating system kernel. '/unix' is created by compiling and linking the operating system source code files. Phase two of the boot procedure starts once the file '/unix' has been loaded into memory and starts to execute.

The first thing that the kernel does is initialize a few hardware interfaces. On machines with memory management hardware the memory management needs to be initialized and on all systems the clock that provides periodic interrupts needs to be initialized. The kernel also initializes a few data structures including the pool of block buffers, the pool of character lists, the pool of inode buffers, and the variable which indicates the amount of main memory.

Following these rather mundane initializations the kernel begins to initialize process 0. Processes ordinarily are created via the fork system call which instructs the system to make a copy of the calling process. Obviously this method is not feasible for creating the first process, process 0. The kernel creates process 0 by allocating a per-user data structure and installing pointers to the data structure in the first slot of the process table. Process 0 is unique for several reasons. First note that there is no code segment for process 0: its entire being is a per-user data structure. All other processes contain code that is executed to perform some function; they are images resulting from the compilation and subsequent execution of a program. Process 0 is just a per-user data structure that is used by the kernel; it is not an image. Also note that process 0 is created anomalously and persists for the life of the system. Finally note that process 0 is truly a system process; it is active exclusively while the processor is in kernel mode. Process zero is called a process only because it is cataloged in the process table. You should keep in mind that process 0 is really a kernel data structure, not a process in the normal sense of the word.

After process zero is created and initialized the system creates process 1 by making a copy of process 0. The copy of process 0 is made by following essentially the same procedure that is followed when a user program executes the fork system call. Although process 1 is hand crafted, at least the hand crafting is beginning to resemble the ordinary process creation scheme.

Initially process 1 is an exact copy of process 0; it has no code region. The first event that occurs after process 1 is created is that it is expanded in size. The size of process 1 is increased by executing the same code that would be executed if the process had issued the break (increase memory allocation) system call. Once again process 1 is acted on anomalously but in imitation of the procedure that is followed by an ordinary program executing a system call. Notice that up to this point both process 0 and process 1 have yet to execute.

The third event in the creation of a viable process 1 is the copying of a very simple program into its newly created code region. The program that is copied into process 1's code region essentially contains the machine instructions to perform the exec system call to execute a program called '/etc/init'.

At this point the initialization of processes 0 and 1 is essentially complete. Process 0 is a per-user data structure that is used by the kernel during the scheduling and process management operations. Process 1 is a viable image that might have resulted from the compilation of a program although it actually was created uniquely by the kernel. Once the UNIX System has initialized a necessary data region (process 0) and a viable first process (process 1) it proceeds to execute the usual scheduling routines.

At this point the initialization of the kernel is complete. However, the initialization of the system is just beginning and we will conclude this section with a description of the first few events in the life of the system. The scheduler is responsible for deciding what process to run and which processes to swap in or swap out. This first time that the scheduler is called, the decision making is very easy, there are no processes to swap, and there is only one process that is anxious to run, process 1. Executing process 1 immediately leads to the exec system call which overlays the original code in process 1 with the code contained in the file '/etc/init'. Now that process 1 has attained its final form we can call it by its usual name, the init process.

The init process is responsible for setting up the process structure of the UNIX System. Init usually is able to create at least two distinct process structures, the single-user mode and multiuser mode. (On some systems init is able to create more than two distinct process environments.) Usually init starts by attaching a shell to the system console and giving this shell superuser privilege. This is commonly called single-user mode. In single-user mode the console is automatically logged in with root privileges and none of the other communication lines will accept logins. Single-user mode often is used to check and repair file systems, and to perform basic system testing functions and other activities that require exclusive use of the computer.

At the conclusion of single-user mode the init process sets up the multiuser process structure. Init does this by creating a getty process for every active communication line. (Getty is discussed in the next paragraph.) Init also creates a shell process to execute the commands in the file '/etc/rc'. The '/etc/rc' file contains a shell script which contains commands to mount file systems, start demons, remove outdated temporary files, and start accounting programs. The commands in '/etc/rc' vary widely from one UNIX System installation to another.

During the life of the system the init process sleeps waiting for the death of any of its children. If one of init's children dies, then init awakens and creates another getty program for the relevant communication line. Thus init not only creates the multiuser process structure, init also maintains that structure during the life of the system (Figure 19.2).

The final actor in the system initialization story is the getty program. Each getty program waits patiently for someone to log in on a particular communication line. When someone does start to log in the getty program performs a few basic adjustments to the line protocol and then execs the login program to actually check the password. If the password is entered correctly, the login program execs the shell program to actually accept commands from the user. When a shell program exits the init program (its only living relative) awakens and fork-execs a new getty program to monitor the line and wait for the next login (Figure 19.3).

19.6 The File System

The hierarchical file system is one of the UNIX System's most important features. The most basic function of any file system is to partition the storage on disks and tapes into named units that we call files. In many systems there are

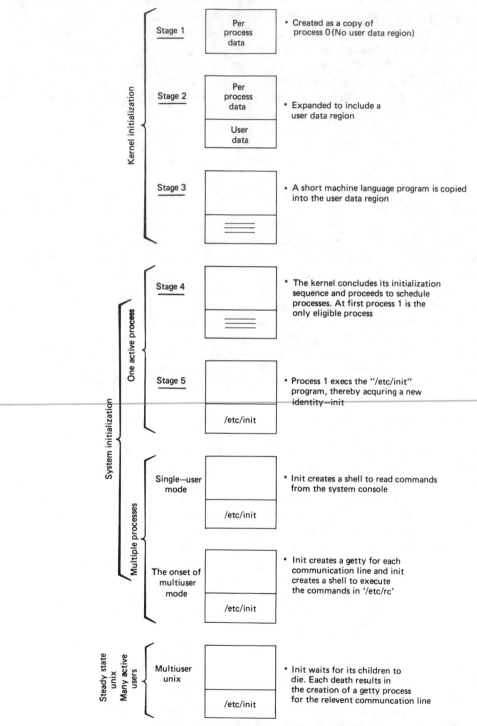

Figure 19.2. The life crises of process 1.

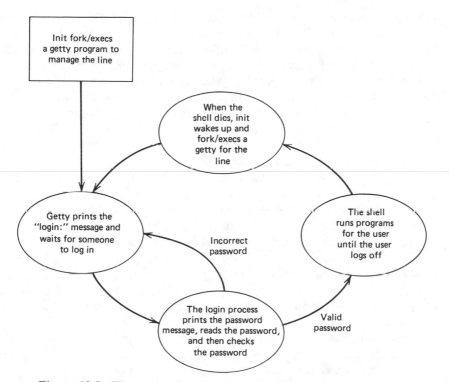

Figure 19.3. The cycle of events for each communication line.

several types of file with distinct access methods for each type. In the UNIX System all files are a simple sequence of bytes. Sometimes files are referred to as text files or binary files but the distinction is the content of the file (text files contain ASCII values only) not the structure of the file or the access method.

From the system user's point of view a directory is a group of files. In some operating systems (other than the UNIX System) all of the files on a storage volume are contained in one directory. Still other file systems, admitting that today's disks store very many files, partition the disk into a number of directories and parcel the files into one of the directories. Both of these methods create a flat file system. Everything is at one level. Flat file systems are usable, but they are messy because each directory contains many types of file.

The UNIX System contains a hierarchical file system. Files are not stored at one level but on multiple levels and the file system supports the illusion of "places" within the system. In flat file systems the directory is the chief organizing structure of the system; the directory contains all of the information about files including their name, length, location, access dates, modes, and types. Because directories in flat file systems contain all of the important information about files they are hidden and protected by the operating system. However, in the UNIX System directories are just files that can be read by any program.

Although directories are the visible structure of the UNIX file system, they are not the repository for all of the information about files. In the UNIX System directories contain just two pieces of information for each file: the file's name and a number which the kernel uses to access the hidden file system structures.

The hidden part of the UNIX file system is the inode. Inodes are where the action really is in the UNIX file system. There is one inode for each file. The inode contains information about the location of a file, the length of a file, the access modes of a file, the relevant dates, the owner, and the like. The casual UNIX System user is well insulated from inodes, at least until the inode structures become inconsistent and need repair.

Let's talk about the internal structure of the UNIX file system starting at the front of every file system (see Figure 19.4). For now we will concentrate on the file system structures that are actually stored on the storage disk. Later in this section we will concentrate on the structures that are stored in memory by the kernel. The first block of any file system is the boot block. For file systems that are involved in bootstrapping the first block contains a short bootstrap program. Typically this bootstrap program reads in a longer bootstrap or perhaps the UNIX System kernel itself. The exact details of bootstrapping are very system dependent. On file systems that aren't involved in the bootstrap process the first block usually is unused.

The second block of a file system is the file system header. The header (also called the superblock) contains a variety of information about the file system. In particular, the superblock contains the size of the file system, the number of inodes in the file system, and several parameters regarding the free list. When a file system is mounted (using the mount command) an entry is made in the UNIX System kernel's mount table and the file system's superblock is read into one of the kernel's large internal buffers. The superblocks of all of the mounted file systems are accessible to the kernel because the kernel needs the information in the superblock in order to access the files and the inodes in the file system.

The inodes are stored on a file system starting at block two. Different sizes of file systems contain different numbers of inodes; the exact inode count is stored in the super block. Since inodes are fixed in size and numbered consecutively from zero it is possible to locate any inode given its inode number.

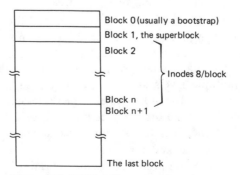

Figure 19.4. The filesystem layout.

Each file is defined by an inode which contains all of the information that the system keeps about each file. The inode contains the mode and the type of the file, the length of the file in bytes, the identification numbers of the owner and the group, the location of the file, and the times that the file was created, last modified, and last accessed. Notice that the inode does not contain the name of a file; the name is stored in a directory.

The location information stored in an inode needs to be examined in some detail. The UNIX System locates files by maintaining a list of the blocks in the file. Some operating systems locate files by maintaining the starting block number and the final block number and the file is stored contiguously on the disk. Contiguous file systems are unpleasant because files cannot grow without bound but are confined by the starting location of the next file. Contiguous file systems tend to waste space because small holes between large files usually can't be used until they are collected during a garbage collection operation. By maintaining a list of the blocks in a file the UNIX System avoids the problems of the contiguous file systems. The blocks in the file may physically be scattered throughout the disk but logically the blocks form a long chain which contains the information in the file.

The key to the location of the file is a list of 13 disk block numbers stored in the inode. The first 10 block numbers in the inode list specify the first 10 blocks in the file. If the file is only four blocks long, then the first four entries in the list contain block numbers and the last nine entries in the list contain zeros. If a file is longer than 10 blocks (5120 bytes) then the eleventh block number is used to specify a disk block that contains a list of the next 128 blocks in the file. This block is known as an indirect block. For files longer than 138 (128 + 10) blocks (70,656 bytes) the twelfth entry in the inode list contains the address of a block which contains the addresses of 128 indirect blocks. This block is known as a double indirect block. Finally, for files longer than 16,522 (10 + 128 + 128 squared) blocks (8,459,264 bytes) the thirteenth entry in the inode list contains the address of a triple indirect block. The maximum number of blocks in a UNIX System file is 10 + 128 + 128 squared + 128 cubed or 2,113,674 blocks, or 1,082,201,088 bytes (see Figure 19.5.)

Fetching information from very large files is harder than fetching information from small files because the indirect blocks need to be fetched in order to determine the addresses of the actual blocks in the file. This overhead is a small price to pay for the ability to accommodate very large files. For example, to entirely read a 10,000 block file the system has to fetch the 10,000 blocks in the file, one double indirect block, and 79 indirect blocks. You should also notice that most of the disks that are available today are much smaller than the 1 billion byte limit on an individual file that is imposed by the UNIX System.

Let's now turn our attention to the directories. A directory is a disk resident file that contains a list of file names and a corresponding list of inode numbers. Programs are prohibited from writing into a directory in order to maintain the integrity of the file system hierarchy; reading of directories is permitted. The system manipulates the directory contents when programs issue requests to

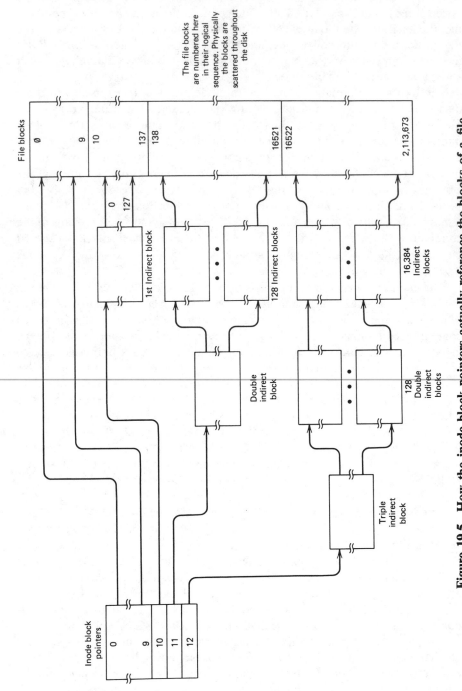

The file blocks are numbered here in their logical sequence. Physically the blocks are scattered throughout the disk

File blocks

0

9
10

137
138

16521
16522

2,113,673

1st Indirect block

0
127

128 Indirect blocks

16,384 Indirect blocks

Double indirect block

128 Double indirect blocks

Triple indirect block

Inode block pointers

0

9
10
11
12

Figure 19.5. How the inode block pointers actually reference the blocks of a file.

create or delete files. Each directory is defined by an inode just as any file is defined by an inode. Directory entries are 16 bytes long: 14 bytes for the file name and 2 bytes for the inode number.

The first two entries in every directory are for '.' and '..'. The '.' entry lists the inode of the directory itself and the '..' entry lists the inode of the parent directory. (Note: in the root directory both '.' and '..' reference the root directory because the root directory has no parent.) These two canonical entries are automatically placed in a directory when the directory is created by the system and they cannot be removed by a user. A directory is considered "empty" when it contains only the '.' and the '..' files.

A path through the file system as viewed from the UNIX System kernel is actually a ricochet between directories and inodes. Consider the path '../a/b'. The path leads from the current directory, to the parent of the current directory, to the parents subdirectory 'a', and finally to the file named 'b' in the directory 'a'. In order to follow this path the system performs the following steps:

1. Fetch the inode for the current directory. (The inode pointer for the current directory is in the user structure.)

2. Use the information in the inode for the current directory in order to fetch and search the current directory for the name '..' and retrieve its inode number.

3. Fetch the inode for '..'.

4. Use the information in the '..' inode in order to fetch and search the parent directory for the file 'a' and retrieve its inode number.

5. Fetch the inode for 'a'.

6. Use the information in the 'a' inode in order to fetch and search the 'a' directory for the file named 'b' and retrieve its inode number.

7. Fetch the inode for 'b'.

8. Access the file 'b'.

This is a lot of work just to fetch a file (see Figure 19.6.). In a flat file system the search for a file is much easier; this extra work by the UNIX System kernel is the price we pay for a hierarchical file system. Following pathnames is a relatively rare event; accessing the files that have already been located is much more common.

Thus far in our discussion of the file system we have been describing the structures that are stored on a disk in order to create the file system structure. These elements are the superblock, the inodes, the directory files, and the ordinary and special files. These elements can be manipulated by the kernel in the ordinary course of operation or they can be manipulated by programs such as fsck and fsdb while the file system is being repaired. Let's now conclude our discussion of the file system with a look at the structures that are maintained in memory by the kernel in order to access the file system (see Figure 19.7).

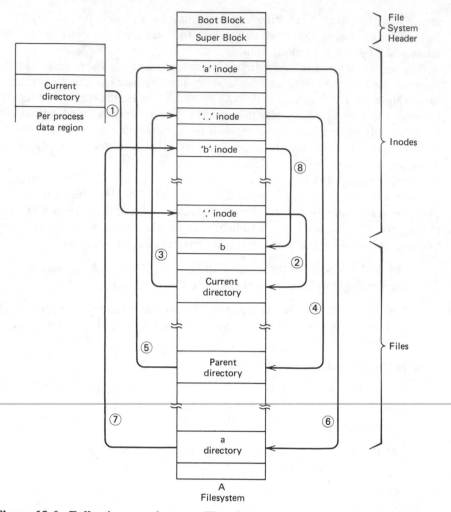

Figure 19.6. Following a pathname. The eight steps (see text) in following the pathname '../a/b'.

We have already mentioned two of the structures the kernel keeps in memory: the superblock of each mounted file system and a table of inodes. The superblock is kept in memory because it contains several key parameters for the file system including most notably the location of the list of free blocks. Each entry in the core inode table contains the key information for accessing a file including the mode of the file and the location of the blocks in the file.

There is one remaining table that the kernel keeps in memory for accessing files – the file table. Each entry in the file table contains a pointer to a particular entry in the inode table and it contains the read/write pointer for the file. The per-user data area for each process contains pointers into the file table for each

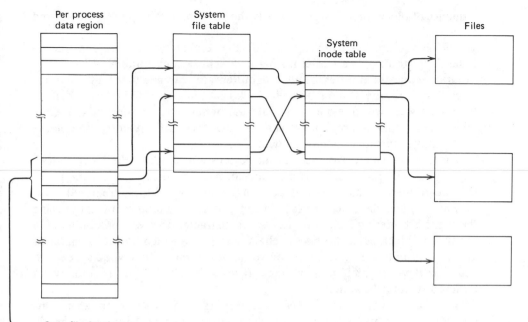

Open file descripters

Figure 19.7. The kernel's data structures for accessing files.

open file and the file table points at the inode table and the inode table actually points at the file.

This seems rather complicated; you might think that the per process data area would contain pointers directly into the inode table. Holding the read/write pointer for the file is the real reason for the file table. When a process with open files forks, the two subsequent processes share a single read/write pointer (stored in the file table) into the file. For example, this feature often is used in the shell. Whenever the shell runs a program it forks, execs the new process, and then waits for the termination of the new process. Meanwhile the new process reads from the standard input and writes to the standard output. The fact that the shell and the child process share the read/write pointers to the standard input and output causes the read/write pointer to be positioned correctly when the shell regains control.

19.7 Peripheral Devices

A peripheral device is a unit that is attached to a computer, usually for performing input or output (or both). Disks, tapes, communication lines, card readers, and printers are typical peripherals. The UNIX System includes two strategies for managing I/O peripherals: the block I/O system and the character I/O system. The block model usually is used for devices that can be addressed as a sequence of blocks of 512 bytes. Usually the block model is applied to disks and tapes.

The point of the block model is to allow the kernel to use buffering in order to reduce I/O traffic. The kernel maintains a set of block buffers. Whenever a program requests a transfer the internal buffers are searched to see if the block is already in memory. If the requested block is not in one of the internal buffers, then the system will free one of the internal buffers and transfer the requested block between the internal buffer and the I/O device. Frequently used blocks tend to stay in memory, thereby reducing I/O traffic.

The character model is used for all devices that don't fit the block model. Usually the character model is used for communication lines, printers, paper tapes, card readers, and so on. Most devices that have a block structured interface also have a character interface in order to access the device without using the kernel's buffering facilities. Accesses to character devices aren't buffered in the systems block pool. Accesses to character devices which transfer a character at a time usually are buffered by the kernel in character lists while accesses to character devices which transfer chunks (usually blocks) of data are usually not buffered at all by the kernel.

There are two major difficulties in developing the I/O portion of an operating system. The first difficulty is the fact that each peripheral requires slightly different management techniques. All of these different techniques need to be programmed into the operating system. The second problem is the fact that the peripherals of most computers are constantly being rearranged. The operating system needs to be modified each time a peripheral device is added or deleted. These two problems are solved in the UNIX System by using individual software modules to control each different type of peripheral and using a set of tables to logically connect the kernel to different device drivers. A more detailed discussion of these techniques is given in the remainder of this section.

A set of subroutines that works within the operating system to supervise the transmission of data between the computer and a particular type of peripheral device is called a driver. The UNIX System is distributed with the drivers for a dozen or so of the more common peripherals. Dozens of other drivers for the more unusual peripherals are available within the UNIX System network.

Getting the correct drivers incorporated into the operating system is the major operation during a system configuration. Operating systems utilize many different approaches to the problem of reconfiguration. The UNIX System kernel is reconfigured by modifying several key program modules and then recompiling. The UNIX System uses two tables, bdevsw and cdevsw, to control the I/O configuration process. These tables usually are contained in a C language source program file named 'conf.c'.

In recent versions of the UNIX System there is a program called config which will automatically create a 'conf.c' file for any given hardware configuration. In earlier versions of the UNIX System the file 'conf.c' has to be modified manually. Besides the bdevsw and cdevsw tables, 'conf.c' usually contains several parameters which control various resources such as the number of the kernel's internal buffers, the size of the swap space, and the lengths of some of the kernel's internal tables.

The heart of the 'conf.c' file is a pair of structures, bdevsw and cdevsw. These two structures are the key to the ability of the UNIX System kernel to adapt easily to different hardware configurations by installing different driver modules.

Let's first examine cdevsw. The cdevsw table is the linkage between the driver modules for the character oriented I/O devices and the UNIX System kernel. Each entry in the table is used to logically connect the system to the drivers associated with a specific major device number. The zeroeth entry in the cdevsw table is for the character I/O device with major device number zero, the next entry is for the character I/O device with major device number one, and so on. This is the table that you must examine when you are creating special device files using the mknod command.

Each entry in the cdevsw table defines the addresses of the driver routines for opening, closing, reading, writing, and controlling the transmission mode for a particular device. The open and close routines perform any special processing that is required before and after data transfers. For example, the open on a telephone communication line might wait for the line to ring and then answer before completing; the close routine on the same line would probably hang up the line. The read and write routines are called from within the kernel to transfer data to and from the device. The read and write routines usually are used in conjunction with interrupt service routines which actually supervise the data transmission. The transmission mode routine is used on communication line devices to adapt the a channel to a particular terminal or line protocol. The transmission mode routine is not used for character devices which aren't sending characters to computer terminals.

The UNIX System drivers are designed so that one driver program can service the requirements of several copies of the associated hardware. For example, on the PDP-11 computer an interface called a KL11 is used to transmit characters to a single terminal. Only one KL11 driver program is needed even if a computer contains several KL11 hardware interfaces. To differentiate between the interfaces the driver routines are passed a number, called the minor device number, which indicates the interface to be used. The interpretation of the minor device number is left to the discretion of the individual drive module. On drivers such as the KL11 driver the minor device number indicates which KL11. Other UNIX System drivers use the minor device number for other purposes. An example is the magtape driver, which uses different minor device numbers to indicate the recording density or whether the tape should be rewound when it is closed.

The names of the driver routines usually start with a standard two character prefix which is a clue to the associated hardware interface. For example, the driver routines for the Digital Equipment Corporation DL11 serial line inter-

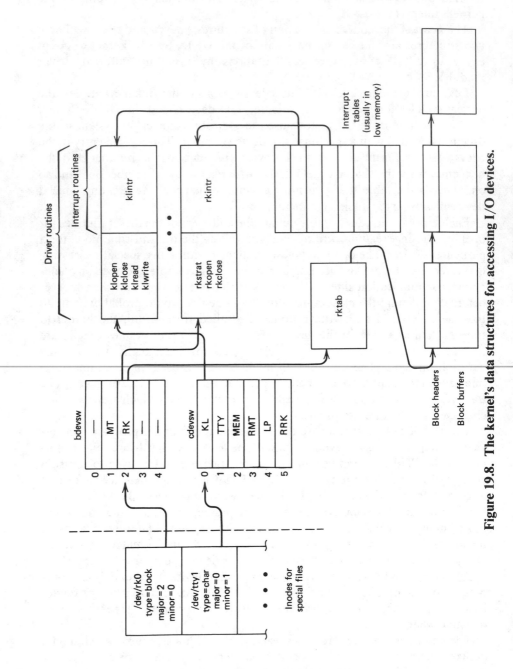

Figure 19.8. The kernel's data structures for accessing I/O devices.

face use the prefix "kl" (because the interfaces formerly were called KL11). The line in the cdevsw table defining the kernel interface to the kl driver is

```
/*0*/ &klopen, &klclose, &klread, &klwrite, &klsgtty,
```

(The ampersand is the C programming language notation for the address of an object.)

Drivers frequently omit certain routines because the associated device doesn't require the operation or doesn't allow the operation. For example, there is no need for a special operation to open or close the UNIX System's memory device and it is obviously impossible to control the transmission characteristics of the memory device since it is not a communication line. When routines are absent from a driver the special routines nulldev or nodev are referenced in the cdevsw table. The nulldev routine is used when a certain operation is not required and the nodev routine used when a certain operation is logically impossible and hence an error. The entry in the cdevsw table for the interface to physical memory is

```
/*8*/ &nulldev, &nulldev, &mmread, &mmwrite, &nodev,
```

This entry indicates that no operation is performed when the memory device is opened or closed and it is an error to attempt to control the transmission mode of the memory device.

The bdevsw table in the 'conf.c' file is used to connect the I/O routines for block devices to the UNIX System kernel. Each entry in the table contains the address of open and close routines, the address of a strategy routine, and the address of a device table. The open and close routines perform any processing that is necessary when the device is first opened and they are often unused (nulldev). The strategy routine is called to perform block reads and writes. The reason that a single routine is called is that the overall access time can be optimized on disks and tapes by arranging the order in which blocks are fetched.

The device table is the central point in performing I/O to block devices. The device table contains pointers to the buffers for the device. Performing an access to a block I/O device occurs in two stages. In the first stage a buffer is allocated and the header of the block is initialized. The header contains the block number on the device as well as several flags and pointers to other headers and a pointer to the actual buffer. The second stage consists of the physical transfer of data between the buffer and the device. The order of the transfers between the buffers and the device may not be the order in which the requests were issued because of the strategy considerations mentioned above.

Many of the peripheral devices that are attached to UNIX Systems use interrupt techniques for transferring data. A hardware interrupt is an electrical signal that causes the processor to stop whatever it is doing and go to an interrupt service routine. The interrupt service routine usually tends to the immediate needs of the peripheral device and then returns control to the interrupted program. Character-oriented devices often interrupt once per character, or occasionally once per line or once per block of data; block-oriented devices usually interrupt once per block of data.

An interrupt handler is the part of a device driver that actually supervises the transmission of data to and from interrupt driven peripherals. These routines are activated when the I/O interface hardware generates an interrupt. In PDP-11 computer systems the addresses of the interrupt service programs must be stored in low memory at specified locations. The address locations are determined by options that are enabled on the actual interface circuit card. Different computers use different techniques for associating specific interrupt handler routines with interrupts from specific classes of I/O devices. Since the PDP-11 stores the addresses in low memory, the UNIX System on PDP-11 computers uses an assembly language file called 'low.s' that specifies the locations of the interrupt service routines.

Abridged UNIX System Manual

This Abridged UNIX System Manual contains citations for the 40 most popular utility programs:

at	file	mv	sort
cat	find	nice	spell
cd	grep	nohup	stty
chmod	kill	od	tail
chown, chgrp	ln	passwd	tee
cp	lpr	pr	time
crypt	ls	ps	tty
date	man	pwd	wc
diff	mail	rm	who
echo	mkdir	rmdir	write

Many UNIX System commands are modified locally in order to provide enchancements; see your local manual for more details. When there are discrepancies between the usage cited here and the usage in your local manual you should probably assume that your local manual is more accurate. A few commands exist in several versions, usually one version used within the Bell System and another version used outside of the system. In all of these cases the external release is described here and a note is placed at the bottom of the citation.

This manual follows the format established by the original UNIX System manuals. In the command synopses, square brackets surround optional command line arguments and ellipses (...) follow arguments that may be repeated. Examples are given for each command. Early examples usually demonstrate the normal use of the command while later examples show the full capabilities of the program.

AT

NAME
at — run shell programs later

SYNOPSIS
at time [date] [file]

DESCRIPTION
The at program is used to execute shell programs sometime in the future. At makes a copy of the file (or of the standard input if no file is mentioned) and then arranges to have the file executed when the time occurs. When the shell program is executed, it will be executed in your current directory with all of the environment variables set to their values when you run the at command. Thus when the command is actually executed the environment will be the same as your environment when you execute the at command.

The time argument to the at command consists of one to four digits optionally followed by an "a" for AM, a "p" for PM, an "n" for noon, or an "m" for midnight. If the time argument is either one or two digits, then the number is assumed to represent hours; if there are three or four digits, then hours and minutes are assumed. If none of the letters follow the digits, then the 24 hour clock is assumed.

The optional date argument takes on one of two forms: a month name followed by a day number or a day of the week. A day of the week may be followed by the word "week", in which case the command will be run a week later than the mentioned day. You can abbreviate the month names or the day names.

EXAMPLES
Run the shell program 'nroffbk.sh' at 2AM on Tuesday:

        at 2 tues nroffbk.sh

Run the shell program 'cmds.sh' on January 2 at 3PM:

        at 3p jan 2 cmds.sh

or equivalently

        at 15 jan 2 cmds.sh

Run the shell program 'cmds.sh' a week from Friday at midnight:

        at 12m fri week cmds.sh

NOTE
If you want to reduce system loading it is better to use at to run large programs during the wee hours of the morning rather than using nice during peak periods to run the programs at reduced priority.

CAT

NAME
cat — concatenate and print files

SYNOPSIS
cat [-u] file ...

DESCRIPTION
The cat program is used for two purposes: printing files on your terminal and combining (concatenating) several files into one using output redirection. The option "-u" is used to suppress the normal block buffering performed by cat.

When you use cat to concatenate files, it is unwise for the output file to be the same as an input file. That is, the commands "cat a b > a" and "cat a b > b" are not likely to work as you would like.

EXAMPLES
Print the 'ch3' file on your terminal:

    cat ch3

Print several files on your terminal:

    cat ch1 ch2 ch3 ch4

Combine several files into the file 'ch1-4':

    cat ch1 ch2 ch3 ch4 > ch1-4

Create an empty file named 'file.new':

    cat /dev/null > file.new

CD

NAME
cd — move to a new working directory

SYNOPSIS
cd [directory]

DESCRIPTION
The cd command is used to move from one directory to another.

EXAMPLES

Move to the '/usr/bin' directory:

    cd /usr/bin

Move to the parent directory of the current directory:

    cd ..

Return to your home directory:

    cd

NOTE

On older systems the cd command is called chdir. The chdir command always requires a directory name argument as it does not recall the name of your home directory.

CHMOD

NAME

chmod — change the access mode of a file

SYNOPSIS

chmod mode file ...

DESCRIPTION

The chmod command is used to change the access mode of files and directories. As discussed in Section 6.5, there are three types of access to a file (read, write, and execute) and three categories of user (the file's owner, the file's group, and all others).

The symbolic mode is usually composed of three parts:

    who op permission.

The following table lists the various codes used to construct the symbolic mode:

Who		Operators	
u	user (owner)	-	remove permission
g	group	+	add permission
o	other	=	assign permission
a	all (ugo)		

Permissions

r	read
w	write
x	execute
s	set user (or group) id mode
t	the save text (sticky) mode
u	the user's present permission
g	the group's present permission
o	the other's present permission

Only the owner of a file or the superuser may change the mode of a file. The set user and group id modes and the save text modes are generally used by the system manager or systems programmers and they won't be discussed here.

Modes may also be specified absolutely by mentioning an octal number in place of the symbolic mode. The absolute form of mode expression is not discussed here; see your UNIX System manual.

EXAMPLES

Make the file 'arli' readable to everybody:

    chmod a + r arli

or, because "a" is the default who part of the symbolic mode, equivalently:

    chmod + r arli

Make the group and other permissions for the file 'britt' the same as the owner's current permissions:

    chmod go = u britt

Make the file 'newsysdb' unreadable and unwriteable by anyone but the owner:

    chmod go-rw newsysdb

Make the file 'ptime' and the file 'qtime' readable and writeable but not executable to everybody:

    chmod a = rw ptime qtime

Make the file 'chbeau.sh' executable:

    chmod + x chbeau.sh

Make it impossible for anyone to create files in the current directory:

    chmod a-w .

CHOWN, CHGRP

NAME

chown, chgrp — change the ownership and group affiliation of a file

SYNOPSIS

chown newowner file ...

chgrp newgroup file ...

DESCRIPTION

The chown and chgrp commands are used to change the owner and group affiliation of files. You might need to do this when you are inheriting files from another user, changing your login name, or transferring files from one system to another.

User names usually are found in the file '/etc/passwd' while group names usually are cataloged in the file '/etc/group'.

EXAMPLES

Change the ownership of the file 'nycal' to the user named "ralph":

```
chown  ralph  nycal
```

Change the ownership of all of the files with the suffix ".n" to the user name "george":

```
chown  george  *.n
```

Change the group affiliation of all of the files whose name starts with the letters "ch" to the group named "elecmicro":

```
chgrp  elecmicro  ch*
```

CP

NAME

cp — copy files

SYNOPSIS

cp file1 file2

cp file ... directory

DESCRIPTION

In its simplest form cp makes a copy of 'file1' using the name 'file2'; 'file1' is not affected by the copy operation. If 'file2' already exists, its mode and ownership are unchanged; otherwise its mode and ownership are copied from 'file1'.

In the second form shown in the Synopsis cp copies the file or files into the named directory while maintaining their original file names.

EXAMPLES

Make a copy of the file 'nuk.abm' in the file 'nk.2':

```
cp  nuk.abm  nk.2
```

Copy all of the files in the 'disarm' subdirectory into the subdirectory 'newlit':

```
cp  disarm/*  newlit
```

Copy all of the files with the suffix '.doc' in the current directory into the 'disarm' subdirectory:

```
cp  *.doc  disarm
```

CRYPT

NAME

crypt — encrypt files

SYNOPSIS

crypt [password]

DESCRIPTION

The crypt program encrypts files in order to ensure privacy. Protecting files with the access privilege system (see chmod) ensures a degree of privacy in the UNIX System. However, encrypted files are considerably more secure than access protected files. The encryption mechanism is governed by a password. The same password is used to encrypt a file or to decrypt an already encrypted file. If the password is not supplied on the command line, then the crypt program will prompt you for the password and turn off echoing while you enter the password. Crypt reads from the standard input and writes to the standard output.

EXAMPLES

Encode the file 'salaryhist', place the encoded version in 'salh.enc', and remove the original file:

```
crypt abracadid  <  salaryhist  >  salh.enc ;  rm  salaryhist
```

Print the original form (the clear version) of 'salh.enc' on the terminal:

```
crypt abracadid  <  salh.enc
```

Recover the clear form of 'salh.enc' and place it in the file 'salaryhist':

    crypt abracadid < salh.enc > salaryhist

In all of these examples the password is supplied on the command line. Alternatively, the password could have been omitted from the command line and crypt would have prompted for it.

DATE

NAME
date - print and set the date and time

SYNOPSIS
date [mmddhhmm[yy]]

DESCRIPTION
The date command generally is used to display the date and time. The superuser is also able to set the date and time using the optional argument. The argument lists the month (01-12), the day of the month (01-31), the hour (00-23), the minutes (00-59), and optionally the last two digits of the year.

EXAMPLES
Display the date:

    date

Set the date to January 21, 1980 at 9:15 AM.

    date 0121091580

NOTE
You must have superuser privilege to set the data.

DIFF

NAME
diff — report differences between text files

SYNOPSIS
diff [-efbh] file1 file2

DESCRIPTION

The diff program is used to compare two files. Diff can be used in a pipeline by using the special name "-" in place of one of the filenames. If the two files are different, then diff usually prints a line which resembles an editor command (to indicate which lines are different) followed by the affected lines from both files.

The following three types of editor pseudo commands are printed by diff:

n1 a n3, n4

> File1 is missing some of the lines that exist in file2. The difference will vanish if lines n3 through n4 from file2 are placed in file1 after line n1 of file1.

n1, n2 d n3

> File1 has some lines which are missing from file2. The differen ce will vanish if lines n1 through n2 are deleted from file1. Alternatively, lines n1 through n2 from file1 can be added after line n3 of of file2.

n1, n2, c n3, n4

> File1 and file 2 have a region that is different. The difference will vanish if lines n1 through n2 of file 1 are changed to lines n3 through n4 of file2 (or vice versa).

For all three types of pseudo command, if n1 equals n2 (or if n3 equals n4) then only one number will be printed. Following the pseudo command the affected lines from the files are printed. Lines from file1 are flagged by placing a "<" at the beginning of each line while lines from file2 are flagged with a ">".

Diff accepts four options:

-e   Produce an editor script for the standard UNIX System editor which will recreate file2 from file1.

-f   Produce a similar script, but in the reverse order. The script produced by the -f option cannot be used by the standard UNIX System editor.

-h   Perform the comparison quickly and on files of unlimited size. Diff is not a good at resynchronizing using the -h option and options -e and -f are not available.

-b   Ignore differences between lines caused by blanks (spaces and tabs).

EXAMPLES

Compare the files 'notes.a' and 'notes.old':

    diff notes.a notes.old

Print an editor script so that 'notes.old' can be recreated from 'notes.a':

    diff -e notes.a notes.old

At some point in the past a file named 'lsfile' was created by executing the command "ls > lsfile". To determine if the directory still has the same contents as when 'lsfile' was created, we want to compare 'lsfile' with the current contents of the working directory:

    ls | diff - lsfile

ECHO

NAME
echo — repeat command line arguments

SYNOPSIS
echo [arguments]

DESCRIPTION
The echo command copies its command line arguments to the standard output. Echo is used for several purposes including printing messages in shell command files, inserting small amounts of known data into a pipe or file, displaying the values of shell variables, and finding out what the shell is doing with command line arguments.

EXAMPLES
Print the message "Hello" on the terminal:

    echo Hello

Place the message "Processing complete" in the file 'pmessage':

    echo Processing complete > pmessage

Display the value of the shell variable $PATH:

    echo $PATH

Problem. When you enter the command "expr \(5 + 7 \) * 3" you expect to see the result "36" but instead you encounter an indecipherable error message.
Solution. Use the echo command to see what arguments the expr command is actually receiving:

    echo \(5 + 7 \) * 3

The output will reveal the problem — the asterisk is expanded into a list of the files in the current directory because of the shell's file name generation process. You must escape the asterisk in order to pass it to the expr program.

FILE

NAME
file — guess the type of the named files

SYNOPSIS
file filename ...

DESCRIPTION
The file command attempts to determine the file type of the named files. For directory files and special files the file command is unnervingly accurate; for other types of files the file command resorts to educated guessing. For ordinary files that appear to contain ASCII text the file command attempts to determine the language; the results often are accurate. For ordinary files that contain binary information the file command attempts to determine if the file is an object file, a library, a cpio image file, or any other file. Files that don't fit any of these categories are usually classified as "data".

EXAMPLES
Determine the file types of all of the files in the current directory:

    file *

Determine the file types of all of the files in the '/usr/bin' directory:

    file /usr/bin/*

Determine the file type of the file named 'unk':

    file unk

FIND

NAME
find — search for files in a subtree

SYNOPSIS
find pathname ... condition ...

DESCRIPTION
The find command searches the file system subtrees specified by the command line pathnames for files that meet the specified conditions. At least one

pathname (often '.') and one condition must be specified. The condition is specified by mentioning one or more of the following:

-atime n
> Specify a file that has been accessed in n days.

-exec cmd
> Specify a command to be executed. The end of the command is indicated with an escaped semicolon. Within the command the argument "{}" is replaced by the current pathname.

-group groupname
> Specify the group affiliation of a file.

-links n
> Specify the number of links.

-mtime n
> Specify a file that has been modified in m days.

-name filename
> Specify a file name using the usual shell metacharacters. The metacharacters must be escaped in order for them to be passed to the find command.

-newer file
> Specifies that the examined files must be newer than the named file.

-ok cmd
> Same as exec except that cmd is printed preceded by a question mark and the operator is given the chance to approve by replying yes or no.

-print The current path name is printed.

-size n
> Specify the size of the file in blocks.

-type c
> Specify a file type: f for an ordinary file, d for a directory, c for a character special file, b for a block special file, and p for a pipe.

-user username
> Specify the owner of a file.

The conditions may be grouped by surrounding them in parentheses, and a condition may be negated using the exclamation point as a not operator.

In the conditions that require a numerical argument (-links, -size, -atime, and -mtime), a number preceded by a hyphen means less than n, a number preceded by a plus means more than n, and a number without a prefix means exactly n. Two conditions side by side are assumed to represent a logical and condition unless the logical or operator -o is used.

Combining a complicated set of conditions using find is more akin to writing a program than entering a command. Casual users (if there are any) should use just one condition at a time followed by -print to print the names of the found files or -exec (-ok) to perform some simple task when the files are found. Searching the entire file system is very time consuming on large systems — you should attempt to limit your searches to as small a subtree as possible.

EXAMPLES

Print a list of all of the files in the current subtree:

```
find . -print
```

The effect of the option -print can be simulated using the echo command:

```
find . -exec echo {} \ ;
```

Find all of John's files that are marooned in George's subtree:

```
find /usa/george -user john -print
```

Find all of the files in John's subtree that are owned by George or Rik:

```
find /usa/john \( -owner george -o -owner rik \) -print
```

Find all of the ordinary files in the entire file system with two or more links:

```
find / -type f -links +1 -print
```

Find all of the files in the file system that are more than 100 blocks long and print a long format listing for each:

```
find / -size +100 -exec ls -l {} \ ;
```

Find all of the files in the file system that haven't been accessed in the last 100 days:

```
find / -atime +100 -print
```

Find all of the special files in the '/usr' subtree or in the '/usr1' subtree:

```
find /usr /usr1 \( -type b -o -type c \) -print
```

Find all of the files in the current subtree with the ".c" suffix:

```
find . -name \ *.c -print
```

GREP

NAME

grep — search for patterns in files

SYNOPSIS
grep [options] expression [file ...]

DESCRIPTION
The grep program searches for text patterns in the named file, or in the standard input if no files are mentioned. The text patterns are indicated by the expression argument, which is a regular expression constructed similarly to regular expressions in the standard UNIX System editors.

Without options the grep program prints each line in the input that contains a text pattern that matches the expression. The options can be used to slightly alter this behavior:

-c Produce a count of lines rather than the lines themselves.

-e expression
  This is almost the same as a simple expression argument. However, since the expression is explicitly introduced with the "-e" option, leading hyphens in the expression are allowed. Normally expressions are constrained to start with some character other than hyphen.

-h When there are several input files the name of each file is usually printed before the matching lines from that file. The "-h" option removes the file names from the output.

-l List the names of the files that contain text patterns that match the expression.

-s Indicate the existence of matches using the exit status of grep. No output is produced. This option is useful for shell programmers.

-v Print lines that don't contain text that matches the expression rather than lines that do contain matching text.

-y Lower case letters in the expression will match upper case or lower case letters in the file.

-n Number the output lines.

EXAMPLES
Print all of the occurrences of the string "Nwords" in a set of files:

 grep Nwords chapt*

List the number of lines that contain the string "Nwords" in a set of files:

 grep -c Nwords chapt*

List all of the files that contain the string "artifact" in the current directory:

 grep -l artifact *

Print and number all of the lines containing the word "bcount" in the file 'rgb.c' or the file 'hsv.c':

 grep -n bcount rgb.c hsv.c

Print all of the lines that don't contain a hyphen in the file 'cmds.sh':

```
grep -v -e - cmds.sh
```

Determine whether any user is logged in on tty30:

```
who | grep tty30
```

<hr>

KILL

NAME
kill — terminate a process

SYNOPSIS
kill [-signalnumber] processid

DESCRIPTION
The kill command usually is used to terminate background processes. In order to terminate a process you need to know its process id number and you need to own the process or be the superuser. You can acquire the process id number for a process using the ps command or you can remember the number that is printed by the shell when you run a process in the background.

Kill usually sends signal number 15, the terminate signal, to the target process. Processes occasionally arrange to catch and ignore signals so it is possible for the specified process to receive the signal without terminating. Other signal numbers can be sent by supplying the signal number on the command line. One very useful signal number is 9, which is a form of the terminate signal that cannot be caught or ignored.

EXAMPLES
Kill process 1103:

```
kill 1103
```

Send signal number 3 (the quit signal) to process 1116. The quit signal will usually cause a termination with a core dump that can be used for debugging:

```
kill -3 1116
```

LN

NAME

ln — create a pseudonym for an existing file

SYNOPSIS

ln file1 [file2]

DESCRIPTION

The ln command is used to establish a new name (a pseudonym) for an existing file. The technical name for creating a pseudonym is linking, hence the name ln for link. If both 'file1' and 'file2' appear in the command, then 'file2' becomes a new name for 'file1'. If 'file2' is not mentioned in the command line, then the pseudonym is created in the current directory with the same name as the last component of the pathname referencing 'file1'.

When a file is known by two (or more) names, both names have equal weight. Even though there are several names, there is only one copy of the data in the file.

EXAMPLES

Create the pseudonym 'softrev' for the file 'techrpt302':

    ln techrpt302 softrev

Create the pseudonym 'mkjuice' in the current directory for the file 'mkjuice' in a distant directory:

    ln ../fruit/tropical/mkjuice

LPR

NAME

lpr — print files

SYNOPSIS

lpr [option] [file ...]

DESCRIPTION

The lpr program is used to print files on the lineprinter. Since the lineprinter cannot be simultaneously shared between several users, the lpr program queues the print requests and arranges for one file to be printed at a time. If there are no files mentioned in the command line then lpr reads the text to be printed from the standard input. Thus lpr can be used as the final stage in a pipeline.

Lpr does not alter the text to be printed in any way; if you want a file to be paginated or titled, you should use the pr command to preprocess the text before handing it to lpr.

On systems with several lineprinters there are usually several versions of lpr, one for each printer. The various versions are often given names similar to lpr: npr, dpr, vpr, ppr, and so on.

The following options are available:

-c   Copy the file immediately to guard against changes that may occur before printing.

-m   Send mail when the printing is complete.

-n   Do not send mail when printing is complete. This is the default condition.

-r   Remove the file when it has been queued for printing.

EXAMPLES

Print 'mydoc' on the lineprinter:

    lpr mydoc

Print a titled version of 'mydoc' on the lineprinter and report the completion by electronic mail:

    pr mydoc | lpr -m

LS

NAME

ls — list the contents of directories

SYNOPSIS

ls [-ltasdriu] [name ...]

DESCRIPTION

The ls command is used to list the files in directories and to list information about files. The options can be used to control the information printed for each file and to control the order of the list. The names can be either the names of directories or the names of files. For each named file the requested information is printed if the file exists. If the file doesn't exist then a brief message is printed. For each named directory the requested information is printed for each file in the directory. If there are no names, then the requested information is printed for the files in the current directory. Thus the command

    ls

is equivalent to the command

    ls .

The list of files is usually ordered alphabetically. Files whose name begins with a period usually aren't listed. The following options can be used to alter this behavior:

-l   Produce a long format listing (see Chapter 7).

-t   Sort the list of files according to the file modification dates rather than alphabetically.

-a   List all files in named directories, including files whose names begin with a period.

-s   Print the sizes of the files in blocks.

-d   For each named directory, list the information for the directory file itself rather than listing the information for each file in the directory.

-r   Reverse the order of the output.

-i   List the i number of each file.

-u   Use the access time rather than the modification time for sorting or output in the long format display.

EXAMPLES

List the files in the current directory:

    ls

List the files in the '/etc' directory:

    ls /etc

See if the file '/usa/bill/kill' exists:

    ls /usa/bill/kill

List the size in blocks of the file '/etc/passwd':

    ls -s /etc/passwd

List the inode number of the file '/etc/passwd':

    ls -i /etc/passwd

List all of the entries, including the entries whose name begins with a period, of the files in the current directory:

    ls -a

List the files in the '/bin' directory according to modification time with the most recently modified files listed first:

    ls -t /bin

List the files in the current directory whose names end in ".doc" with the oldest (least recently modified) files listed first:

    ls -rt *.doc

List the files in the current directory whose names end in ".doc" with the most recently accessed listed first:

    ls -u *.doc

List all of the files in the current directory whose names begin with "chapt" in reverse alphabetic order:

    ls -r chapt*

List in long format all of the files in the parent directory.

    ls -l ..

List in long format the parent directory. The "-d" option is used to force the listing of the directory itself and to suppress the listing of individual files in the directory.

    ls -ld ..

NOTE
Many installations have augmented their ls commands with several additional options. See your local UNIX System manual for more details.

MAN

NAME
    man — print entries from the UNIX System manual

SYNOPSIS
    man [option] [section] title

DESCRIPTION
    The man command is used to locate and print citations from the UNIX System manual. It is used primarily by users to produce manual sections when needed as a quick reference when a printed manual is unavailable. The system administrator uses man to produce printed copies of the manual for dis-

tribution to the user community. A regular printed manual is more convenient but less up-to-date than repeated use of the man command.

The man command recognizes several options:

-t   Produce output using the troff formatter suitable for phototypesetting.

-n   Produce output using the nroff formatter on the standard output.

-e   Use eqn (or neqn when the -n flag is present) as an additional text preprocessor.

-w   Print the pathnames of the manual entry but don't print the entry.

The section argument specifies which section in the manual to search for the entry. Manual entries describing the commands are in section 1. If the section argument is omitted, then the all eight sections of the manual are searched.

EXAMPLES

Print the manual entry for the ls command:

```
man -n ls
```

Print the manual entry for kill:

```
man -n kill
```

Two citations will appear for the above command: one citation for the kill command in section 1 of the UNIX System manual and one citation for the kill system call in section 2 of the UNIX System manual. If you only want the citation for the kill command enter the command

```
man -n 1 kill
```

Print the pathnames for the kill citations:

```
man -d kill
```

NOTE

The man command commonly used within the Bell System uses options different from the man command described above, which is usually used outside the Bell System.

MAIL

NAME

mail — send mail to users or read your own mail

SYNOPSIS
    mail username ...
    mail [-rpq] [-f mailfile]

DESCRIPTION
When usernames are mentioned as arguments to the mail command then mail is sent to the named users (the first command in Synopsis, above). In all other cases the mail command is used to read your own mail.

Let's first discuss sending mail to other users. Mail acquires the message from the standard input. You may prepare the message in advance using a text editor and use the input redirection capabilities of the shell, or you can type the message interactively and then strike Control-D (EOF) to terminate input. If the named users cannot be located (i.e., you probably mistyped the username), then the message is saved in the file 'dead.letter' to allow you to determine the correct user name and then retransmit the message.

The mail command works differently when you use it to read your mail. When you log in the shell will inform you of the presence of mail by printing the message "You have mail". Mail accepts four command line options to help you read your mail:

-f filename
    This option specifies that the named file is the source of the mail; ordinarily the file is in the '/usr/mail' directory.

-p   Print all of the messages without pausing; ordinarily the messages are printed one at a time and you are prompted between messages for a disposition command.

-q   Ordinarily an interrupt merely causes mail to stop printing the current message. However, when the "-q" option is used the program will terminate when an interrupt is received.

-r   Print the oldest messages first; ordinarily the newest messages are printed first.

Mail ordinarily stops after printing each message and waits for you to enter a disposition command. The following disposition commands are recognized:

<newline> or +
    Print the next message.

d   Delete the message.

m usernames
    Forward (mail) the message to the named users.

p   Print message again.

s [file]   Save message in the named file ('mbox' is used by default). A header will be placed in front of the message to identify the message.

w [file]   Save the message in the named file omitting the header.

-       Go back to previous message.

<Control-d> or q
> Place undeleted mail back in mailbox and exit.

? Print a help message. (Some installations use the asterisk in place of the question mark to produce a help message.)

You can usually read your mail without using any of the command line options and only using the <newline> and the "d" dispositions.

EXAMPLES
Send Tom, Dick and Barry the message in 'msgfile':

    mail tom dick barry < msgfile

Read your mail:

    mail

Enter "d" to delete a message and strike return to type the next message.

MKDIR

NAME
mkdir — create a directory

SYNOPSIS
mkdir dirname ...

DESCRIPTION
The mkdir command is used to create directories. You must have write permission in the parent directory in order to create a directory.

The entries '.' and '..' are automatically installed in directories when they are created.

EXAMPLES
Create a subdirectory named 'newsub':

    mkdir newsub

Create a directory named '/usa/kc/games/numoo':

    mkdir /usa/kc/games/numoo

MV

NAME
mv — move and rename files

SYNOPSIS
mv file1 file2
mv file ... directory

DESCRIPTION
The mv command is used to manage files. In its simplest form the mv command changes the name of a file. Mv can also be used to move a file (or a group of files) from one directory to another. Movements within a file system are actually sophisticated renaming operations; movements from one file system to another involve an actual transfer of data.

In the first form of the mv command, 'file1' is renamed 'file2'. In the second form of the mv command, the named files are moved into the named directory. The files retain their original names.

If 'file2' already exists and is write protected, mv will print the access mode of the file and read a line from the standard input. A "y" will cause the operation to proceed while "n" (or anything else) will halt the movement. If 'file2' already exists and is not write protected, mv will replace it with 'file1'.

EXAMPLES
Rename the file 'newdb' to 'olddb':

    mv newdb olddb

Move the file named 'rjstat' from the current directory into the 'rjefiles' subdirectory:

    mv rjstat rjefiles

Move the file named 'ddstat' into the 'rjefiles' subdirectory under the new name 'xddstat':

    mv ddstat rjefiles/xddstat

Move all of the files in the 'rjefiles' subdirectory into the 'oldrje' subdirectory of the parent directory:

    mv rjefiles/* ../oldrje

NICE

NAME
nice — run a command at reduced priority

SYNOPSIS
nice [-increment] command [arguments]

DESCRIPTION
The nice command is used to reduce the priority of a process in order to reduce the demands that the process places on the system. Nice typically is used with time consuming background processes in order to keep them from degrading system performance.

The optional increment argument is used to specify the amount of priority reduction. The lowest priority attainable in the UNIX System is achieved with an increment of 19 and a barely perceptible decrease in priority is achieved with an increment of 1. If no increment is specified, then a default of 10 is assumed.

While ordinary users can only decrease the priority of their process, the superuser can run jobs at increased priority by specifying a negative increment.

EXAMPLES
Run a process called 'bigjob' in the background at low priority:

    nice bigjob &

Run 'bigjob' at the minimum priority:

    nice -19 bigjob

Run a process called 'importjob' at maximum priority:

    nice --19 importjob

Note that you must be superuser to specify a negative increment (-19 in this case).

NOTE
All UNIX System processes compete for resources, even when they are scheduled at low priority. Running processes at slack periods (see the at command) is a more effective way to reduce system load than running processes at low priority during peak periods.

NOHUP

NAME
nohup — run a program that is immune to hangups

SYNOPSIS
nohup command [arguments]

DESCRIPTION
Normally any commands that you have started in the background will be sent the hangup signal when you log off the system. Most programs exit when they receive the hangup signal. The nohup command is used to initialize processes so that they ignore the hangup and quit signals. Thus any commands you run in the background using nohup will not die when you log off of the system.

Nohup will direct the standard output to the file 'nohup.out' unless you use output redirection to specify some other disk file. Commands run using nohup should not need to interact with a terminal.

EXAMPLES
Nroff a file in the background using nohup so that you can log off while the processing is being performed:

```
nohup nroff -ms chapt?.n > chaps.nr &
```

OD

NAME
od — dump a file

SYNOPSIS
od [format] [file] [offset]

DESCRIPTION
The od (octal dump) program is used to produce a dump of the named file (or the standard input if no file is specified). The format argument allows you to control whether the file is dumped in octal words (the default), octal bytes, ASCII bytes, hexadecimal words, or decimal words. The file is normally dumped starting at the beginning unless an offset is supplied.

The following format control arguments are recognized:

-b   Interpret bytes in octal.

-c   Interpret bytes in ASCII.

-d   Interpret words in decimal.

-o   Interpret words in octal.

-x   Interpret words in hexadecimal.

When bytes are interpreted in ASCII the following escapes are used to represent certain common nongraphic characters:

\0   null

\b   backspace

\f   formfeed

\n   newline

\r   carriage return

\t   tab

During ASCII interpretation, bytes that are nongraphic and not listed in the above table are represented using three-digit octal numbers.

The offset is used to control the distance from the beginning of the file where the dumping starts. If no file is mentioned, the offset must start with a plus sign. Otherwise the offset can start with an ordinary number. The offset is interpreted as an octal number unless a period is attached to the end. Thus the offset "10" is interpreted as decimal 8 while the offset "10." is interpreted as decimal 10. If the offset is suffixed with a "b" then the number is taken to mean blocks of 512 bytes, otherwise the offset is in bytes. Thus the offset 20 is interpreted as decimal 16 bytes while the offset 20b is interpreted as decimal 16 blocks.

EXAMPLES

Dump the file 'a.out' in octal word format:

    od a.out

or equivalently:

    od -o a.out

Dump the file 'a.out' in octal byte format:

    od -b a.out

Dump the file 'a.out' in hexadecimal word format starting at block 10 (in decimal):

    od -x a.out 10.b

or equivalently:

> od -x a.out 12b

Dump the file 'a.out' in decimal format starting at the sixteenth byte:

> od -d a.out 16.

PASSWD

NAME
passwd — change your login password

SYNOPSIS
passwd [name]

DESCRIPTION
The passwd command is used by ordinary users to change their own login passwords and by the superuser to change the passwords of ordinary users. When invoked by an ordinary user, the program prompts for the old password to verify that the authorized user is actually changing the password, then the program prompts for the new password, and then the program prompts again for the new password to make sure that the password was entered correctly. Echoing is suppressed during the password entry to improve security.

The superuser uses passwd to install a password while creating an account. Also on some systems the administrator periodically changes user passwords to improve security. An encoded version of all passwords is kept in the file '/etc/passwd'.

EXAMPLES
Change your own login password:

> passwd

PR

NAME
pr — paginate, title, and format files

SYNOPSIS

pr [option] [file ...]

DESCRIPTION

The pr command is usually used to prepare files for printing. Pr paginates files, supplies headings, partitions a file into columns, and adjusts for varying page lengths or widths. If none of the options are specified, then pr produces single column output, 66 lines per page, with a short header and a short trailer, of the named files or of the standard input if no files are named. The standard header contains the date, the name of the file, and the page number. If the output of pr is a terminal, then messages are suspended during output.

The following options can be used to adjust the format of the file.

-h   Use the following argument in the header in place of the file name.

-ln   Produce pages that are n lines long. The default is 66 lines.

-m   Print all files simultaneously, one file in each column.

-n   Produce n column output. The default is single column output.

+n   Begin output starting at page n. The default is to start at page 1.

-sc   In multiple column output, separate the columns with the character c (usually a tab character) rather than with the appropriate amount of white space. If c is missing, a tab is assumed.

-t   Do not produce the header or the trailer.

-wn   During multiple column output, use the number n for the page width rather than the default of 72.

EXAMPLES

Print a file in the conventional format on the lineprinter:

    pr myfile | lpr

Columnate the output of the ls program (headers are removed to make output to the terminal less likely to scroll out of view):

    ls | pr -6t

Print 'myfile' starting at page 10 and place the output in the file 'myfile.end':

    pr +10 myfile > myfile.end

NOTE

Many systems have augmented the pr command to provide several additional options.

PS

NAME
ps — print the status information for processes

SYNOPSIS
ps [options] processid

DESCRIPTION
The ps command is used to print information about the active processes. Ps does for processes what ls does for files. Without options the ps command prints the following information for all your personal processes: the controlling tty name, the process number, the cumulative execution time, and an approximation of the command line. The following options can be used to modify the action of the ps command:

-a   Print information about all processes with a controlling tty, not just your personal processes.

-k   Use information from the file '/usr/sys/core' for the examination. This option often is used by the system administrator following a crash — ordinary users don't usually need this feature of ps.

-l   Produce a long format listing. Most of the information presented in a long format ps listing is too technical to be of much use for ordinary users.

number If a process number is mentioned, then the information for that process is produced.

-x   Print information for processes that aren't associated with a controlling terminal.

EXAMPLES
Produce a list of the current processes:

ps

Produce a long format list of the information for the current processes:

ps -l

Produce a list of all of the processes on the system:

ps -ax

Print some information about process 3402:

ps 3402

NOTE
The UNIX System manual explains the format of the long listing for the ps command. Also note that the ps command commonly used in the Bell System uses different options than those described here for the ps command commonly used outside the Bell System.

PWD

NAME
pwd – print the name of the working directory
SYNOPSIS
pwd
DESCRIPTION
The pwd command prints the full path name of the current directory.
EXAMPLES
Print the name of the working directory:

    pwd

RM

NAME
rm – remove files
SYNOPSIS
rm [-fri] file ...
DESCRIPTION
The rm command is used to remove files. To remove a file, you must have write permission in the directory that contains the file but you do not need to have write permission for the file itself. If you don't have write permission for the file, rm will print the file mode and wait for you to enter "y" or "n" to indicate whether you really want to remove the file.

Three options are available:

-f   The force option removes files without regard to whether you have write permission on the file — the usual query for approval to remove write protected file does not occur.

-i   The interactive option causes rm to ask you whether you really want to remove each named file. Reply "y" or "n".

-r   The recursive option is used to remove an entire subtree of the file system. The file name argument should be the name of a directory; that directory and all of its files, subdirectories, and so on, will be removed. The "-i" option can be used with "-r" in order to make the recursive remove a bit more controlled.

EXAMPLES

Remove the file 'mydocs':

    rm mydocs

Remove several files:

    rm nicotine caffeine tar

Remove all of the files in the subdirectory 'xyresp':

    rm xyresp/*

Remove all of the files in the subdirectory 'xyresp' interactively:

    rm -i xyresp/*

Remove all of the files in the subdirectory 'zzresp' without querying for write protected files:

    rm -f zzresp/*

Remove the subtree headed by the '/usa/kc/nudocs' directory:

    rm -r /usa/kc/nudocs

RMDIR

NAME

rmdir — remove directories

SYNOPSIS

rmdir dirname ...

DESCRIPTION

The rmdir command removes empty directories. By definition, an empty directory is one that contains only two entries, '.' and '..'. In order to see a list of all of the files in a directory you should use the command

    ls -a dirname

If there are just the two entries, '.' and '..' then the directory is empty. To remove a directory you must have write permission for its parent directory.

EXAMPLES

Remove the '/usa/kc/games/numoo' directory:

    rmdir /usa/kc/games/numoo

Remove the 'sortsh' subdirectory:

    rmdir sortsh

SORT

NAME

sort — sort and/or merge files

SYNOPSIS

sort [-cmu] [-tc] [-bdfinr] [+pos1 [-pos 2]] ... \
    [-o outfile] [file ...]

DESCRIPTION

The sort program orders the lines of the input files and then writes the rear-ranged lines to the standard output or to the named output file if the "-o" option is used. Ordinarily the entire line is the sort key. However, if the position options are used, then the sort key is restricted to the indicated fields of the line. There can be several position options to indicate several sort keys; later keys are used only when the earlier keys compare as equal. As a last resort, lines that otherwise compare equal are ordered with all positions significant.

The following five options are used to control the general behavior of the sort program. (The six ordering options will be discussed shortly.)

-c   Check the input file to verify that it is sorted according to the rules. No output is produced unless the file is not properly sorted.

-m   Merge the input files. Presumably the input files are already sorted.

-o outfile   The output is written to the named file rather than to the standard output.

-tc   The character c is taken as the field separator. Blanks (spaces and tabs) are ordinarily used as the field separator.

-u   Suppress all but one in a set of equal lines. For the purposes of this option, equal lines are defined as lines that compare as equal within all of the active sort keys. Fields outside of the sort keys as well as ignored characters (see the "-b" and the "-i" options) do not participate in the judgment of equality.

If no positions are indicated, then the sort key is the entire line. By using the position indicator +pos1 a sort key can be constrained to start at the indicated position. The position indicator pos2 constrains a sort key to stop just before the indicated position. If -pos2 is missing, then the sort key stops at the end of the line. The position indicators have the form "m.n" where "m" indicates the number of fields to skip from the beginning of the line and "n" indicates the number of characters to skip further. The position indicator "+5.2" indicates that a sort key starts after skipping five fields and then the next two characters. The position indicator "-0.2" indicates that a sort key ends after skipping zero fields and then two characters. If the "n" part of a position indicator is missing, then zero is assumed.

There are six options for controlling the ordering of items. If these six options appear before any position indicators, then they are global options. The six ordering options also can be placed following the position indicators in order to change the default ordering for that particular field.

-b   Ignore leading spaces and tabs when making a field comparison.

-d   Enable dictionary-style ordering rather than the default ASCII collating sequence. Only letters, digits, and blanks are significant in field comparisons.

-f   Fold upper case letters into lower case letters for the purpose of field comparisons. In the output the original case is retained.

-i   Ignore characters outside of the ASCII range 040-0176 in non-numeric comparisons.

-n   Perform numeric comparisons. A number may have leading blanks, an optional minus sign, and zero or more digits with an optional decimal point. The ordering is according to the numeric value, not the dictionary ordering or the ASCII collating sequence.

-r   Order the items in decreasing order. Normally items are ordered in increasing order.

EXAMPLES
For the first few examples, assume that the file 'tdata' contains the following four words, each on a separate line: "apple", "Balloon", "apple", and

"Apple". We are using an example with duplicates because handling duplicates is one of the major problems in controlling the sorting process.

Sort 'tdata' and place the output in 'tdata.1':

```
sort -o tdata.1 tdata
```

The ordering produced will be "Apple", "Balloon", "apple", "apple" because in the ASCII sequence upper case letters precede lower case letters.

Sort 'tdata' without regard to capitalization:

```
sort -f tdata
```

The ordering produced is "Apple", "apple", "apple", "Balloon". The three apple words are ordered by the last resort rule; when lines compare as equal order them with every position on the line significant.

Sort 'tdata' and discard equal lines:

```
sort -u tdata
```

The ordering produced will be "Apple", "Balloon", "apple".

Sort 'tdata' without regard to capitalization and discard equal lines, producing the upper case line if both cases are present:

```
sort -f tdata | sort -muf
```

The first sort in the pipeline orders the lines into the ASCII collating sequence while the second sort in the pipeline merges the already sorted data, discarding the trailing duplicate lines. Merging never alters the order, hence merging with a single file allows one to predict what items will be discarded (the subsequent items) when the "-u" option is present. The ordering produced is "Apple", "Balloon".

Sort 'tdata' to produce all of the unique words. When a word is present in both the capitalized form and the lower case form, the capitalized word should follow the lower case word in the final list:

```
sort -u  + 0f  + 0r tdata
```

This is essentially a two pass sort because there are two sort keys, each key being the entire line. The ordering in the second key is used only to resolve entries that compare as equal under the ordering of the first key. In our example the three apple words will compare as equal because of the "f" option following the first position indicator. The second key specifies a reverse sort (the "r" option) that will place the capitalized apple word following the lower case apple word, and the "-u" option will discard the duplicate lower case apples. The ordering produced is "apple", "Apple", "Balloon".

For the following few examples, assume that the file 'numbs' contains the following three lines: "ab: 40", "cd:-20" and "ab:.30".

Sort 'numbs' in dictionary order:

```
sort -d numbs
```

The order produced will be "ab: 40", "ab:.30", "cd:-20". The colon, hyphen, period, and plus sign are all ignored in dictionary ordering.

Sort 'numbs' by the second field (fields are separated by colons):

    sort -t: +1 numbs

The order produced will be "ab: 40", "cd:-20", "ab:.30" because in the ASCII sequence space precedes the hyphen, which precedes the period.

Sort 'numbs' according to the numerical ordering of the second field:

    sort -t: +1n numbs

The order produced will be "cd:-20", "ab:.30", "ab: 40".

Sort 'numbs' primarily according to the first field and secondarily according to the reverse numerical ordering of the second field:

    sort -t: +0 -1 +1rn numbs

The order produced will be "ab: 40", "ab:.30", "cd:-20".

SPELL

NAME
spell — check spelling in text files

SYNOPSIS
spell [options] [file ...]

DESCRIPTION
The spell program extracts all of the words from the named files, or from the standard input if no files are named, and looks them up in a dictionary. All of the words that are not in the dictionary and cannot be derived from the dictionary words by applying standard inflections, prefixes, and suffixes are listed on the standard output as possible misspellings. Some of the words flagged by spell are correct while certain errors in the text are not detected. However, even though spell is not perfect, it is a valuable aid for locating many spelling errors.

Spell supports three options:

-b   Check British spelling.

-v   Print all words that aren't in the dictionary along with possible derivations.

-x   Print every possible stem for each word.

These options seldom are used by most users.

EXAMPLES

Check for misspelled words in a set of text files:

    spell xydocs?

Check for British spelling in the same set of text files:

    spell -b xydocs?

STTY

NAME

stty — set or display terminal options

SYNOPSIS

stty [options]

DESCRIPTION

The stty command is used to control various options so that the system can handle your terminal correctly. One reason for the stty command is that there are many types of terminal and they all need slightly different treatment. Another reason for stty is to allow you to customize certain UNIX System features (the assignments for the erase and kill control characters). If no options are specified, then stty will report on the current settings of a few key options.

Obviously stty is one of the most machine dependent utility programs. The summary of options that follows is for Version 7 of the UNIX System running on the Digital Equipment Corporation series of minicomputers. UNIX Systems on different machines are likely to have different or additional settings, and new settings are possible as a result of advances in computer terminal and interface electronics.

The following options are commonly used to control the handling of your terminal:

even (-even)
>   Enable (disable) even parity for serial transmission.

odd (-odd)
>   Enable (disable) odd parity for serial transmission. Both even and odd parity are often disabled: only one (odd or even) should be enabled at any given time.

raw (-raw)

> Enable (disable) raw input mode. In raw input mode the system doesn't perform the normal input processing, in particular the erase, kill, interrupt, quit, and eof characters are delivered to running programs and all characters are delivered with the parity bit in place. Your terminal handler is not usually in the raw input mode.

cooked   Same as -raw.

cbreak   Input characters can be read one at a time. Erase and kill are ineffective but interrupt, quit, and eof work as usual.

-cbreak   Input characters are available only when you strike the newline (or return) at the end of the line. Erase, kill, interrupt, quit, and eof all work normally. This is the normal mode for most UNIX System activities.

-nl   Allow either carriage returns or newlines to indicate the end of input lines.

nl   Only allow newlines to indicate the end of input lines.

echo (-echo)

> Echo (do not echo) each character as it is typed. The -echo mode is used only during the entry of passwords and other sensitive information or on terminals that always echo locally.

lcase (-lcase)

> Map (do not map) upper case input to lower case and map (do not map) lower case output to upper case. The lcase mode is only used on terminals that don't have lower case letters; the mode -lcase is used on most terminals which support both upper and lower case.

tabs (-tabs)

> Preserve tabs (replace tabs with spaces) on output. The -tabs option is used on terminals that don't know how to expand tabs, the tabs option is used on terminals that understand the dynamics of the tab character.

ek   Set the erase character to # and the kill character to @.

erase c   Set the erase character to c (c stands for any keyboard character). A control character can be indicated by preceding the character with a (escaped from the shell) caret.

kill c   Set the kill character to c.

cr0 cr1 cr2 cr3

> Carriage return delay (0, 0.08, 0.16, and 0 seconds, respectively). Some terminals require a slight delay after they receive a carriage return. Most terminals use the cr0 setting.

nl0 nl1 nl2 nl3
> Newline delay (0, x, 0.1, and 0 seconds, respectively). The nl1 delay is column dependent and is occasionally used on printing terminals.

tab0 tab1 tab2 tab3
> Tab delay specification: tab0 specifies no delay, tab1 specifies a column dependent delay, tab2 specifies a .1 second delay, and tab3 is the same as -tabs, that is tabs are replaced by spaces.

ff0 ff1   Form feed delay (0 and 2 seconds, respectively).

bs0 bs1   Backspace delay (0 and 0.05 seconds, respectively).

hup (-hup)
> Hang up (do not hang up) the dataphone connection when it is closed for the last time.

0   Hang up the dataphone connection immediately.

50 75 110 134 150 200 300 600 1200 1800 2400 4800 9600
> Set the baud rate.

EXAMPLES

Print a summary of the current options:

    stty

Set the computer's communication interface to 300 baud:

    stty 300

Set the erase character to Control-h:

    stty erase \^h

Set the kill character to Control-u:

    stty kill \^h

Direct the computer to expand tabs to spaces during output:

    stty -tabs

Set the erase and kill characters to their defaults, # and @, respectively:

    stty ek

TAIL

NAME
tail — type the end of a text file

SYNOPSIS

tail [offset] [file]

DESCRIPTION

The tail program prints the last part of the named file or the last part of the standard input if no file is mentioned. If no offset is mentioned, then tail prints the last few (usually 10) lines of the file.

The offset argument is used to control how much of the end of the file is printed. When the offset argument is introduced by a hyphen the offset is relative to the end of the file; when the offset is introduced by a plus sign the offset specifies an amount to skip from the beginning of the file. The offset can be specified in units of lines, blocks (512 bytes), or characters by using the modifiers "l", "b", and "c", respectively. If no unit is mentioned, lines are assumed.

EXAMPLES

Print the last few lines of the file 'wrdstr.1':

    tail wrdstr.1

Print the last 200 characters of 'wrdstr.1':

    tail -200c wrdstr.1

Print all but the first 500 lines of the file 'bell.5.1980':

    tail +500 bell.5.1980

Print the last 23 lines of a long format listing of the '/bin' directory:

    ls -l /bin | tail -23l

TEE

NAME

tee — duplicate the standard input

SYNOPSIS

tee [-i] [-a] [file ...]

DESCRIPTION

The tee program duplicates the standard input. The tee in a pipeline is the equivalent of a tee fitting in a plumber's pipeline. Tee usually is used when you want to place the output of a program in a file and see it too, although tee also can be used in pipelines to save intermediate stages of processing that would normally be invisible.

The "-i" option instructs tee to ignore interrupts and the "-a" option instructs tee to append its output to the output files rather than overwrite the output files.

EXAMPLES

Save the output of the spell program in a file and simultaneously view the output on the screen:

```
spell ch1.doc | tee ch1.errs
```

Save the output of the wc program in a file and simultaneously append the output in another file and also see the output on the terminal:

```
wc ch1.doc | tee -a ch1.logerrs | tee ch1.errs
```

TIME

NAME
time — time a process

SYNOPSIS
time command [arguments]

DESCRIPTION
The time command allows you to time a process. When the process is complete the time program prints three indications: the total elapsed time, the execution time of the process, and the system time of the process. The total elapsed time is accurate to the second while the execution time and the system time are measured in sixtieths of a second. The times can depend on a variety of random factors including most notably the system load.

EXAMPLES
Time the who process:

```
time who
```

Time the ls program producing a long format listing of the '/bin' directory:

```
time ls -l /bin
```

TTY

NAME
tty — print the name of the special file for the terminal

SYNOPSIS

tty

DESCRIPTION

The tty command prints the name of the special file that is used as the standard input. If the standard input is not a file, then the tty command prints a message similar to "not a tty".

EXAMPLES

Print the name of the terminal's special file:

tty

WC

NAME

wc — count words, lines, and characters in files

SYNOPSIS

wc [-lwc] [file ...]

DESCRIPTION

The word count program is used to count units of text in text files. The usual case is for wc to report the number of lines, words, and characters in its input files, or in the standard input if no files are mentioned in the command line. The options can be used to direct wc's attention to count just words (-w) , lines (-l), or characters (-c).

EXAMPLES

Count the lines, words, and characters in 'mydoc':

wc mydoc

Equivalently one could use the command:

wc -lwc mydoc

Count the number of words in 'mydoc':

wc -w mydoc

Count the number of files in the current directory:

ls | wc -l

WHO

NAME

who — list the users who are using the system

SYNOPSIS

who

DESCRIPTION

The who command produces a list of all of the people who are currently logged onto the system. The list contains the login name, the time of login, and the terminal for each user.

The special command "who am i" ("whoami" on some systems) usually produces your login name.

EXAMPLES

List the current users:

who

List your login name:

who am i

WRITE

NAME

write — engage in a typed two-way conversation

SYNOPSIS

write username [ttyname]

DESCRIPTION

The write command allows you to initiate (or respond to) a conversation with another logged in UNIX System user on your system. To initiate a conversation with a person whose username is "tom" you should enter the command

write tom

Usernames can be inferred using the who command or by examining the file '/etc/passwd'. If Tom is logged on at several different terminals, then you can use the command

write tom tty50

to write to tom using the '/dev/tty50' connection.

Once you have entered the command a message similar to "Message from ralph on tty30" will appear on Tom's terminal. Tom should drop what he is doing and enter the command

write ralph

to complete the connection. At this point anything that Tom or Ralph types will appear on both of their terminals. In order to reduce the level of confusion only one user should type at a time. Usually the person who initiated the conversation will type a message and then type an "o" to signify "over." Then the other party will type a message followed by "o". This is similar to the protocol used in CB radio communication. At the conclusion of a conversation you should enter an "oo" to signify "over and out" and you should strike Control-d to stop the write program.

GLOSSARY

Access Mode. (also called access privilege) The protection information for a file. In the UNIX System, files can be read, written, or executed by the file's owner, members of the file's group, or others. The access mode details the operations allowed (reading, writing, or executing) by the three classes of users (owner, group, and others). In a shared computer system access modes ensure a degree of privacy and safety for the user's files.

Acoustic Coupler. A device which converts electrical signals to telephone tones and vice versa. *See* Modem.

Application Program. A computer program for a specialized purpose, such as an accounting program.

Argument. Additional information that is passed to a command. The command name and its arguments are separated from one another by spaces and/or tabs. Arguments usually are used to direct the operation of a command.

ASCII. American Standard Code for Information Interchange. A standard code used with most computers and data terminals.

Assembly Language. A programming language that relates directly to the native instruction set of a particular computer. Assembly language programs occasionally are used in situations where efficient routines are necessary. The disadvantage of assembly language programming is that assembly language programs are difficult to write and they are not transportable from one type of computer to another.

Background Process A process that runs unattended in a manner that allows other programs to be initiated and interacted with while the background process is running. Some background processes are started during the UNIX System bootstrap in order to perform system management functions while other background processes are started interactively by users to perform personal work.

Batch processing. A noninteractive approach to data processing. In a batch system programs are formally submitted for execution by users, and then the programs are scheduled for execution by the operating system. The scheduling may lead to considerable delays (often hours) between the time a program is introduced to the system and the time a program actually starts to execute in order to optimize machine utilization.

Baud Rate. The transmission rate between computers and/or communication equipment or devices, measured in bits per second. The baud rate divided by 10 is a rough measure of the characters transmitted per second.

'/bin'. On most UNIX Systems this is the directory that contains the most frequently used commands.

Binary. A number system using the number 2 as its base. In binary the digits are zero and one. Binary is important in computers because computers are constructed from logic elements which take on one of two states, corresponding to the binary digits zero and one.

Binary File. Files that contain codes that are not part of the ASCII character set. Binary files utilize all 256 possible values for each byte in the file. Unfortunately they cannot be typed on your terminal because most of the 256 values are not printable ASCII characters. Binary files can be examined using the od program to convert the binary codes into printable ASCII equivalents.

Bit. A binary digit, the smallest unit of data.

Bit Bucket. The UNIX System bit bucket is a special file named '/dev/null/'. In computer jargon, a bit bucket is a place where output can be sent in order to discard the output, or a place where input can be acquired in order to acquire nothing. *See* Null Device.

Block Special File. A special file that provides an interface to a device which is capable of supporting a file system.

Booting. The process of starting the system.

Bourne Shell. The shell program used in Version 7 of the UNIX System. Named after its author, S. R. Bourne. *See* Shell.

Break Key. A key on the terminal keyboard which sends an unmistakable code to the host computer. During the login process the break key may cause the UNIX System to change its communication speed in an attempt to synchronize speeds with your terminal.

Buffer. A place where data are stored temporarily.

Bug. An error in a computer program or in the computer hardware.

Byte. A specified number (usually eight) of bits. Most of the mass storage devices and I/O devices that are available today are designed to transfer sequences of 8-bit bytes.

Character. The symbols corresponding to the keys on the terminal keyboard including all alphanumerics, punctuation marks, and other special symbols. Characters are usually stored in a single byte.

Character Special File. A special file that provides an interface to an I/O device. The character interface is used for devices that cannot support a file system and as an alternate interface to devices capable of supporting a file system.

C-Language. A general purpose programming language that is the primary language of the UNIX System. It has been classified as not a very high level language but has been praised for its economy of expression, absence of restrictions, and generality. C was developed by D. M. Ritchie.

Command. An order directing the system to perform some function. Some commands are handled internally by the shell, although most commands result in the execution of a program.

Command File. An ordinary file that contains shell commands. The term command file is usually used when the file contains just one or a few commands; the term shell program usually is used when there are a lot of commands or when the shell's facilities for looping and conditional execution are used.

Command Interpreter. A component of an operating system which decodes and executes the commands entered by the user. The UNIX System command interpreter is called the shell.

Command Name. The first word of a command. The words following the command name are called the arguments. Sometimes the command name is referred to as the zeroeth argument because in programs the subsequent arguments are numbered consecutively beginning with one.

Compiler. A computer program that translates a text file containing a program written in some high level programming language into a machine language output that can be executed. On UNIX Systems the machine language output from a compiler is called an object file.

Concatenate. The act of combining several files, one after the other. This operation usually is performed using the cat program.

Conditional. A programming language construct that causes a statement (or statements) to be executed only if a certain condition exists.

Context Search. Searching for a body of text in a given file by entering a text pattern you want the system to locate. You can perform a context search within the editor or you can perform context searches using the grep command.

Control Character. Control characters are embedded in text in order to control various functions, such as cursor movement or printing functions. A control character is typed at a terminal by depressing the control key (CTRL) and an alphabetic key simultaneously.

Control-d. *See* EOF character.

CPU. (Central Processing Unit) - The control, arithmetic, and logical unit of a computer.

Crash. An unexpected interruption of computer service, usually due to a serious hardware or software malfunction.

CRT. (Cathode Ray Tube) - A television screen on which information can be displayed.

Current Directory. The directory whose files are directly accessible. At all times in your interactions with the UNIX System there is a current directory; the name of the current directory can be printed using the pwd command and you can move to another directory by using the cd command.

Current Subtree. The subtree whose root is the current directory, that is, the current directory, all of its subdirectories and files, their subdirectories and files, and so on.

Cursor. A special symbol on a display terminal which indicates the position where the next character will appear. The cursor is usually a small box or underline, and it may be blinking.

Data. The basic elements of information which can be processed or produced by a computer.

Data Processing. Using machines (usually computers) to manipulate information. The term data processing is usually used to connote business activities using computers.

'/dev'. The directory where special files usually are located.

Diagnostic. An error message produced by a program, often an error message that is intended to provide information relating to a bug in the program or a problem in the program's environment.

Dialogue. A conversation between the user and the UNIX System. In the usual UNIX System dialogue the shell displays a prompt, the user then enters a command followed by a return, the command is executed, consequently the shell displays another prompt.

Dial-Up Terminal. A terminal that is connected to a computer via the public switched telephone network.

Directory. A group of files. Directories are used to organize and structure the file system. Without the organization provided by the UNIX System's hierarchical directory system it would be very difficult to manage the thousands of files that exist in typical UNIX System installations. The ls command is used to list the files in a directory. When you first log onto the system you are in your home directory. You can move to another directory by using the cd command and you can print the name of the current directory by using the pwd command.

Disk. The medium that is used in a disk drive. Disks are usually platters covered with a magnetic material. Disks are classified as rigid or flexible (floppy) according to the rigidity of the platter. Rigid disks usually have a greater storage capacity than floppy disks.

Disk Drive. A hardware device that uses a rotating magnetic media (a disk) to store information; a type of mass storage device.

Disk File. A named collection of information that is stored on a mass storage device. Disk files are said to be nonvolatile because they are retained even when operating power is removed from the mass storage device.

Display Terminal. A computer terminal that uses a CRT as the output device.

Echoing. The UNIX System's repetition of the user's typed input. The characters that you type are normally sent to the UNIX System and then echoed so that they appear on your terminal. Echoing is occasionally turned off (for instance, when you enter your password).

Edit. To change or alter information. Often used in reference to changing the text in a text file by using a text editor.

Editor. *See* Text Editor.

Electronic Mail. A system which transmits information (memos, messages, letters, etc.) to other users of the system or to users on other systems.

End of File (EOF) Character. Control-d is the UNIX System's end of file character. (It is activated by depressing the control key and the alphabetic "d" key simultaneously.) Since the shell normally stops processing when it encounters the end of file, one way to log off the UNIX System is to strike Control-d in response to a shell prompt.

Erase Character. The erase character will erase previously typed characters on your current input line one at a time. It is assigned initially to the sharp key (#); it can be reassigned to another key using the stty command.

'/etc'. The UNIX System directory that contains miscellaneous files that are used for system administration.

'/etc/passwd'. The UNIX System file that contains the major login information (password, login name, user number, home directory, and the name of the user's shell) for each user of the system.

Execute. The act of performing the instructions stored in an ordinary file.

Execute Permission. For ordinary files execute permission is an access mode that allows you to execute the file. For directory files execute permission is an access mode that allows you to search them in the course of resolving a pathname.

Execution Time. The time the computer requires to complete a given command.

Fifo. Fifo stands for First In First Out. In the UNIX System a fifo is a named permanent pipe. A fifo allows two unrelated processes to exchange information using a pipe connection. Normal pipes work only with related processes. Not all systems have fifos.

File. A named collection of information. Files usually are stored on a mass storage device and UNIX System files are collected into groups called directories.

Filename. The name that is used to identify a particular file.

Filename Generation. The procedure that the shell follows to expand command line words containing metacharacters into the corresponding list of filenames. For example, in a directory containing the files 'x.doc' and 'nm.doc' the shell file name generation process expands the word "*.doc" into the list of files 'nm.doc' and 'x.doc'.

File System. The collection of files and file management structures (inodes) on a mass storage device. In the UNIX System the file system is hierarchical.

Filter. A program that reads its information from the standard input and writes its results to the standard output.

Foreground Process. A process that is run interactively. There may be several active background commands, but under normal circumstances there is just one active and perhaps several inactive foreground processes.

Flag. *See* Option.

Graphics. The use of diagrams and other visual displays.

Group. Several users who are members of the same department, working on the same project, or related in other ways. Each UNIX System file is associated with a certain group and members of that group have specified privileges for accessing the file.

Hardware. The mechanical and electronic elements in a computer system.

Hardwired Terminal. A terminal that is attached to a computer by dedicated wires.

Header. A record at the beginning of a file that details the sizes, locations, and so on, of the information that follows in the file.

Hexadecimal Radix. A numerical system where the base is 16 and the digits are 0, 1, 2, 3, 4, 5, 6, 7, 8, 9, A, B, C, D, E, and F.

Hierarchy. Any system of persons or things that can be ranked or ordered one above the other. The UNIX file system is hierarchical.

High Level Language. A general term for programming languages which support an abstract view of the process of computing, in contrast to assembly languages which relate directly to a particular computer architecture. C, FORTRAN, BASIC, and Pascal are examples of high level languages.

Home Directory. The directory the user is placed into at the conclusion of the login process.

Inode. The key internal structure for managing files in the UNIX System. Inodes contain all of the information pertaining to the mode, type, owner, and location of a file. A table of inodes is stored near the beginning of every file system.

Input Redirection. The shell's reassignment of the standard input to a file other than the terminal. *See* Standard Input.

Interactive Computer System. A conversational system that allows for a continuous dialogue between the user and the computer.

i-number. A number specifying a particular inode on a file system.

I/O. A general term to describe the process of transmitting information between a computer and peripheral devices such as the mass storage devices, terminals, and printers.

I/O Device. A peripheral device to which information can be transmitted from the computer (i.e., printer, terminal, disk, etc.). In the UNIX System I/O devices are accessed via special files.

Kernel. The memory resident part of the UNIX Operating System, containing all of the UNIX System functions that are needed immediately and frequently. The kernel supervises the I/O transactions, manages and controls the hardware, and schedules the user processes for execution. The UNIX System kernel is compiled from about 10,000 lines of C language code and about 1000 lines of assembly language code. In the UNIX System the kernel is endowed with relatively few features (compared to other operating systems) so that these features may be provided more conveniently by individual utility programs.

Kill Character. The kill character allows a user to erase the entire current line. It is initially assigned to the commercial at (@) key; it can be reassigned to another key using the stty command.

Login. The procedure that provides access to the system for authorized users.

Login Directory. *See* Home Directory.

Login Name. The name that a user uses during the login process.

Logout. The procedure that informs the system that the user will be exiting and placing no further demands on the system.

Machine Language. The native language of a computer.

Macro Package. In the UNIX System, the term macro package usually is used to describe a set of high level nroff/troff text formatting commands. The built-in nroff/troff commands are very low level and inconvenient; macro packages introduce a more convenient set of text processing functions.

Mail. *See* Electronic Mail.

Mass Storage Device. A unit for storing large amounts of information; usually a disk, tape, or cartridge unit. The information stored on mass storage devices is accessible to the CPU, although the access time is much longer than that for information stored in the main memory. Information is stored magnetically on most mass storage devices. Also called the secondary store.

Memory. A device into which information can be copied, stored, and retrieved at a later time. Usually the term refers to the main memory of a computer, which is an electronic device capable of storing moderate quantities of information that are accessible very rapidly by the CPU. Main memory is also called the primary store.

Metacharacter. Keyboard characters which have special meanings in certain situations. For example, the asterisk can be used to match any sequence of characters when you are entering a shell command such as "ls *.c". If you wish to use metacharacters without invoking their special meanings, you must use quotation.

Modem (modulator-demodulator). A device that translates data signals from a form compatible with data processing equipment into a form that can be transmitted long distances, usually over public telephone lines.

motd (Message of the Day). A text file ('/etc/motd') in which the system administrator places timely messages. On most systems the motd file is printed when you log in.

Multiprogramming. The ability to run several programs or routines simultaneously on a single computer.

Multiuser. Able to support several users simultaneously.

Named Pipe. *See* Fifo.

Null. A term that is often used to indicate emptiness or even nonexistence.

Null Device. The UNIX System null device is called '/dev/null'. When you direct output to the null device it is discarded; when you read input from the null device you immediately encounter an end of file. Output occasionally is directed to the null device in order to discard it, and input occasionally is read from the null device in order to read nothing.

Null String. A text string that does not contain any text. The length of a null string is zero.

Object File. A file containing machine language instructions that can be executed by a computer. In the UNIX System an object file is the result of a compilation.

Octal Radix. A numerical system where the base is 8 and the digits are 0, 1, 2, 3, 4, 5, 6, and 7.

Operating System. A program for managing the resources of a computer. Operating systems simplify housekeeping duties such as input/output procedures, process scheduling, and the file system.

Option. An argument that alters the operation of a command. Usually options are single characters preceded by a hyphen. For example, in the shell command "ps -l" the option is the letter "l" which directs the ps command to perform a long format list of processes rather than the usual short form list.

Ordinary File. Ordinary files are used for storing data. Ordinary files often contain programs, documents, letters, data bases, and other types of information.

Output Redirection. The shell's reassignment of the standard output connection to a specific file. *See* Standard Output.

Password. A unique set of letters or digits which a user enters during an identification process.

Pathname. A path through the file system that leads to a file. It is formed by listing directory names separated by /'s in order to define the path. For example, the pathname '/usr/bin/lex' specifies a path that starts in the root directory, leads to the 'usr' directory, then to the 'bin' directory, and then finally to the file 'lex'.

Permissions. The access modes associated with a file. *See* Access Mode.

Permuted Index. A keyword form of indexing used to locate entries in the Unix User's Manual.

Pipe. A connection between the standard output of one program and the standard input of another program. For example, the shell command to create a pipe between the ls command and the wc command is "ls | wc".

Pipe Fitting. A pipe connection.

Pipeline. A group of commands connected by pipe connections.

Primary Store. *See* Memory.

Printer. A device connected to a computer system for producing printed output.

Printing Terminal. A computer terminal that uses a print mechanism for output. Whereas the term printer usually is used to describe a device that is optimized for producing printed output, the term printing terminal is used to describe a printing device that is optimized for interacting with a computer.

Process. A program that is being executed. An entry in the system's process table.

Process Identification Number. A unique process id number is assigned to each process by the UNIX System kernel. The identification numbers for the current processes are printed by the ps command. When you run a program in the background the shell prints its pid number.

'.profile'. A file of shell commands that may reside in a user's home directory. If there is a '.profile' in a home directory, then the shell will execute the commands in it before executing commands interactively from the terminal each time the user logs on. Commands in '.profile' are often used to initialize shell variables (e.g., the search string), set the terminal handler's modes, and so on.

Program. A sequence of computer instructions for performing some useful function.

Prompt. A message printed by a program to indicate that the program is ready to accept another command from the user. The prompt for the shell can be changed by assigning a value to the variable $PS1. The default prompt for the UNIX System shell is either a sharp, a percent sign, or a currency symbol ($) on most systems.

Quotation. The process by which metacharacters are prevented from having their special meaning.

Read. The act of acquiring information, usually from a file or I/O device.

Read Permission. Allows a person to execute a program that reads data from a file.

Regular Expression. A regular expression specifies a set of strings of characters.

Search String. The UNIX System shell maintains a search string that directs the shell to search in a certain set of directories for each command that is entered. The search string list usually includes the current directory, the

'/bin' directory, and the '/usr/bin' directory. The search string can be altered by assigning a new value to the variable $PATH.

Secondary Store. *See* Mass Storage Devices.

Shell. A command programming language that provides an interface to the UNIX Operating System. As a command language it interactively accepts commands from users and arranges for the requested actions to occur. As a programming language it contains control flow and string valued variables. The program which implements the shell is called '/bin/sh'.

Shell Program. A program written using the shell programming language. Shell programs can be written and executed interactively, although most shell programs are stored in ordinary files.

Software. Programs and programming facilities that are stored in a computer accessible medium.

Source Code. The text version of a program. A compiler transforms source code into object code.

Single user. Able to support just one user. In the UNIX System single-user mode is usually entered just after the system is booted and it is usually used for file system repair and maintenance and other functions where one person requires exclusive use of the computer. Even when it is in single-user mode, the UNIX System is able to run several processes (multiprogramming).

Special File. Special files are used in the UNIX System to provide an interface to I/O devices. Each UNIX System contains at least one special file for each I/O device that is connected to the computer. Special files can be accessed using the same techniques that are used to access ordinary files. Special files usually reside in the '/dev' directory and there are two types, block special files for devices which can support file systems and character special files for everything else.

Standard Error. The place where many programs place error messages.

Standard I/O. Many programs need to read commands and data from the user, write messages to the user, and write error messages. Therefore, the shell prepares three standard I/O connections for each program, the standard input, the standard output, and the standard error. The standard channels usually are connected to the user's terminal although they can be reassigned using redirection.

Standard Input. The source of input for many programs. *See* Input Reassignment.

Standard Output. The place where many programs place their text output. *See* Output Reassignment.

Subdirectory. A directory below another directory in the file system hierarchy. For example, the directory '/usr/bin' is a subdirectory of the '/usr' directory.

Subtree. A branch of the UNIX file system.

Superuser. A special privilege level that exists in the UNIX System to allow system managers to perform certain functions that are denied to ordinary users. The superuser is not constrained by the normal file access mode system.

Swapping. Occasionally more processes are executing than can be stored in main memory. When this occurs the excess processes are stored temporarily on a mass storage device, a procedure known as swapping. The act of transferring a process from main memory to mass storage is called swapping out; the opposite procedure is called swapping in.

Swap Space. The region on a mass storage device where processes are stored after they are swapped out.

Syntax. The rules that govern the construction of sentences in a language. In computers the term syntax is used to describe the rules for writing legal statements in programming languages or command languages.

System. An assembly of components united by some form of regulated interaction to form an organized whole.

System Call. A request by an active process for a service by the UNIX System kernel. The UNIX System contains system calls to perform I/O, to control, coordinate, and create processes, and to read and set various status elements of the system.

Tape Drive. A type of mass storage device which uses magnetic tape to store information.

Terminal. An I/O device containing a typewriter keyboard and either a display device or a printer. Terminals usually are connected to a computer and they allow a person to interact with a computer.

Text Editor. A general purpose program used to prepare text files. A text editor enables a user to enter and correct text. Most editors contain commands to locate specific lines or words in the text and commands to add, delete, change, and print lines in the text.

Text Formatter. A program that is used to prepare text for final publication or printing. Formatting smooths margins, aligns tables, controls spacing and titles, and so on. The basic UNIX System text formatting programs are nroff, troff, eqn, neqn, and tbl.

Text File. A file comprised solely of ASCII characters.

Time Sharing. A technique developed to share a computer's resources among several users, so that each user is given the illusion of having exclusive use of a computer. This is accomplished by switching very rapidly from one task to another so that it appears that all of the activities are occurring simultaneously.

The UNIX Programmer's Manual. (also referred to as UNIX User's Manual). The UPM describes the specific features of the UNIX System. There are appropriate manuals for each version of the UNIX System.

User. Someone who uses the UNIX System.

'/usr'. A general purpose directory that is the head of a subtree that contains most of the UNIX System software and documentation.

'/usr/bin'. A directory that usually is used to store the less frequently used UNIX System utility programs.

Utility. A standard routine developed to perform generic data processing tasks.

Variable. A symbol whose value is allowed to change. In the shell variable names are preceded by a currency symbol except during assignment operations. Some of the standard shell variables are $PATH, $PS1, and $TERM.

Word Processing. A generic term that connotes working with text data using a computer to produce documents. The software components of a word processing system usually include a text editing program and a text formatting program.

Write. The act of sending data to a file or I/O device.

Write Permission. Allows a user's programs to write data to a file.

Zeroeth Argument. *See* Command Name

Index